THE LIFE AND TIMES
OF THE
WESTERN
MOVIE

THE LIFE AND TIMES
OF THE
WESTERN
MOVIE

JAY HYAMS

GALLERY BOOKS
An Imprint of W. H. Smith Publishers Inc.
112 Madison Avenue
New York City 10016

To my mother and father
brother and sister
and Deborah L. Weiss

Copyright 1983 by W. H. Smith. All rights reserved. No part of this book may be produced or transmitted in any form or by any means, without written permission from the Publisher.
Published by Gallery Books, an imprint of W. H. Smith Publishers Inc.
112 Madison Avenue
New York, New York 10016

Manufactured in Hong Kong

Edited by Hedy Caplan
Designed by Alan Mogel
Production by Lori Stein
1 2 3 4 5 6 7 8 9 10

Library of Congress Cataloging in Publication Data

Hyams, Jay, 1949–
    The Life and times of the western movie.

    1. Western films—History and criticism.   I. Title.
PN1995.9.W4H92 1983   791.43′09′093278   83–11244
ISBN 0-8317-55458

Photo research by Deborah L. Weiss

Page 1: *McCabe rides into Presbyterian Church in*
McCabe and Mrs. Miller *(Warner Brothers, 1971).*
Pages 2–3: She Wore A Yellow Ribbon *(RKO, 1949).*
Pages 4–5: Rough Night in Jericho *(Universal, 1967).*

John Wayne holds forth in
Rooster Cogburn *(Universal, 1975).*

Preface

The first true movie was a western, and the history of western movies is in large part the history of moviemaking in the United States. It has become popular recently to declare westerns "dead," by which is meant that no new ones are being made. That is not true, of course, and in their long history, westerns—and the American film industry—have had to suffer many droughts.

This book provides an overview of the more than eighty years of western movies, from their beginning, in 1903, to the present. I hope that the book will give you some insight into the changes that have taken place in both the films and in our way of looking at the West and at ourselves. I also hope that reading the book will increase your enjoyment of the films.

The book is arranged chronologically, each chapter covering, roughly, one decade. The films discussed within each decade are organized according to some shared attribute. Thus, some films are grouped according to theme, some according to director, some according to actor, some according to scriptwriter. More than four hundred films are covered. There is an index at the end of the book to help you locate particular films; in the text the main entry for each film is given in bold type. Alternate titles, including the titles used in Great Britain, are given in parentheses following the title; also given are the distributor and year of release for each film. Abbreviations have been used for the names of some distributors. These include AIP (American International Pictures); CIN (Cinema Releasing Corporation); EMB (Embassy Pictures); MGM (Metro-Goldwyn-Mayer); NGP (National General Pictures); and RKO (RKO Radio Pictures).

Contents

The Professionals

The Way It Should Have Been

Living Legends

*"Little by little,
the look of the country changes
because of the men we admire."*
Hud

Introduction

Sometime during the fall of 1901, Robert Leroy Parker and Harry Longabaugh (better known as Butch Cassidy and the Sundance Kid) spent a few weeks in New York City in the company of Sundance's girlfriend, Etta Place. No one in the crowded city recognized the famed outlaws, even though their exploits as train and bank robbers had put them at the top of the most-wanted list. Their pockets were full of cash (they had recently pulled off a very profitable railroad heist), and they ate in the best restaurants, slept in the finest hotels, and took in a few operas (blue-eyed Sundance was very fond of Wagner).

As they made their way through the busy streets, stepping over the trolley tracks and watching out for the occasional oncoming horseless carriage, Butch and Sundance were passing through a world on the verge of enormous change. President Theodore Roosevelt's reassuring grin was leading America into an exciting new century, lit with electric light. Butch and Sundance were convinced that there was no room for them in the new age. Indeed, they felt that the United States had grown too small for them, and when they left New York, it was on a ship headed for South America.

The story of what happened to these former members of the Wild Bunch in South America is lost in legend. Some historians claim they died there, shot down by the Bolivian army, but there is no proof of that, and other sources hold that they both made it safely back to the United States. What happened to them in South America is not as important as the fact of their going. The notion of heading for the territories south of the border was not unique to Butch and Sundance. Even before the turn of the century, many westerners—and not all of them outlaws—had started looking for a new frontier. They were tired of tripping over fences and getting hung up on the badges of the marshals, sheriffs, Texas Rangers, range detectives, and Pinkerton men who were eagerly bringing law and order to the West; they were weary of getting cut up on

Paul Newman as Butch Cassidy and Robert Redford as the Sundance Kid in Butch Cassidy and the Sundance Kid *(20th Century-Fox, 1969).*

barbed wire, of sniffing "stinking woolies" (sheep), and of bumping into sodbusters and hayshakers. And they were looking for work. A series of severe winters and summer droughts during the 1880s had changed the cattle industry forever. The days of easygoing free enterprise, of cattle drives and cow towns, were over. Corporations, most of them owned and run by businessmen in the East—or in Europe—had taken over, and "civilization" had spread across the country. The wild times were finished, and restless cowpunchers, seeking adventure or just looking for the way of life they felt suited for, took off to be Rough Riders, or to take part in the Boer War, or to see what things were like down in Australia—or in South America.

The period of the old West had lasted barely the length of a man's life, roughly from 1840 to 1890, and Butch and Sundance were not the only Americans to lament its passing. Even as the nation looked forward to the new century, it looked back with growing nostalgia at what had passed away—or at what it imagined had passed away, for well before the old West was no more, it had been made into a national legend.

The popularity of Owen Wister's novel *The Virginian*, first published in 1902, demonstrates the power of that legend. Wister dedicated the book to his former Harvard classmate Theodore Roosevelt, and in his foreword he explained that men like the soft-spoken, gentlemanly, and courageous Virginian no longer existed—theirs was a "vanished world." The character of the Virginian, the idealized cowboy hero with his mixture of innocence and bravado ("When you call me that, *smile!*") gripped the nation's imagination, and the book was an immediate best-seller. It was not, however, the first western novel.

As early as 1860, the publishing house of Beadle and Adams had begun publishing dime novels, which, in the tradition of James Fennimore Cooper's "Leather-Stocking Tales," had glorified the frontier. Written according to set formulas by a staff of prolific writers, dime novels established the basic form of the western

saga. The heroic escapades of such characters as Deadwood Dick and Hurricane Nell thrilled thousands of avid readers. The heroes of these pulp westerns were not all imaginary, however—some were living men.

Such writers as Prentiss Ingraham and Edward Zane Carroll Judson (known by his pseudonym, Ned Buntline), while turning out hundreds of dime novels about imaginary characters, created a few living heroes, too. Many of the men made into folk heroes by these frontier press agents have maintained their created fame, and it is no longer possible to determine just where the truth ends and the legend begins. Under the guidance of Buntline and Ingraham, William F. Cody became Buffalo Bill; James Butler Hickok became Wild Bill; and Wyatt Earp got his famous Buntline Special, a revolver with a twelve-inch barrel, with which Earp supposedly coldcocked ruffians.

Buntline made Cody the hero of a series of dime novels and gave him the lead in his play *The Scouts of the Plains* (1872). Ten years later, Cody opened his Buffalo Bill's Wild West, which brought to life the

world of the dime novels. Spectators were dazzled by displays of crack shooting, horseback riding, and attacks on stagecoaches by howling Indians; Annie ("Little Sure Shot") Oakley blasted glass balls as fast as they could be tossed in the air; Sitting Bull went through his paces as a noble red man; Wild Bill Hickok reenacted thrilling moments from his career as a gunfighter. Buffalo Bill's was only the first Wild West show, and soon many others were traveling across the nation and visiting Europe, their names echoing the heroes of dime novels: Pawnee Bill, Broncho Ben, Cherokee Ed, and Lone Star May.

The dime novels and the Wild West shows sold Americans a glorious past and provided all the ingredients for the legend of the West. The American Revolution (which, in comparison with the action of the West, seemed distant and foreign, with too many wigs and too great a concern for paperwork) was pushed aside and replaced with a new American heritage—the endless plains, a lone rider, and a galloping horse.

At about the same time that Buffalo Bill was slaughtering Indians and other ne'er-do-wells in Buntline's play, the galloping horse—so essential to the West—had become the subject of a little wager. Leland Stanford, the governor of California, one of the men responsible for both the Central Pacific and the Southern Pacific railroads, and founder of Stanford University, bet a friend $25,000 that at some point during a horse's gallop all four of its legs are off the ground. It was a difficult theory to prove with the naked eye, so Stanford, being a man of means, hired an eccentric English photographer, Eadweard Muybridge (he had changed his name from Edward Muggeridge), to solve the problem. Muybridge lined up a series of twelve cameras with tripwires set out across a racetrack. As the running horse passed each camera, it tripped the cord and a picture was taken. The resulting series of photographs, when placed together in proper sequence, won Stanford his bet and gave Muybridge an idea.

Muybridge invented a device for projecting his animated pictures on a screen and showed it to Thomas

MISS ANNIE OAKLEY, THE PEERLESS LADY WING-SHOT.

Opposite top: Series of photographs by Eadweard Muybridge. On the bottom row, the horse's hooves do indeed all leave the ground at once.
Opposite bottom: Theodore Roosevelt fell in love with Buffalo Bill Cody's phrase "Rough Riders" and used it for his cavalry in the Spanish-American War.
Left: Poster for Annie Oakley.

Cripple Creek Bar-Room *(Edison, 1898).*

Edison, the American inventor responsible for so much of the modern world's gadgetry. It wasn't long before Edison had combined Muybridge's invention with other developments in the film industry and come up with his kinetoscope viewer, a kind of peepshow machine. For a penny, the viewer could squint through a slit in the top of the machine and watch a minute-long flickering motion picture. It was quite a success, and penny arcades with rows of the machines sprang up all over the country.

Edison next invented a projector that allowed audiences, rather than single viewers, to watch movies. Armed with camera and projector, Edison and his competitors set about making movies. But what to photograph? The thrill of the new machine was the display of movement, so the novice filmmakers aimed their cameras at anything that moved: prizefighters, acrobats, vaudeville acts, marching armies. The fact that Edison's company was located in New Jersey didn't keep him from coming up with western subjects. Annie Oakley made her film debut in 1894, and the same year saw such Edison short subjects as *Sioux Indian Ghost Dance; Indian War Council;* and *Bucking Bronco,* in which a Colorado cowboy named Lee Martin rode a horse named Sunfish, while another cowboy stood by and fired a pistol for encouragement. In 1898, Edison came out with a movie called *Cripple Creek Bar-Room,* in which a few denizens of the "West" (photographed somewhere in New Jersey) languished in front of a bar.

By the turn of the century, the infant film industry was on the skids. The novelty of the movies had worn off, and the public was tired of the same dreary scenes in which not much ever happened. The moviehouses had gained bad reputations both as firetraps (the nitrate-based film frequently blew up) and as locations of sin and vice (miscreants were taking advantage of the darkness). Serious actors refused to appear in such a base form of entertainment, and films were most often used to mark the end of vaudeville shows—the appearance of the film meant it was time to go home.

Films might have disappeared altogether had it not been for an inventive engineer working for Edison. Edwin S. Porter was interested in the possibility of telling stories with films. In 1902, using bits and pieces of stock film combined with some new material, Porter created a film called *The Life of an American Fireman.* It was longer than previous films, running for almost an entire reel (1,000 feet of film), and it made good use of the close-up and the exciting device of a scene of dire peril with help on the way.

The Life of an American Fireman was reasonably successful, and its popularity made Porter think. In 1903, he made a film for the Delaware, Lackawanna and Western Railroad, and the railroad, pleased with Porter's product, agreed to let him use the trains and the rails for any other film he might care to make. He

was mulling this over when a certain Billy Martinetti—an acrobat, scene painter, and general handyman—remarked, "Gee, I know a fellow who used to be in *The Great Train Robbery* when it was on the road."

Martinetti was referring to a four-act play by Scott Marble that had first opened in New York City in 1896. In the best Wild West show tradition, the cast of the play included Indians (with such names as Crazy Dog, Split Bark, and Hailstones-in-His-Stomach) and cowboys (with such names as Dashing Charlie, Dead Shot Harry, Alkali Ike, and Broncho Bill).

Porter liked the idea. The play wasn't important, but the title was great. After all, weren't outlaw gangs like the Wild Bunch holding up trains every day? Porter gathered up a group of actors and set out for the wilds of New Jersey to make his movie.

The Great Train Robbery was not the first film with a western subject, and it may not have been the first film to tell a story, but it was a fantastic success, and it stands as a landmark of moviemaking. Porter's twelve-minute film changed movies forever. It also changed America, for it brought to life the American West in a way that outdid the antics of Wild West shows. It was as though what had been lost had been rediscovered—the real West was over, but another, even more exciting West was just beginning. In leaving the country, Butch and Sundance had acted too hastily. All their crimes would gladly have been forgiven had they only agreed to play themselves on the silver screen. As it was, their film had to be made by others.

The Silent West
1903–1928

The Great Train Robbery

It took Edwin S. Porter two days to film *The Great Train Robbery* (Edison, 1903). The completed film ran nearly 800 feet—twelve minutes running time—and was composed of fourteen separate scenes. The plot was dramatically simple and made use of so many devices that have since become standard in western movies that, when viewed today, it is difficult to believe that it was the first western. It's all right there: the ruthless villains who tie up the telegraph operator, stop the train, and cold-bloodedly shoot down the valiant train guard; the saloon scene, with a tenderfoot who is made to "dance" by a bully blasting away at his feet; the dramatic chase, with sixguns blazing and riders tumbling from their saddles; the final shootout, which ends with all the badmen dead. The film races along from its first scene to its last, holding the viewer's attention with mounting suspense.

Porter "wrote" (the silent film had no subtitles), directed, photographed, edited, and may even have acted in the film (some film historians claim to recognize him in the role of the dancing tenderfoot). He was pleased with what he had done, but he wasn't sure audiences would appreciate his creativity. The success of his previous 800-foot film, *The Life of an American Fireman,* had not convinced him that people would sit still for long films, and he was even more concerned with how they would respond to some of his film editing. The portly, mustachioed filmmaker was not a great artist, but he was a masterful technician. He had been working for the Edison Company since 1896, and, like the man he worked for, he was always on the lookout for innovations. In *The Great Train Robbery* he made use of all his latest tricks. Chief among these was concurrent action, cutting from one scene to another and trusting that the viewer would understand that the two events were occurring simultaneously. Porter had invented what would become the western cliché of "meanwhile, back at the ranch," and he wasn't sure audiences would follow the crosscutting. He also threw in a dramatic close-up of one of the bandits—played by an actor named George Barnes—raising his pistol and firing it directly at the audience. Porter didn't know exactly what to do with this close-up, so he just tacked it on to the end of the movie (the Edison Company distributors later gave exhibitors the choice of using it either to begin or end the film).

To be on the safe side, it was decided to try out the film at the Eden Musée on 14th Street in Manhattan. Porter had worked there as a projectionist, and Barnes had been friendly with the owners. When the film was announced, the audience didn't respond well to the title—the play it was stolen from had been popular, but the clientele of the Eden Musée was not particularly cultured, and the title sounded suspiciously serious.

The lights were turned down, the film began, and Porter, listening to the audience's reactions, learned immediately that his fears had been unfounded. The audience began to shout, to yell, "Catch 'em!" "Get 'em!" They were the first audience yelling at the first good guys in hot pursuit of the first bad guys, and they were excited. Some of them stood up. And when the film was over, they wouldn't leave the theater. They nearly rioted. They wanted to see it again, and it was run again. And again.

After that first showing, Edison and Porter decided to see how a more sophisticated audience would respond, so they took it to the Hammerstein Theater, a vaudeville house on 42nd Street and Broadway. The Hammerstein's audience was known for its tough-to-please taste: they got up and walked out on anything they didn't like. When the picture started, the audience stood up and headed for the exits. But they kept looking back at the screen, and finally they went back to their seats. They sat there and stared. They didn't yell, but when it was over they gave it a long, loud round of applause.

The subsequent success of *The Great Train Robbery* was phenomenal; it was the most famous and profitable film until D. W. Griffith's *The Birth of a Nation* in 1915. Part of its popularity can be attributed to its topicality—as the Edison Company's ads stated, the film dealt with "a sensational and highly tragic subject . . . and only recently the East has been shocked by several crimes of the frontier order." But canny businessmen realized that the film was more than a documentary based on current events. It had struck a vein in the American public, and it convinced many entrepreneurs that fortunes were to be made making and distributing films. *The Great Train Robbery*—the first western film to tell a story (the first successful *film* to tell a story)—led to the creation of the American film industry. The birth of westerns was the birth of movies.

Broncho Billy Anderson

Although he worked in the film industry for another dozen years, Porter never made another film to equal his masterpiece. He spent most of his time making experimental films, such as *The Dream of a Rarebit Fiend* (1906), based on a popular cartoon strip by Winsor McCay ("Silas"), in which he used trick photography to demonstrate the sort of nightmares brought on by the insatiable desire for Welsh rarebit. Having made a lot of money from his endeavors—and invested it wisely—Porter retired from films in 1915. Unfortunately, he lost all his wealth in the stock market crash of 1929. When he died in 1941, his passing went unnoticed by press and public alike.

For a short period of time following *The Great Train Robbery*, the new West of the movies lived side by side with what remained of the old West. Buffalo Bill Cody, ever the showman, appeared in *The Life of Buffalo Bill* (1909); *Buffalo Bill's Far West and Pawnee Bill's Far East* (1910); *The Indian Wars* (1913), a remarkable film that included among its cast many of the soldiers and Indians who had actually participated in the final battles of the Indian wars—only fragments of the film have survived; *Sitting Bull—The Hostile Indian Chief* (1914); and *Patsy of the Circus* (1915). Emmett Dalton, youngest of the Dalton brothers, appeared in *Beyond the Law* (1915), which was not to be his last experience in filmmaking. Even Mark Twain made it into a film—*A Curious Dream* (1907). Everyone wanted to make movies. A truly homemade movie was *The Bank Robbery* (1908), which starred a real outlaw and was directed and photographed by the lawman who had finally put him behind bars. William

("Uncle Billy") Tilghman is rarely mentioned in movies—*Cattle Annie and Little Britches* (1981), in which Tilghman is played by Rod Steiger, is an important exception—but he was a true hero of the West, the kind of lawman famous in his time for both his honesty and his fearlessness. Al Jennings was a very inept bandit, but publicity did a great deal for him, and his name was well known. The two men, marshal and bandit, made *The Bank Robbery* in Cache, Oklahoma, where Jennings had attempted to commit most of his crimes.

Aside from the unusual cast and director, the film is noteworthy because it was the first two-reel western. By rough estimate, over 3,500 multireel westerns have been made since. The film is not remarkable as an example of the filmmaker's art. Tilghman's aim with a camera did not match his skill with a Colt, and the wary lawman evidently felt it was best to maintain a good distance from the action, so most of the film is

Preceding pages: *Scene from* The Great Train Robbery (Edison, 1903): *a dummy, substituted for one of the engineers, is thrown off the train.*
Above: *Broncho Billy Anderson in* Broncho Billy's Bible (Essanay).

shot from far, far away. No attempt was made to identify the famed outlaw—he's just one more face seen fleetingly, if at all, amid the gang of desperadoes.

Although catchy names and distinctive garb had been essential to the heroes of Wild West shows, the heroes of early western films were unidentified—they were not given any screen credit—and they wore in their films pretty much what they usually wore, which, being of the period, was actually quite realistic. Not counting the crowd of passengers on the train, Porter had used as many as forty actors to make *The Great Train Robbery*. They were given no credit, of course, but not all of them have been forgotten. The dramatic close-up of him firing his pistol at the audience has preserved the name of George Barnes. The locomotive driver was played by an actor—and former locomotive driver—named Tom London. His role in *The Great Train Robbery* was only the first of his more than 2,000 appearances in movies—probably the most ever made by an actor. (His last picture was *The Lone Texan*, made in 1959.) And somewhere in *The Great Train Robbery* (he may have performed as many as four roles) is a fellow named Gilbert M. Anderson.

Anderson (born Max Aronson—he changed his name in the hope of getting into vaudeville) was supposed to play the part of one of the mounted robbers. When Porter asked the aspiring actor if he could ride a horse, Anderson shot back, "I was born in the saddle." It was an exaggeration. Although born in Little Rock, Arkansas, and raised in St. Louis, Missouri, Anderson was not an accomplished horseman. When he tried to mount his horse from the wrong side, he was promptly thrown to the ground. He may have been given a role on foot, or he may have been allowed to try his luck again in the saddle—one of the bandits makes a very convincing fall during the final chase scene—either way, Anderson was in the film.

He was amazed at the success of *The Great Train Robbery*, and he determined that his future lay in the movies. On the basis of his part in the film (he undoubtedly also exaggerated his importance in the making of it), Anderson got himself jobs as a director for various film companies. Then, in 1907, he formed a partnership with George K. Spoor, a theatrical booking agent. They called their company Essanay (S and A, after Spoor and Anderson), and they went to California to make short comedy films starring Ben Turpin. Their first endeavor was *Ben Gets a Duck and Is Ducked* (1907), in which Turpin, playing a poor soul with a great hunger, dives into a lake after a duck.

But G. M. Anderson wanted to make westerns. He was aware of the westerns being made by other filmmakers, and he thought there was one thing wrong with all of them—they all lacked a central character, someone for whom the filmgoer could root. A popular actor was the last thing filmmakers wanted, for an actor with a following could demand a higher salary. But Anderson was sure that a hero was needed, and, after moving his company to Niles, California, about 400 miles north of Los Angeles, he looked around for someone (presumably someone with equestrian talents) to take the part. Finding no one to his liking, Anderson chose himself for the role.

He lifted the plot for his first movie, *The Bandit Makes Good* (Essanay, 1908), from a story by Peter B. Kyne. Its leading character was named Broncho Billy. Anderson liked the name and christened himself Broncho Billy Anderson (he later dropped the H to become Bronco Billy Anderson). Between 1908 and 1915, he turned out more than 375 one- and two-reel Broncho Billy westerns, a new film each week, with himself as writer, director, and star. The budget for each film was about $800; each one grossed nearly $50,000. It was quite a racket, and the films made Broncho Billy a popular attraction—and made G. M. Anderson the first movie star, the first actor to be given screen credit. As the first star, Anderson was also the first actor to use stuntmen as stand-ins for all those hard falls.

The Broncho Billy films were the first western serials. Their plots owed a lot to the plots of pulp westerns, and so did their titles: *Broncho Billy and the Baby*, *Broncho Billy and the Greaser*, *Broncho Billy's Love Affair*, *Broncho Billy's Oath*, *Broncho Billy's Mexican Wife*, *Broncho Billy's Leap*, *Broncho Billy's Christian Spirit*, *Broncho Billy's Bible*, *Broncho Billy's Last Spree*, *Broncho Billy's Christmas Dinner*. The character that Anderson created became a staple of westerns—"the good badman," the tough and courageous loner with a dubious past who is shy around womenfolk, lives by his own code, and inevitably does what is right, even (or particularly) when it involves great personal sacrifice. There was no consistency to the films—sometimes Broncho Billy was a doctor, sometimes he was an alcoholic; sometimes he was married—sometimes he was even killed off in the end. No matter what befell him, Broncho Billy was back the next week, hale and hearty (Anderson was a rather plump man), in a new film.

Anderson eventually tired of life in the saddle. Competition from other makers of westerns—particularly William S. Hart—was getting stiff, and, perhaps more important, he was having disagreements with his partner, Spoor. Relinquishing his cowboy role, he made a few comedy films with Stan Laurel, including *Lucky Dog* (1917), notable because one of the minor characters was a certain Oliver Norwell Hardy (it was not until 1926 that Laurel and Hardy were made a team). In 1918, Anderson tried to make a comeback, but feature films (of four or even five reels) were taking over. He made one, *The Son-of-a-Gun*, but it didn't do well, and its failure ended Anderson's screen career. He produced a few more comedy films and disappeared.

Above: *Broncho Billy film in which he plays a lawman with a large star. On the door at left is the symbol of the Essanay Company—putting the company's emblem in frames of the film helped prevent pirating.* Left: *D. W. Griffith as an actor in Edwin S. Porter's* Rescued from an Eagle's Nest *(Edison, 1907).*

For nearly forty years, no one heard from G. M. Anderson. In 1957, after a nationwide search, he was finally located and awarded an Oscar, for Special Contribution to Motion Pictures. In 1965, he was given a small part in a western—a talkie, of course—*The Bounty Killer*. Anderson lived out his last days in a dingy hotel a few blocks from the Paramount studios, watching westerns on television. He liked them and thought they weren't so very different from his Broncho Billy films, just a tad more realistic. As he said of his films, "In those movies, a blank used to turn a corner and kill a man." He also gave his opinion of western-movie audiences: "People don't care why the stagecoach goes over the cliff as long as it goes over."

Griffith and Ince

Anderson was right: excitement is an important part of western movies. Edwin S. Porter knew that, too, and in 1907 he made what he thought was quite an exciting little film with a western setting called *Rescued from an Eagle's Nest*. The plot of the film concerns an eagle that snatches away a farmer's young son and carries him to an aerie high in the mountains; the father takes off in pursuit and rescues the child after a grueling battle. The film was not remarkable in and of itself, but it is important in the history of films because the daring father who tangled with the large stuffed bird was D. W. Griffith.

Griffith did not want to be an actor in films. He wanted to be a serious actor—on the stage. He had come to the Edison studios in the hope of selling a scenario for the opera *Tosca*. The scenario was rejected, but Porter liked Griffith's looks and offered him the lead in his movie. In need of cash, Griffith accepted. He didn't stay long at Edison, however, and the next year he was working for another company, Biograph, where he teamed up with a cameraman named Johann Gottlob Wilhelm ("Billy") Bitzer. Together, the two men set about making movies, and their creativity changed the making of films from a rough process into an art.

The westerns Griffith made are usually neglected in favor of his other films, particularly his monumental *The Birth of a Nation* (1915). But that film made use of many of the techniques and themes Griffith first developed in westerns.

Griffith's most famous westerns—*The Last Drop of Water* (1911); *Fighting Blood* (1911), the first film version of a Zane Grey novel; and *The Battle at Elderbush Gulch* (1913)—share many similar plot elements. Griffith loved the last-minute rescue and the scene of the besieged cabin (both of which he used to great effect in *The Birth of a Nation*). He also loved the close-up, and he provided Bitzer with plenty of interesting faces to focus in on: Lillian and Dorothy

Gish, Mae Marsh, Mary Pickford, Lionel Barrymore, Charles West, Alfred Paget, and Harry Carey, who was soon to earn greater fame working with John Ford.

Griffith was an artist. He spurned scripts and followed his instincts. The fame of his films rests on his editing, and during his career he perfected many methods and invented others, including the fade-in and fade-out, the long shot, the moving-camera shot, the flashback, crosscutting, and montage.

Griffith threw away a lot of film, and had the industry followed his lead, it might have drowned itself in expenses. That it did not is due in large part to one of Griffith's contemporaries, Thomas Ince.

Like Griffith, Ince wanted to be an actor; unlike Griffith, he was usually cast as the heavy. He, too, left acting to work behind the camera, but he approached his work differently. Ince was a businessman. Sent out to California in 1911 to make westerns by the New York Motion Picture Company, he immediately set about organizing his productions. The first thing he did was to reconnect the western movie with its roots by hiring the Miller Brothers' 101 Ranch, a traveling Wild West show that included cowboys, trick riders, Indians, horses, buffalo, cattle, tepees, stagecoaches, and all the related costumes and props. In 1913, he established his so-called Inceville, a piece of land larger than Manhattan Island with perfect terrain for his films. Ince directed a few films himself, but he soon hired other directors and took control of the entire production of the films. He demanded detailed shooting scripts, with every scene and every camera angle planned—and approved by him—well before a foot of film was shot. He demanded tight production schedules. He demanded supervision over every aspect of every film's production, planning, and budgeting for the greatest efficiency. The assembly-line techniques that he introduced and his idea of giving the business end of moviemaking control over the eventual products led to the studio system.

In 1903, when Edwin S. Porter made *The Great Train Robbery*, he shot his outdoor sequences near Dover, New Jersey. The locale didn't look very western, and the local telegraph poles are clearly visible in some of the scenes. Five years later, when D. W. Griffith filmed his first western for Biograph, *The Redman and the Child*, he, too, took his camera and crew to New Jersey. New York City was the center of the film business, and New Jersey was its bucolic backyard. Things might have stayed that way had not Thomas Edison grown impatient with his competitors. Edison was a shrewd businessman, and he was fond of monopolies. He believed that since he had invented the camera he should benefit from its use.

In 1909, he joined his company with the other big companies of the day—Kalem, Lubin, Vitagraph, Biograph, Selig, Essanay (Broncho Billy's outfit), Klein,

Scene from The Battle at Elderbush Gulch *(Biograph, 1913).*
The puppies precipitate the battle with the Indians. Sally
(Mae Marsh) goes to visit her uncle and takes along her
beloved puppies. She has the misfortune of arriving while
the local Indians are celebrating their Feast of the Dogs.

and the French firms Méliès and Pathé—to form the Motion Picture Patents Company. The express purpose of the Patents Company, better known as the Trust, was to monopolize filmmaking in the United States. No one other than the ten members of the Trust was to use Edison's equipment to make films.

It didn't work. The small, independent companies went west. There already were some companies working on the West Coast (Biograph had set up a studio in Los Angeles as early as 1906). They were there for the weather, the vaunted 350 days of annual sunshine. But the West Coast—and in particular Los Angeles—had another appeal for the companies fleeing the Trust: it was near the Mexican border. If representatives of the Patents Company suddenly appeared, the unauthorized filmmakers could grab their equipment and head for the border. Los Angeles even had a third attraction: labor was nonunion and cheap.

By 1913, there were nearly sixty studios operating on the West Coast. The film industry, following the path of the pioneers, had moved west, and the individual studios, growing in size and importance, eventually eclipsed the Trust.

Nineteen thirteen was a good year for westerns, including Thomas Ince's *The Heart of an Indian*, a tragic tale, very sympathetic to the Indians, told in two reels; *Broncho Billy's Oath*, a standard two-reel product of the Essanay Company; D. W. Griffith's *The Battle at Elderbush Gulch*, a thrilling two-reeler with an impressive climax—the last-minute rescue of a cabin

surrounded by Indians; and Cecil B. De Mille's first film, *The Squaw Man*.

The Squaw Man ran for six reels and is frequently credited as the first major Hollywood production. Actually, it was preceded by *Arizona*, a film made by the All Star Feature Corporation. But *Arizona* was not a hit, and *The Squaw Man* was an enormous success, the first big blockbuster, and it established Hollywood as the center of the nation's—and the world's—film industry.

The story of *The Squaw Man* concerns a high-born Englishman, James Wynnegate, who leaves England when he is accused of a crime and takes off for the American West. While there, he marries an Indian. When his brother—making a deathbed confession—clears his name, Wynnegate inherits an earldom and accidentally shoots his wife. (In the play, she decides she cannot go back to England and become a countess and so commits suicide.) He returns to England with his half-breed son.

The star of *The Squaw Man* was Dustin Farnum. De Mille used Farnum again the following year as the hero in *The Virginian*. The Selig Company hired Dustin's brother William for a version of the Rex Beach novel *The Spoilers* (1914), a film about claim-jumping in Alaska that is famous for its final fistic battle. It is difficult to keep track of the various versions of these three films—De Mille made three versions of *The Squaw Man*, including another silent version in 1918 and a talkie in 1931; *The Virginian* of 1914 was only

Dustin Farnum as an Englishman out West in The Squaw Man *(Famous Players-Lasky, 1914).*

the first of four versions; and *The Spoilers* was filmed no fewer than five times: in 1914, 1923, 1930, 1942, and 1955.

William S. Hart

The Squaw Man was based on a play by Edwin Milton Royle. *The Virginian,* based on the Owen Wister novel, had also been made into a play. An actor named William S. Hart played important roles in both (while performing in the stage version of *The Virginian* he had complained to Wister about the plot of the book—he didn't think any westerner would help hang a friend). In 1912, Hart was playing in *The Trail of the Lonesome Pine* (De Mille made it into a movie in 1916). He went with the play on the road to Los Angeles, and while there he visited Thomas Ince. Hart first met Ince during the winter of 1903, when the two of them, both between acting jobs, shared a room in a cheap hotel in New York City. Hart was a stage actor, but his real love was the West, and he had passed the time telling Ince stories about the Indians and their tragic fate and the lawmen and their heroic exploits. Ince listened—he may have had little choice—and he remembered.

When Ince met him again in 1912, Hart was still full of the West. Hart made Ince promise him a chance to make westerns. Two years later, Hart reappeared, eager to take Ince up on his promise. Begrudgingly—westerns were in a slump in 1914—Ince gave him a chance, and Hart became one of the director-actors under Ince's tight control.

William Surrey Hart was 44 when he began his film career. He had been a successful actor on the stage for twenty years, and he brought to his movies all the acting methods he had used in the ponderous melodramas of that period. He was a serious man, and he wasn't drawn to moviemaking just in the hope of making money (he was consistently bilked by Ince)— he came to deliver a message, his version of the old West, the West he had known as a child. He was born in Newburgh, New York, but his family had moved west, and he had passed his early years in the Dakota Territories, where he claimed to have spent time among the Sioux and to have befriended the local lawmen. He had seen gunfights in the streets of western towns, had spent time as a cowhand, and he had something to say about the West.

The character that Hart evolved was a continuation of Broncho Billy's good badman. The Hart hero was a man with a past, a man outside the law who, usually because of a woman's gentle affections, ends up protecting the innocent, defending the oppressed, and casting aside his former ways in favor of a new life (in the company of the female). Hart was physically perfect for the part; his long, bony, sad face seemed to

William S. Hart bursting through a door to confront the villains in a scene from Tumbleweeds *(United Artists, 1925).*

Scenes from four versions of The Spoilers. Opposite top: *1914.* Opposite bottom: *Near the end of the famous fight, 1930.* Above: *Dealing with claim jumpers in 1942.* Left: *Jeff Chandler (left) and Rory Calhoun in the 1955 issue.*

27

express constant nostalgia or remorse, and he was adept at manipulating his clear, sharp eyes—to show he was thinking, he would squint more narrowly; to show he was angry, he would glare.

Hart's westerns are noted for their "realism," and Hart is frequently credited with making the first "adult" westerns. The realism had nothing to do with the plots or with Hart's emotive acting. Rather, Hart's films seem realistic because his version of the West is encased in layers of dust. There are pigs and chickens running wild in the muddy streets of Hart's towns. The buildings—knocked-together shabby shacks—visibly lean against one another, and the saloons have dirt floors. And when Hart rode into town, half-hidden by the dust kicked up by his horse, he didn't just lope into the nearest saloon to slake his thirst; rather, he would thoughtfully lead his horse to a water trough. (Horses were very important to Hart. His favorite was named Fritz, and he gave Fritz screen credit. Hart was a very sentimental man.)

The mud and the dust were actually common features of early western films. Filmmakers had not yet thought to water down the dirt streets; it had not yet occurred to them that the West should look like anything other than what it really looked like. Hart's films get credit for their realism probably because so many of them have survived.

Hart's westerns were "adult" in the sense that they dealt with serious, if not grim, subjects. When Hart unholstered his twin Colts and, hugging his weapons close to his chest, burst in upon the villains, he was the embodiment of the avenging angel. However realistic the settings, costumes, and weapons, Hart's films had a strong sense of the melodramatic. His *Wild Bill Hickok* (1923) begins with a subtitle in which he apologizes to the audience for not resembling in any way the subject of the film. He did not think it necessary to apologize for the fact that the plot in no way approached the truth.

Hart made many westerns between 1914 and 1925, including *The Passing of Two Gun Hicks, The Conversion of Frosty Blake, Truthful Tulliver, The Disciple, The Square Deal Man, The Sheriff's Streak of Yellow, The Narrow Trail* (a tribute to Fritz), *Blue Blazes Rawden, The Toll Gate, The Aryan, Hell's Hinges, The Primal Lure,* and *Tumbleweeds.*

One of the best of these is *Hell's Hinges* (Triangle, 1916), in which Hart plays a character named Blaze Tracey, described by a subtitle as "the embodiment of the best and worst of the early west." The title of the film comes from the nickname of the town, "a town known on the government surveyor's maps as Placer Centre, but throughout the length and breadth of the sun-baked territory as just plain Hell's Hinges, and a good place to 'ride wide of.' "

To this "gun-fighting, man-killing, devil's den of

The interior of the Palace of Joy Saloon, headquarters of iniquity in Placer Centre, the town better known as Hell's Hinges (Triangle, 1916). Hart is seated at center; note the dirt floor.

iniquity that scorched even the sun-parched soil on which it stood" are sent a weak-willed minister (his mother chose the calling for him—he would rather pass his time with women and wine) and his virtuous sister, Faith. The local gang leader, Silk Miller ("mingling the oily craftiness of a Mexican with the deadly treachery of a rattler") wants Blaze to help drive the minister out of town, but at first sight of Faith, Blaze is touched by her sincere goodness and, eventually, is converted to God's way. As he himself reports, "When a woman like her says there's a God, there is one, and He sure must be worth trailin' with."

The minister is corrupted by the evil elements in the town (who while away their free time in the Palace of Joy Saloon) and joins with them when they decide to burn down the church. There follows a desperate battle between the crowd of godless villains and the small group of decent citizens. The minister is killed, the church is set afire, and the God-fearing folk are run out of town into the desert. Blaze, of course, was out of town during all this commotion. Returning, he is apprised of current events, becomes enraged, kills Silk Miller, and burns the entire town to the ground. Then he and Faith head out toward the mountains to make a new future.

Hart's career in films was marked by conflicts with his producers, who wanted him to trade some of his realism for a little of Tom Mix's showmanship. His personal life had its problems, too. He lived with his sister, and when he finally wed, at age 51, his marriage lasted only a few months. The virtuous Hart was even slapped with an embarrassing paternity suit—he was, of course, found to be blameless.

In 1919, when Douglas Fairbanks, Charlie Chaplin, D. W. Griffith, and Mary Pickford got together to form United Artists, they invited Hart to join them. He declined the offer, but it was for United Artists that he made his greatest film, *Tumbleweeds* (1925).

A poignant tale about the end of the West and the end of the freedom-loving cowboys (the "tumbleweeds" of the title), the film tells the story of the 1889 land rush in the Cherokee Strip of Oklahoma. The film begins as the cowhands round up the last cattle, abandoning the land to make room for the settlers. "Boys," exclaims Hart in a subtitle, "it's the last of the West," and he and his pals remove their hats to mark the moment. Throughout the film, Hart strides about bolt upright, his chest pulled in as though he were inhaling the last of some beloved breeze. There are villains, of course, and there is a girl. One of the villains wants the girl, and both of the villains want to steal the best land. When Hart first meets the girl he is, naturally, bewildered, and he decides to take off for South America, where there are cows, which are much "more reliable than women." The villains' plot is foiled, but not before a dramatic reenactment of the land rush and a

Opposite top: *While working on* Three Word Brand *(Paramount, 1921), Hart gives actress Jane Novak a kiss (they were engaged at the time). In the film, Hart plays three roles—the hero, and the hero's father and brother.* Opposite bottom: *Jane Novak and Tom Mix.* Above: *Hoot Gibson, at right, with a pal, sharing a Coke and some strong glances.*

breathtaking horse race by Hart, his horse hitting the ground hard, clods of earth flying and dust enveloping him. At one point, as he rides along the edge of a ridge, the picture is shot from beneath, and horse and rider seem to leave the ground. He wins the race, gets the land and the girl, but the penultimate scene is one of implied sorrow—a tumbleweed caught in barbed wire.

Although it is unmistakably a Hart western, there are indications in *Tumbleweeds* that Hart, in accordance with the demands of his producers, was trying to make this film more colorful than his usual productions. In the film Hart has a sidekick, named Kentucky Rose, a clowning character who frequently consults a handless pocketwatch; and at one point, Hart makes a dramatic getaway by polevaulting over a fence onto his horse. The humorous sidekick and the circus acrobatics were not vintage Hart; they were more suited to Tom Mix.

Tom Mix began making films before Hart did, and Mix's career outlasted Hart's by a decade. Mix represented a different sort of western hero. He did not play a good badman. If the character Mix played had any past at all, it was as a Boy Scout with a chest laden with merit badges. He was a skilled horseman, and he had a sense of showmanship and flair that made Hart seem tired and staid.

Mix's films were the forerunners of the so-called B westerns, films that eventually occupied the B, or secondary, position in a double feature. The once-a-week Broncho Billy films had shown the way. Like the Broncho Billy films, the B westerns owed their plots to pulp westerns, and these simple plots served only as an excuse for Wild West show action—trick riding, pistol twirling, and the accurate throwing of lariats. B western heroes assumed Wild West show attire—they frequently wore white and always wore outfits that would have immobilized a working cowhand.

The heroes of B westerns rarely fired guns (some, like Hoot Gibson, didn't usually wear them—Gibson had to borrow a firearm from a pal when one was needed). They usually roped the villain rather than shooting him, but when they did resort to gunplay these heroes did not need to aim their revolvers. Nor were they forced to rely on gunpowder—or so it seemed—preferring to fling the bullet out of their gun with a fast, downward slashing movement. They trusted in their virtue to guide the projectile—not to the villain's heart, but to his gunhand, cleanly knocking away his weapon without breaking the skin.

As time passed, the differences between the B westerns and other western films became more pronounced. Tom Mix was joined by Hoot Gibson, Ken Maynard, and a host of others who eventually included such heroes as Gene Autry, Tex Ritter, Roy Rogers, The Lone Ranger, and Hopalong Cassidy. With the coming of sound, a new breed of star arrived, those happy-go-lucky singing cowboys.

Many actors and directors got their start in B westerns (also called programmers, or serials), and many of the films are well-made and entertaining. Before television finally laid them to rest, B westerns had evolved a fantasy world, with airplanes, trains, cars, horses, sixshooters, cowboy hats, and business suits all united by the joyous cowboy tunes.

Hart's subtle nod to Tom Mix's flamboyance did not save him. *Tumbleweeds* was his last film. It was not a success, and Hart retired to his ranch to write novels and his autobiography. He occasionally worked as a consultant on western films, and his voice was frequently heard complaining about the lack of authenticity in the films made by other men. The truth is that he had been overtaken by more than Tom Mix.

Silent epics

When William S. Hart had asked Thomas Ince for the opportunity to make westerns, Ince had hesitated because westerns were in a slump; they didn't seem to have anything new to offer. Hart—and Mix—had made the western popular again, but by 1923, twenty years after the first western, westerns were again falling out of popularity. Only fifty westerns were made in 1923. But one year later, in 1924, there were 125. The reason for the renewed popularity was *The Covered Wagon* (Paramount, 1923), which leapt over the dashing personalities of Hart and Mix and united the western with American history.

The plot of *The Covered Wagon* is not very dramatic; it is a love triangle (the good guy and the bad guy are after the same girl), and when viewed today the film seems actionless. But it was the first western epic, and its documentarylike style gave it the feel of authenticity and brought to life, in an inspiring way, the hardships and courage of the pioneers.

Directed by James Cruze and photographed in Nevada, the film chronicles the 2,000-mile journey of a wagon train along the Oregon Trail in 1849. Aside from the love triangle, the film does not concern itself as much with individuals (there are two drunken scouts to provide humor) as with the wagon train, the long line of wagons winding across the plains. There are attacks by Indians, brush fires, a buffalo hunt, and the fording of a swollen river. The courageous settlers are the heroes, but the dominant characters in the film are the landscapes—the vast plains and the mountains—

The Iron Horse *(Fox, 1924).*

33

and the wagon wheels, forever rolling forward.

For all its faults, *The Covered Wagon* proved that there was much more to westerns than the pathos of Hart and the showmanship of Mix. Hart, of course, didn't like the film. He claimed that it contained errors "that would make a western man refuse to speak to his own brother." He was particularly piqued by a scene in which the wagon train camps in a closed canyon (easy prey to the marauding Indians) and the scene of the river fording, in which, Hart pointed out, the cattle were kept in their neck yokes. But Hart's lamentations did nothing to diminish the popularity of the film, and it marked the way for many westerns to come. Will Rogers paid it great tribute by making fun of it in *Two Wagons, Both Covered*, in which the unfortunate pioneers fall victim to land speculators.

The Covered Wagon was ten reels long; in 1924, William Fox's Fox Film Corporation (which joined with Twentieth Century in 1935 to form 20th Century-Fox) outdid it with another epic about a conveyance that settled the West—the twelve-reel *The Iron Horse*, the story of the construction of the Union Pacific Railroad.

The Iron Horse was made on a truly epic scale. Aside from the main actors, its cast listed "A Regiment of United States troops and cavalry; 3,000 Railway Workmen; 1,000 Chinese Laborers; 800 Pawnee, Sioux, and Cheyenne Indians; 2,800 horses; 1,300 buffalo; 10,000 Texas steers." Director John Ford assembled this enormous cast in the Nevada desert. There were so many people that it was necessary to print a daily newspaper to record such events as births, deaths, and marriages.

Like *The Covered Wagon*, *The Iron Horse* uses a simple plot (a son's search for the man who murdered his father) to unite the story, but Ford masterfully combines the personal story with the historic, giving the action of the film a sense of mythic importance, of national destiny. The film begins and ends with Abraham Lincoln, who expresses his desire to see the nation united by the railroad, and although it is not always historically accurate, the film is exciting and includes one of Ford's most dramatically staged Indian attacks.

The Iron Horse was John Ford's forty-ninth movie and his fortieth western. He was 29 years old, having started in movies in 1914. *The Iron Horse* is one of the three Ford westerns from the silent period that survive today (the other two are *Straight Shooting* and *Three Badmen*). It is also the longest film Ford ever made. After *Three Badmen* (1926) Ford left the western for other films. When he returned thirteen years later, he was to change it forever.

Cruze's *The Covered Wagon* led to more than just *The Iron Horse*. In 1924, a sequel to *The Covered Wagon, North of '36*, was made, directed by Irvin Willat. In 1925, Cruze himself made another western epic,

Opposite top: *Harry Carey in* Straight Shooting
(Universal, 1917). Opposite bottom: *Ricardo Cortez*
as a rider in The Pony Express *(Paramount, 1925).*
Above: *Fording a river in* North of '36 *(Paramount, 1924).*

The Pony Express, a film that foresaw the "company" epics (such as *Union Pacific, Wells Fargo,* and *Western Union*) soon to come. *The Pony Express* is also interesting because its villain, a thief and murderer, goes free at the end. The year 1925 also included Hart's epic, *Tumbleweeds.* The last in this series of silent epics appeared in 1927: *The Vanishing American.*

Directed by George B. Seitz, **The Vanishing American** (Paramount) relates no less than the history of the West from prehistoric times to the present. The screenplay, by Ethel Doherty, was based on a novel by Zane Grey; the star of the film was Richard Dix. When it was made, it was intended to portray the heroic and tragic story of the American Indian, but when viewed today its concern with superior races seems like an adumbration of fascism. The theme of the film is that one race replaces another, the stronger defeating and replacing the weaker. It begins with a prologue in which one race overtakes another, from cavemen to basket weavers to cliff dwellers. And then, "from no man knows where" (as a subtitle says), the Indian appears and destroys the cliff dwellers—but not before one of the cliff-dwelling priests puts a curse on the Indians: "May the Father drive you into darkness, as you drive us. May He send a stronger race to grind you into dust and scatter you through the four worlds of lamentation." It isn't long before Coronado and his band of explorers arrive. The Indians, although they suffer at the hands of unscrupulous agents, are not wiped out, and they survive to take part in the First World War.

Not all silent westerns were so somber. Aside from the humor in Tom Mix, Hart made a few humorous films, as did Douglas Fairbanks, such as *Manhattan Madness* (1916). Even Buster Keaton went west in *Go West* (1925), in which he plays a character named Friendless who befriends a cow named Brown Eyes.

The great epics of the mid-twenties, dramatic celebrations of the nation's past, thrilled audiences and gave the western a new hero—the West itself. Broncho Billy and William S. Hart had helped mold the man of the West, the tough individualist with a keen sense of honor and a personal code of ethics, the lone man on a horse—the American hero. Equal to the man was the terrain he moved through, America just as America thinks of itself—beautiful but rugged, open, with room to roam freely and to play out an endless store of history and legend.

For a short period, however, the western's dependence on the outdoors seemed to spell its doom. For in 1927, in a film called *The Jazz Singer,* Al Jolson turned to the audience and *said,* "You ain't heard nothin' yet, folks."

Top: *Director George B. Seitz, in white shirt and hat, discussing a drum with Navajo Indians on location for* The Vanishing American *(Paramount, 1927). Right:* Buster Keaton as Friendless in Go West *(MGM, 1925).*

Iron Men and
Iron Horses

1929–1939

"The thrill of it all!"

The advent of motion pictures with sound delighted moviegoers but presented problems to the makers of westerns. It was one thing to record sound within the four walls of a studio set; how could it be done outdoors? The man who showed the way was Raoul Walsh, who had been active as both a director and an actor since 1909. (He played John Wilkes Booth in *The Birth of a Nation.*) Walsh was a colorful man. As a youth he had gone to sea, traveled in Europe, and taken part in Texas cattle drives. He dressed like a cowboy, was suitably lanky, rolled his own Bull Durham cigarettes, and was fond of strong drink.

In 1929, Walsh went to Zion County, Utah, to film *In Old Arizona* (Fox)—had it been 1979, he would have gone to Spain. He set up his microphones in trees and under rocks and went about making the first outdoor talking picture. It was also the first sound western about the Cisco Kid, the character from O. Henry's story "The Caballero's Way." The film had no chase scene—that would have been too difficult to record—and more than half an hour of it takes place within a cabin, but it proved that westerns could be as noisy as other films.

Walsh had originally intended to both direct and star in the film, but while he was driving through the desert one night, a jackrabbit jumped through the car's windshield. The flying glass injured Walsh's right eye, ending his acting career. The lead in the picture was given to Warner Baxter, who was awarded an Academy Award for his performance as Cisco.

Walsh eventually wearied of the constant round of treatments for the injured eye, and he had it removed, adding an eyepatch to his already imposing presence. He claimed women were afraid of him.

There was more to be heard in westerns than galloping horses and gunshots. The same year as *In Old Arizona,* the first talking version of *The Virginian* appeared, allowing audiences to hear the Virginian's immortal line, slightly reworded from Wister's novel: "If you want to call me that, *smile!*" The line was spoken by Gary Cooper.

The Virginian (Paramount, 1929), directed by Victor Fleming (who ten years later directed *Gone with the Wind*), was not Cooper's first film. It wasn't even his first western. Beginning as a cowboy extra in 1925, he had moved quickly to leading roles, and by the time of *The Virginian,* he was a popular star. Although he acted in many nonwesterns during his thirty-six-year career as an actor, it was in westerns that he made his greatest mark, and in retrospect his arrival nearly equals the arrival of sound. Tall and soft-spoken, Cooper embodied the western hero, and when he died, in 1961, some people declared the western itself dead.

Cooper directed the famous line to the villain, Trampas, played by Walter Huston in his first western appearance. Richard Arlen played the Virginian's pal, Steve, and Mary Brian played the schoolmarm, Molly Wood. The plot of *The Virginian* concerns cattle rustling in Wyoming. As foreman of the Box H Ranch, the Virginian is forced to take part in the lynching of Steve, when the latter is discovered stealing cattle for Trampas. The Virginian and Trampas eventually get to shoot it out.

Although it is not clear in the movie, and even in the novel it is not explicitly stated, the story of *The Virginian* is set against the Johnson County War, the famous Wyoming cattlemen-versus-homesteaders conflict that has been used as the general theme for a number of westerns, including *Shane,* another film with a one-name hero. The war itself reached its most dramatic moment in April of 1892, when the wealthy cattlemen (who believed the small landowners were rustling their cattle) prepared a list of the men they wanted killed and hired fifty gunmen to invade Johnson County. More than fifty years after the first talking version of *The Virginian,* the story of the Johnson County War provided the plot of *Heaven's Gate.*

Not far behind Gary Cooper was John Wayne, who began his career in films as a prop man, and had his first role (unbilled) in 1928. Like Cooper, Wayne worked as a stuntman and had small parts in films, including a few by John Ford. When one-eyed Raoul Walsh went looking for a leading man for his upcoming film, *The Big Trail* (Fox, 1930), Ford recommended Wayne to him. At that time, Wayne was still Marion Michael Morrison, and Walsh later claimed credit for naming him John Wayne—he said he had named him after General Anthony "Mad Dog" Wayne. (Marion Michael Morrison was already known as Duke, a childhood nickname he had been given because of his fondness for a dog of that name.) Cast as the star of *The Big Trail,* Wayne played the part of Brick Coleman, a trapper who acts as scout for a wagon train on the Oregon Trail while seeking revenge for his brother's murder. The film made use of all the epic ingredients made famous by *The Covered Wagon*—an Indian attack, a buffalo hunt, the crossing of a swollen river. Unfortunately, the film was made in a 70mm widescreen process, and movie theaters were just installing the equipment for sound—only a dozen theaters were equipped to show the wide-screen films. (It was eventually rereleased in 35mm.) That fact and Wayne's stilted acting are usually given as explanations for the film's poor showing at the box office. After his part in *The Big Trail,* Wayne was relegated to B westerns—he even played the part of a singing cowboy ("Singin' Sandy") in *Riders of Destiny* (1933). Wayne languished in B westerns until John Ford chose him for *Stagecoach* in 1939.

Preceding pages: *The stagecoach in Monument Valley in* Stagecoach *(United Artists, 1939). Note the snow.* Above *(left to right): Warner Baxter, Dorothy Burgess, and Edmund Lowe in* In Old Arizona *(Fox, 1929).* Left: *Gary Cooper (standing at left in white shirt); Eugene Pallette (holding bedroll); and Richard Arlen (standing in black) in* The Virginian *(Paramount, 1929).*

The Big Trail was not the only film made in 1930 for the wide screen. King Vidor's *Billy the Kid* (MGM, 1930) relied on its 70mm Realife format to such an extent that the film has almost no close-ups, which only adds to its feeling of stark loneliness. The script for the film was based on *The Saga of Billy the Kid* (1926), written by Walter Noble Burns, and Vidor hired William S. Hart as technical adviser. Hart contributed a gun used by the real Billy, and the seedy clothing, dusty streets, and rickety towns may be the result of Hart's influence. For even greater realism, the film was shot on the actual locations of the Lincoln County War, the New Mexico conflict in which Billy the Kid came to fame. The film's dark mood is more the result of Vidor's direction than its authentic scenery: its sinister ambience foreshadows Vidor's *Duel in the Sun* (1946). Vidor's West seems barren and harsh, a lawless place where death is brutal and commonplace. The ending of the film, in which Garrett (Wallace Beery) lets Billy (Johnny Mack Brown) escape over the border into Mexico, contradicts both history and the sense of the film—it also anticipates the ending of Ford's *Stagecoach*. (The film was made with an alternate, more historical ending in which Billy is killed by Garrett, but this ending was used only in the European release of the film.)

(King Vidor, who had made his first full-length film, *The Turn in the Road*, in 1919, died in 1982. His last role in a film was the part of a senile grandfather in 1982's *Love and Money*.)

Another innovation in sound occurred in 1930 in **The Indians Are Coming** (Universal, 1930). Chief Thunderbird spoke in his native Sioux, the first instance of Indian language in a western.

When Edna Ferber's *Cimarron* was published in 1930, it became an instant best-seller, and in 1931, with all the suitable fanfare, the film version appeared, enjoyed great success, and won the Academy Award as best picture—the only western, thus far, to do so. *Cimarron* (RKO, 1931), directed by Wesley Ruggles, begins with the Cherokee Strip land rush (the event that ends Hart's *Tumbleweeds*) and follows the subsequent history of Oklahoma as experienced by one family. The hero of the film, Yancey Cravat (Richard Dix), is the personification of the pioneer spirit, a man who moves on as soon as he senses civilization is settling in around him. Cravat explains his wanderlust with a quote from *The Merchant of Venice:* "Why should a man, whose blood is warm within, sit like his grandsire cut in alabaster?" Cravat's idealism, his determined efforts as a lawyer and editor in support of unpopular causes, his heroism as a pistoleer, and his eloquence as a poet made him precisely the kind of larger-than-life character that must have settled the West. Cravat was matched with a patient and understanding wife (Irene Dunne).

Cimarron was the last big-budget epic western for

Opposite: *John Wayne in* The Big Trail *(Fox, 1930).* Above: *Walter Huston (right) and Harry Carey (second from right) in* Law and Order *(Universal, 1932).* Left: *George O'Brien in the first talking version of* The Riders of the Purple Sage *(Fox, 1931).*

quite a while. When the Depression took hold, westerns fell out of favor as audiences sought more light-hearted entertainment, saved money by tuning in their radios, and showed their preference for another—far more contemporary—type of film: the gangster film.

By 1931, gangster films were more popular at the box office than westerns, and they held their lead until the end of the decade. Gangster films had more to say about the world Americans were facing—a grim world of poverty and lawlessness. There was no room in the gangster's world for a hero like Yancey Cravat. There was nowhere to move on to—there was nothing over the horizon but more of the same dust bowl, more of the same despair. The heroes of gangster films were the villains: tough individuals who had fought their way to the top, men whose brutality was a reflection of a brutal society. The women in gangster films, sexy gun molls, were more interesting and more contemporary than the demure females of the plains.

The prolific author W. R. Burnett turned out many popular novels and stories that were made into films, including *The Asphalt Jungle*, *The Dark Command*, *High Sierra*, *Little Caesar*, and *Saint Johnson*. *Little Caesar* was made into the most popular gangster film of the period; *Saint Johnson* was made into one of the best and most neglected westerns of all time, *Law and Order* (Universal, 1932), directed by Edward L. Cahn.

John Huston wrote the screenplay for *Law and Order*, based on Burnett's *Saint Johnson*, but although the hero's name is Frame ("Saint") Johnson, his character is clearly based on Wyatt Earp. Walter Huston played Johnson, and Harry Carey played a character named Ed Brandt—based on Doc Holliday. The movie ends with one of the best film versions of the gunfight at the O.K. Corral. (The film was remade in 1953 with Ronald Reagan in the lead role.)

The real Wyatt Earp died in January of 1929. He had spent a lot of time during his last years hanging around movie lots. He was a friend of both William S. Hart and Tom Mix—they both served as pallbearers at his funeral—and he was occasionally called on to supply his expert advice.

Earp was convinced that the public would be interested in hearing his life story. He put together a long manuscript, but he couldn't interest any publishers in his tale. Then, in 1928, he met Stuart N. Lake. Lake listened to Earp's story, wrote it all down, and in 1931 published *Wyatt Earp: Frontier Marshal*. Earp did not live to see the book—nor did he get a chance to enjoy the four films that were based on it.

The first of these, *Frontier Marshal*, appeared in 1934, released by Fox and directed by Lewis Seiler. This first adaptation of Lake's book is notable for a performance by Irene Bentley in which she goes out of her way to imitate Mae West. The cast also includes Berton Churchill who, as the town mayor, is the villain (five years later Churchill performed a similar role as the banker in *Stagecoach*). The film includes at least one error—gleefully noted by critics. A letter going from Tombstone to another town is stolen by a bandit who robs the stage going *into* Tombstone.

Another, much better *Frontier Marshal* appeared in 1939, again released by Fox. Directed by Allan Dwan, it starred Randolph Scott as Wyatt, Jon Hall as Virgil Earp, and Cesar Romero as Doc Holliday. The gentlemanly, Virginia-born Scott, whose career in films began in 1929 after a fortuitous encounter with Howard Hughes on a golf course, was on his way to becoming a western star. (He had helped Gary Cooper with his accent in *The Virginian*.) Although an excellent film, *Frontier Marshal* was lost in the crowd of westerns that came out that year. But it was not the end of Lake's book. Both Ford's *My Darling Clementine* (1946) and Louis King's *Powder River* (1953) were based on the book. It's a shame Earp didn't live to enjoy his fame.

The Arizonian (RKO, 1935), directed by Charles Vidor, while not based on Lake's book, dealt with a very Earp-like marshal cleaning up a nasty town named Silver City. Richard Dix plays the reform marshal who has the ability to disarm villains simply by staring at them and can convert outlaws with nothing more than his virtuous presence.

King Vidor returned to the western with *The Texas Rangers* (Paramount, 1936), which claimed to be based on incidents from the files of the Rangers. The plot, however, is quite standard: two former outlaws (Fred MacMurray and Jack Oakie) join the Rangers and have to hunt down their old partner (Lloyd Nolan). The Rangers resemble frontier G-men, except, of course, that the FBI, ever cautious about hiring the right men, would never have pinned badges on men with criminal records.

Zane Grey novels enjoyed their usual popularity during the thirties. *The Riders of the Purple Sage* (Fox) made its sound appearance in 1931 (Tom Mix had starred in a silent version in 1925), but perhaps the best Zane Grey western of the period was *To the Last Man* (Paramount, 1933), which stars Randolph Scott and Richard Dix. The film was directed by Henry Hathaway, who had worked as assistant director on a 1923 silent version of the same story directed by Victor Fleming. Grey's novel is based on the Graham-Tewksbury feud, which took place in Pleasant Valley in the Tonto Basin of Arizona from 1886 to 1892. What began as a spat between cattlemen and sheepmen grew to become a vicious feud that wiped out the two warring clans. *To the Last Man* anticipates the Tollivers-versus-Falins feud of *The Trail of the Lonesome Pine* (Paramount, 1936), which included in its cast Henry Fonda,

Production still of Sylvia Sidney and Henry Fonda in The Trail of the Lonesome Pine *(Paramount, 1936).*

already on his way to becoming one of America's greatest actors.

The Last Round-Up (Paramount, 1934), directed by Henry Hathaway, starred Randolph Scott and included as the villain the venerable star of silent films Monte Blue. The film is based on Zane Grey's *The Border Legion*—it got its new title from a popular song on the radio. *The Last Round-Up* is of particular interest because, like many westerns before and after it, it was declared by critics to be the last of a dying breed—westerns, they said, were truly on their way out, having been replaced, of course, by the gangster film. The truth is that the end of Prohibition, in 1933, had taken away a lot of the gangster film's power, and although the mid-thirties saw few important westerns, the decade ended in a flood of them that increased their popularity and prepared the way for the forties.

Viva Villa! (MGM, 1934) is an outstanding film, and although it does not deal with the American West, it stands as an early indication of what Hollywood had in store for Mexican politics. Wallace Beery's performance as Villa—at once a foolish, childishly romantic freedom fighter and a ruthless killer—is gripping, and the direction of the film, begun by Howard Hawks and finished by Jack Conway, is at times haunting. But it is the film's location that is important. The revolutionary period in Mexico, with its divided loyalties and opportunities for constant gunplay, would soon provide Hollywood with exactly what it had provided numerous former cowpunchers and outlaws—virgin territory, an escape from the overly civilized life north of the border, and a chance to continue a way of life.

In *The Plainsman* (Paramount, 1936), Cecil B. De Mille brought the epic back to the western. The film begins with President Abraham Lincoln being reminded by his wife that they are going to be late for the theater if he doesn't get a move on, and it maintains its guise of history by assembling a lot of famous names from the old West: Gary Cooper plays Wild Bill Hickok; Jean Arthur plays Calamity Jane; James Ellison is Buffalo Bill Cody and Helen Burgess is Mrs. Buffalo Bill; even General Custer takes part, played by John Miljan. The hero, Hickok, dies at the end, and, in the film's nicest scene, his body seems to melt into the ground—the legend of Wild Bill becomes part of the land itself.

Wells Fargo (Paramount, 1937), directed by Frank Lloyd, celebrates a business venture that helped settle the West. The film was Joel McCrea's first western (he plays opposite his real wife, Frances Dee), and tells the story of twenty-five years of the company's history, beginning with the original decision to run passengers across the country. De Mille must have been impressed with McCrea's performance for he chose him to star in *Union Pacific* (Paramount, 1939), the story of the transcontinental railroad. De Mille took some of his action sequences from Ford's *The Iron Horse* and added some of his own, including a spectacular train wreck, a train holdup, and the destruction of a saloon.

The railroad and the destruction of a saloon figure largely in *Dodge City* (Warner Brothers, 1939), Errol Flynn's first western—in fact, the first of three Warner Brothers westerns that have a lot in common: they were all directed by Michael Curtiz, and they all have screenplays by Robert Buckner and music by Max Steiner. And all three star Errol Flynn and share an aggressive disdain for history.

Dodge City begins in Kansas in 1866 with Colonel Dodge and a group of businessmen on their way to name the new city. The train—variously referred to as a "snortin' teapot" and a "coffeepot on wheels"—races a stagecoach and wins, prompting Colonel Dodge to exclaim, "Iron men and iron horses—that's progress!" In epic fashion, a golden spike is used to unite the rail lines that meet at the location of the new town. But the town does not respond well to its prosperity, and by 1872 (as a subtitle informs the viewer) it has become "a town with no ethics but cash and killings." But then Flynn arrives in town, an Irish soldier of fortune with the name Wade Hatton. He has an interesting past, having served as a soldier in India, a cowboy in Texas, a Cuban revolutionary, and a soldier for the South during the Civil War. He even has two sidekicks—Rusty and Tex.

The monstrous saloon brawl for which the film is famous and which appears as stock footage in many other films (mostly comedies) begins when the band in a local saloon plays a Northern song and Hatton's boys retaliate with a rousing chorus of "Dixie"—a musical confrontation Curtiz made better use of in his *Casablanca* (1943).

When a school picnic collides with a street gunfight and a little boy is killed, Hatton takes on the role of sheriff, changing his fringed frontiersman shirt for a well-ironed red one and pinning the badge on his gunbelt. Just when he has cleaned up the town and is about to take off with his new wife (Olivia De Havilland), Colonel Dodge reappears to report that Virginia City now needs his help. So Flynn and his bride happily cancel their honeymoon plans and set out for Virginia City.

Only Flynn arrives, and to get there he has to first dig his way out of Libby Prison, for *Virginia City* (Warner Brothers, 1940) is not about cleaning up another dirty western town—it is a tale of the Civil War. (De Havilland never makes it to Virginia City—she is replaced as heroine by Miriam Hopkins—but she returns in the next film.) Flynn is a Northern officer, Randolph Scott is his counterpart in gray, Humphrey Bogart is a Mexican bandit (with a vaguely suitable accent) named John Murrell, and all three are after $5 million in gold

Top left: *Wallace Beery (left) as Pancho Villa and Leo Carrillo as General Sierra divide up some spoils in* Viva Villa! *(MGM, 1934).* Left: *Bob Burns (left) and Joel McCrea in* Wells Fargo *(Paramount, 1937).* Top: *Gary Cooper in* The Plainsman *(Paramount, 1936).* Above: *Brian Donlevy (center) and gang in* Union Pacific *(Paramount, 1939).*

Below *(left to right): Alan Hale, Errol Flynn, and Guinn "Big Boy" Williams in* Dodge City *(Warner Brothers, 1939).* Bottom: *Miriam Hopkins and Errol Flynn in* Virginia City *(Warner Brothers, 1940).* Right: *Ronald Reagan (center), Errol Flynn (to Reagan's left), and Raymond Massey in* The Santa Fe Trail *(Warner Brothers, 1940).*

bullion that Confederate sympathizers out West have offered the cause of the South. Flynn's mission is to make sure the gold never reaches Dixie (as it turns out, it never reaches anyone).

The third western in the series, *The Santa Fe Trail* (Warner Brothers, 1940), begins with the West Point class of 1854, which is distorted to include as graduates Phil Sheridan, James Longstreet, Jeb Stuart, and George A. Custer (most attended West Point; no two graduated at the same time). Flynn, as always the hero, plays Stuart; he has, as his humorous sidekick, a man with great promise for the future: George A. Custer, played by Ronald Reagan.

The two good-natured former classmates, one from the South and one from the North, agree not to let politics come between them; instead, they bicker over possession of the hand of De Havilland. Flynn wins, and Reagan laments, "I guess we can't all have charm and good looks, too." The plot of the film concerns a more serious matter: John Brown, his seizure of the arsenal at Harpers Ferry, and his subsequent capture and hanging. Raymond Massey plays a convincingly possessed Brown ("I am a David armed with power and the glory!"), but the film stumbles in its treatment of him, vaguely suggesting that he was nothing more than a religious fanatic. Nor does the film bother to point out the importance of Harpers Ferry—it ends with Flynn's marriage to De Havilland, a small union overshadowed by the historic division about to take place.

Virginia City was not Bogart's only western. In *The Oklahoma Kid* (Warner Brothers, 1939), directed by Lloyd Bacon, he plays a villain named Whip McCord. James Cagney, looking very much like a kid, plays the title role. Cagney and Bogart both felt better suited to gangster films, and they found their cowboy getups quite humorous. But they wear their garb well, and their edge-of-hysteria acting adds charm to the film. Like Curtiz's three films, *The Oklahoma Kid* has a rousing Max Steiner score, and the screenplay was written by Robert Buckner (among others). The film has a lot of action and not a little humor, such as when Cagney rides into a town and politely asks directions of a man tacking up a wanted poster that has Cagney's face on it and the legend "$500 Reward." At another point, Cagney lulls a Mexican infant to sleep by singing "Rockabye Baby" in Spanish. Al Jennings, the inept bank robber who had starred, long distance, in *The Bank Robbery* (1908), was technical director for this film. Bill Tilghman, the brave lawman who had filmed *The Bank Robbery*, was dead. He had been shot down by a drunken, trigger-happy bootlegger in 1924.

There is a more direct variety of humor in *Destry Rides Again* (Universal, 1939), directed by George Marshall, the film that established sex and humor as elements of the Hollywood West. The novel, by Max Brand, had already been made into a film in 1932, starring Tom Mix, and it was destined to be remade in 1955, but the 1939 version remains the best. Marlene Dietrich plays Frenchy, a dangerous woman—"a tough cookie"—who spends her time destroying men in the Last Chance Saloon, the biggest bar in the town of Bottleneck. She and her compatriots are taking over the territory. Because it suits them, they appoint a local drunk sheriff, but the sheriff sends for young Thomas Jefferson Destry, Jr., son of the famous lawman who cleaned up Tombstone. As the drunk exclaims, "When he gets here, Destry will ride again!"

Thomas J. Destry, Jr. (James Stewart), whose hobby is carving napkin rings, arrives on the stagecoach and climbs out carrying a parasol and a canary (mercifully, they aren't his). He then ambles over to the Last Chance—and orders himself a glass of milk!

The sexy humor of the film did not please everyone. The Hays Office, with its charge of maintaining decency in films, had been around since 1922. In 1939, because of complaints from religious groups, it started to get tough. David O. Selznick had to fight quite a battle to keep the "damn" in Rhett Butler's "Frankly, my dear, I don't give a—." Selznick won. But the Hays Office had its way with *Destry Rides Again*. It permitted the scene in which Dietrich pushes money into her cleavage but censored her accompanying line, "There's gold in them thar hills."

By the end of the thirties, the western was back in vogue. The last year of the decade experienced a flood of good westerns, including *Destry Rides Again*, *Dodge City*, *Frontier Marshal*, *Union Pacific*, *The Oklahoma Kid*, *Jesse James*, and *Stagecoach*. Because it was such a popular film, *Stagecoach* is frequently credited with bringing the western back to popularity, but it was only one of many, and it neither revived the western nor made John Wayne a star (*Red River* is the film usually credited with making Wayne's fame). *Jesse James* and *Stagecoach* are similar in that the villains of both films are bankers. In that sense, they are recognizable products of the Depression. In a larger sense, they both anticipate the westerns of the forties and fifties by using the setting of the old West to examine contemporary American society.

"His times produced him" is the epitaph for the famous outlaw in *Jesse James* (20th Century-Fox, 1939), directed by Henry King. The war (the Civil War) taught him to kill, and when he returned home to take up his life as a peaceful farmer, unscrupulous bankers and railroad men took away his land and drove him to outlawry. *Jesse James* is a lot like another Fox film of the same period: *The Grapes of Wrath*. Both were produced by Darryl Zanuck; the screenplays for both were written by Nunnally Johnson (Hal Long worked with Johnson on *Jesse James*); and Henry Fonda had

James Stewart as Thomas Jefferson Destry, Jr., and Marlene Dietrich as Frenchy in a production still from Destry Rides Again *(Universal, 1939).*

important roles in both. In *Jesse James*, Fonda plays Jesse's brother, Frank. Jesse is played by Tyrone Power, and the remarkable cast includes Randolph Scott, Nancy Kelly, Henry Hull, Brian Donlevy, John Carradine (as Bob Ford), Lon Chaney, Jr., Donald Meek, J. Edward Bromberg, and George Chandler. The story follows the James brothers from the Civil War to Jesse's death. Fonda repeated his role as Frank James in *The Return of Frank James* (20th Century-Fox, 1940), directed by Fritz Lang, which included a number of actors from *Jesse James:* Hull, Carradine, Meek, Bromberg, and Chandler. It was also Gene Tierney's first film. *The Return of Frank James* begins with film from the end of *Jesse James*, the kind of solid connection most sequels lack.

Stagecoach (United Artists, 1939) ranks among John Ford's greatest films, and many critics consider it the best western ever made. The story of a group of disparate people thrown together in a small space and faced with a common danger has been repeated many times, particularly in such "disaster" films as *Airport, The Towering Inferno,* and *The Poseidon Adventure.* But Ford's story is far more complete: each of the characters and each element in the film tells a different part of the same story. Like the musical score for *Stagecoach,* which is composed of themes taken from American folksongs, Ford's version of the West combines American ideas and values in a coherent vision, giving us the West just as our folklore would have it. The various themes of the film—the journey from civilization to wilderness; the importance of names and family relationships; pride and social prejudice—all overlap to create a unified whole.

The passengers on the Overland Stage going from Tonto to Lordsburg include Dr. Josiah Boone (Thomas Mitchell), a whiskey-sodden physician "who couldn't cure a horse"; Samuel Peacock (Donald Meek), a whiskey drummer immediately befriended by the good doctor; Dallas (Claire Trevor), a prostitute run out of town by the righteous harridans of the Law and Order League; Mrs. Lucy Mallory (Louise Platt), a pregnant wife going to join her cavalry-officer husband; Major Hatfield (John Carradine), "a notorious gambler" and a southern gentleman who takes the trip only to protect Mrs. Mallory, whom he sees as "an angel in the jungle"; Henry Gatewood (Berton Churchill), a banker absconding with his bank's money; and Sheriff Curly Wilcox (George Bancroft), who rides shotgun next to the stage driver, Buck (Andy Devine). This group is joined by the Ringo Kid (John Wayne).

Everyone on the stage has a name (no one ever gets poor Peacock's right), a past, and a social standing within the group. Even the horses pulling the stagecoach have names, and Buck calls them out one by one when urging the horses to move faster (the sheriff throws stones at them). Geronimo's name strikes fear, but he and his ferocious Indians remain faceless, an ever-present danger that is just one more part of the savage landscape. The Plummer brothers, who murdered the Ringo Kid's father and brother, are a part of Ringo's fate, something he must deal with. As he says, "I used to be a good cowhand, but things happen." The real villain of the film is the banker, who expresses himself in such phrases as "What's good for the banks is good for the country" and "What this country needs is a businessman for president." He is arrested when he proudly announces his name.

Stagecoach was Ford's first use of Monument Valley, an area he was to return to so frequently that its landscape would become an integral part of the western film. It was also Ford's first use of John Wayne since their silent-film days. Like Monument Valley, Ford used Wayne again and again after *Stagecoach*—after having neglected him for years. Ford reused many of the actors in *Stagecoach* in later films in the same way that he reused hymns ("Shall We Gather at the River" was a favorite) and pieces of folklore. The famous "deadman's hand," aces and eights—the hand Wild Bill Hickok was supposedly holding when he was killed in Deadwood, South Dakota—is dealt to Luke Plummer in *Stagecoach* and to Liberty Valance in *The Man Who Shot Liberty Valance.* In Ford's films, items of American folklore are used to create a sense of destiny and to make his films seem like poetic lessons in America's emotional history.

A large part of the excitement in *Stagecoach* is due to the stunts, many of which were performed by Yakima Canutt, the man most responsible for developing the art of the stuntman. Some of the stunts he created—such as falling between the horses and letting the stagecoach roll over him—have become classics. During his long career as a stuntman, stand-in, and second-unit director of action sequences, Canutt has thrilled audiences and made a lot of the people he works with very nervous.

Although it was nominated for many Oscars, including best picture and best director, *Stagecoach* had the misfortune to come out the same year as *Gone with the Wind, Wuthering Heights, The Wizard of Oz, Mr. Smith Goes to Washington, Ninotchka,* and *Goodbye, Mr. Chips.* Thomas Mitchell (who also played Scarlett's father in *Gone with the Wind*) won an Oscar for best supporting actor for his role as Dr. Boone in *Stagecoach.* The New York Film Critics named Ford the year's best director, and *Stagecoach* received merit of another sort when Orson Welles said that he had spent hours—he saw it more than forty times—watching *Stagecoach* before directing *Citizen Kane.*

Stagecoach did not please everyone, however. William S. Hart was still keeping his sharp eyes trained on westerns, and he found fault with Ford's film,

Stagecoach (United Artists, 1939): George Bancroft, John Wayne, Andy Devine, and Vester Pegg.

pointing out that no Indians would have wasted their time chasing the stagecoach. According to Hart, they would simply have shot the horses.

Fortunately, Hart's last words were not complaints. In 1939, *Tumbleweeds* was rereleased with the addition of an eight-minute prologue, spoken by Hart himself. Audiences finally had a chance to hear his voice, which had been trained by years as a Shakespearean actor. It was a beautiful, resonant voice, and it is a moving speech, Hart delivering his own epitaph. Dressed as he did in his films, and looking older but no less noble, he stands on a hill in front of a large tree (the sound equipment picked up the wind rustling through the leaves and occasional birdsong). He explains the history of the Cherokee Strip land rush, what it meant to the settlers and what it meant to the Indians who had to give up the land. He explains that a "sooner" was someone who went out to claim land before the signal gun was fired to begin the land rush. And then he talks about himself. He gives the excuse of injuries suffered and old age (he's moving toward that "last great roundup into eternity") for no longer making films. He says that he misses Fritz. The prologue is not without humor, and its sincerity reveals Hart as a man of great dignity and grace. At the end, he shudders and exclaims—speaking of his career and of the great joy he had making his films—"The thrill of it all!"

The stagecoach and a cavalry escort ride into Monument Valley in Stagecoach *(United Artists, 1939).*

Adventurers
and
Scoundrels

1940–1949

"I sure like that name. Clementine."

My Darling Clementine

Little Bend? Greasewood City? These sad little burgs with their painfully honest names could exist in only one man's West: the West of W. C. Fields. In *My Little Chickadee* (Universal, 1940), directed by Edward Cline, Fields, as a roving snake-oil vendor, has the misfortune of encountering a certain Flower Belle—Mae West. When Joseph Calleia, playing the part of a masked bandit, inquires, "I wonder what kind of a woman you are," West, without hesitation, rolls back at him, "Too bad I don't give out samples."

A free sample would have been asking too much, but a pinup might have satisfied some of Calleia's curiosity. The forties saw a number of memorable films—*Citizen Kane, The Grapes of Wrath, The Maltese Falcon, Casablanca*—but the most popular picture, at least for the men in uniform, was a rear view of Betty Grable in a bathing suit and high heels, smiling over her shoulder.

Sex symbols in bathing suits and tight sweaters were appreciated by the soldiers overseas, but the women left at home—many of whom had jobs and a new sense of responsibility and value—wanted to see women in more fulfilling roles. Hollywood, short on male actors, gladly complied, turning out vehicles for such actresses as Joan Crawford, Bette Davis, Barbara Stanwyck, and Gene Tierney.

The war killed the Depression, and those at home had money to spend with very few luxuries to spend it on. But they could always go to the movies. Amid the comedies, melodramas, war films, and musicals, westerns stayed alive, but like the rest of the country, the old West was changed by the war.

Due as much to prohibitive production costs as to changes in attitude, the epic westerns that had typified the thirties gave way to "smaller" films in which panoramic action was replaced by activity on a more intimate level. Characters became inward-looking and not always sure of themselves; they were frequently forced to face personal crises before confronting the villain. Relationships between men and women and, in particular, among groups of men were examined. Eventually, this introspection gave way to the so-called psychological westerns of the fifties.

Attitudes toward sex went through the same changes in westerns that they went through in American society. Women were given more important roles than they had had previously, and, particularly in such films as *The Outlaw* (1943) and *Duel in the Sun* (1946), they were revealed to have bodies and their own powerful sexuality.

The end of Prohibition had begun the downfall of the western's greatest rival, the gangster film. It was replaced in large part by films celebrating the exploits of law-enforcement agencies, such as the FBI. But some of the gangster's appeal was transferred to the western hero: he was made more understandable. The good badman, who inevitably does right and gets the girl, was replaced by the likeable badman, whose career is interesting, whose character is intriguing and multifaceted, and who sometimes gets killed. Two movies directed by Raoul Walsh for Warner Brothers provide a unique example of the gangster-western relationship.

In 1941, Walsh directed *High Sierra*, the story of a gangster, Roy Earle (Humphrey Bogart), whom the "syndicate" gets out of prison so that he can pull off a big job. He is accompanied by a loyal gun moll named Marie (Ida Lupino). The heist goes according to plan, but the money is lost, one of the robbers squeals, and Earle, spurned even by the syndicate, is chased down and finally killed by the police.

In 1949, Walsh made *Colorado Territory*, the story of an outlaw, Wes McQueen (Joel McCrea), who escapes from a Missouri jail and goes to Colorado where he joins up with his old gang. They decide to pull off one last job. McCrea is accompanied by Virginia Mayo as a blond, barefooted half-breed. The train holdup goes according to plan, but things don't work well afterward, and McCrea and Mayo die under a hail of gunfire.

The two films are indeed similar—the screenplays for both are based on the same novel, W. R. Burnett's *High Sierra*. John Huston adapted it for *High Sierra*, and John Twist and Edmund H. North used it for *Colorado Territory*. *High Sierra* is sometimes referred to as "the last swallow of the gangster summer"; *Colorado Territory* proved the adaptability of westerns—and of the novels of W. R. Burnett.

With the addition of psychology, sex, and fuller characterizations, the western emerged from the forties with a new vitality and a new role. No longer merely a simple-plotted vehicle for exciting action, the western proved itself capable of telling any story. The old West could be used to deliver a warning about fascism, as in *The Ox-Bow Incident* (1943), or it could be used as the setting for a Broadway musical, as in *Oklahoma!* (1943). It could be humorous or ironic, full of gunfire or without a single shot fired. It could turn history into legend, as in *My Darling Clementine* (1946), or it could celebrate national values by personifying them, as in *Red River* (1948).

The forties were a period of strong national identity. Aaron Copland's *Appalachian Spring* (1944) uses themes from traditional American folk tunes in the same way that Ford uses them for the musical scores in his movies. The nation needed great strength to fight the world war, and it found it mirrored in the heroic men and women who had won the West.

The "war" of the West was the Civil War, a par-

ticularly vicious conflict because it divided families and personal loyalties. Many elements of the old West have their roots in the period of the Civil War. The blue uniforms of the Indian-fighting cavalry—worn by many former slaves and many former Confederate soldiers—are symbolic of law and order but also of the eastern government. The gentlemanly conduct of the traditional cowboy is southern in its heritage—as is the traditional "walkdown" gunfight, which was born of the code duello. The Mississippi riverboat gambler with his fancy clothes and his tendency to cheat appears in saloons all the way to the Barbary Coast. And many famous outlaws learned their disrespect for the government and its employees while fighting for the Cause.

Not all the battles of the Civil War were fought by uniformed soldiers. West of the Mississippi, particularly in Missouri and Kansas, the war was fought by bands of guerillas, organized gangs that, in alleged support of one side or the other, pillaged and burned, ambushed and lynched. The lawlessness and butchery gave Kansas the epithet "Bleeding" and created hatreds in the area—and in the men who took part—that did

not end with the war. The most infamous of these guerilla bands was led by William C. Quantrill, and among those who rode with him were Frank and Jesse James and Cole and Jim Younger.

Quantrill's most notorious act was his raid of Lawrence, Kansas, in 1863, during which his men slaughtered the defenseless townspeople. This event is the highlight of **The Dark Command** (Republic, 1940), directed by Raoul Walsh (the raid of Lawrence was directed by second-unit director Yakima Canutt). The film stars John Wayne (his first film with Walsh since *The Big Trail*), Claire Trevor (who had played opposite Wayne in *Stagecoach*), and Walter Pidgeon in the role of the vicious Quantrill. Opposing Quantrill are Wayne; his sidekick, George "Gabby" Hayes; and Roy Rogers (who, according to a Republic advertisement for the film, "rides like he was part of the horse").

The screenplay for the film was based on a novel by W. R. Burnett, and Walter Pidgeon's performance as the power-mad Quantrill is the best in the film. Some of its power may be attributable to Burnett, who knew how to describe the lure of power.

Preceding pages: *Humphrey Bogart (left) and Walter Huston in* The Treasure of the Sierra Madre *(Warner Brothers, 1947).* Above: *Mae West and W. C. Fields in* My Little Chickadee *(Universal, 1940).*

Stuart N. Lake, the man whose biography of Wyatt Earp was made into four films, was also interested in powerful men. *The Westerner* (United Artists, 1940), directed by William Wyler, is based on his story of Judge Roy Bean, "the law west of the Pecos."

There really was a Judge Roy Bean, just as there really was a Lily Langtry. Bean's courtroom was his saloon—which was not at all unusual in the West (John Ford's *The Man Who Shot Liberty Valance* provides a good example of the saloon as civic center). Bean had only one lawbook, and he interpreted it to his own liking. The justice he handed out was frequently eccentric, occasionally humorous, and always harsh. His character was made even more intriguing by his all-consuming love for Lily Langtry, the English actress known more for her beauty than her thespian skills. He named his saloon The Jersey Lily, and the town where he held court is still known as Langtry, Texas.

Walter Brennan's performance as Bean in *The Westerner* won him an Academy Award as best supporting actor. The hero of the film is Gary Cooper, whose portrayal of a quiet cowhand provides the perfect foil to Brennan. Falsely accused of stealing a horse, Cooper is about to experience one of Bean's summary sentences ("The larceny of an equine is a capital offense, but a horse thief always gets a fair trial before he's hung," states Bean) when he discovers Bean's passion for Langtry and promises him a lock of her hair. Back on his own, he allies himself with the local homesteaders in their fight with the cattlemen and Bean. There is a final shootout between Cooper and Brennan, but Brennan gets to meet Lily before he dies.

The Westerner was the film debut for both Forrest Tucker and Dana Andrews. The script, based on Stuart N. Lake's story, was written by Niven Busch and Jo Swerling. In retrospect, one can see in *The Westerner* the seeds of Busch's later screenplays, his so-called psychological westerns.

Just as there really was a Lily Langtry and there really was a Judge Roy Bean, so were there a Lola Montez and a Black Bart. Montez was born Irish (her family name was Gilbert), but she wanted to be a Spanish dancer, so she changed her name to Lola Montez and took up a life of amorous adventures. She had legendary affairs with Franz Liszt and Alexandre Dumas père before becoming the mistress of King Louis I of Bavaria. Lola's capricious politics led in no small way to the revolution of 1848, after which she was banished. She appeared in California shortly after the gold rush, still kicking up her pudgy legs and enjoying all manner of scandal. (Her dancing was not always appreciated out West, and she received more rotten eggs than roses.) It is unlikely that she ever ran into the notorious Black Bart—she died in 1861 and he didn't begin his career of stagecoach depredations until 1875—but that is more her loss than his, for Black Bart

Top: *Gary Cooper on the set of* The Westerner *(United Artists, 1940).* Right: *Walter Brennan in* The Westerner. Opposite: *Dan Duryea (right) as Black Bart in* Black Bart *(Universal, 1948).*

(his real name was Charles E. Boles) was a very unusual highwayman. On at least two occasions, he left something in return for the cash he stole—doggerel verse, the best-scanning of which runs:

> I've labored long and hard for bread,
> for honor and for riches,
> but on my corns too long you've tred,
> you fine-haired sons of bitches.

He signed his work "Black Bart, the Po-8."

Lola meets Black in *Black Bart* (Universal, 1948), directed by George Sherman. He saves her life in a holdup, she thanks him, and he allows, "It's nothing any other red-blooded hero wouldn't have done." That is probably true, but in the film, Black Bart (Dan Duryea) teams up with another outlaw (John McIntire) in a plot to undermine the Wells Fargo Company—an ambitious undertaking that would have shocked the demure Charles E. Boles. Lola Montez (Yvonne De Carlo) cannot prevent this madness. The film has the proper mood of humor, but it ends with needless violence: the villains are shot down as they flee a burning shack. The camera looks away, sparing viewers the spectacle of their death, and focuses on the flames.

The real Black Bart, after twenty-seven successful robberies of Wells Fargo stages, was caught and sent to prison. On his release, he promised he would not hold up any more stages or write any more verse. Leg-

end has it that Wells Fargo agreed to pay him a lifetime monthly pension of $125—provided he left their stages alone.

White-collar crime was not unknown in the old West, and *The Baron of Arizona* (Lippert, 1949), directed by Samuel Fuller, tells the story of James Addison Reavis (1843–1914), an ambitious con man who tried to swindle his way into ownership of most of the state of Arizona. An employee of the Federal Land Office in Santa Fe, New Mexico, Reavis forged documents in an attempt to lay claim to 66,000 square miles of the state of Arizona. Reavis was both debonair and punctilious. He took the time to enter a monastery in Spain just to get at some ancient documents (which he then forged); he went to South America and Mexico to make important alterations and emendations in land-grant titles; and he convinced his Spanish-American wife, a simple and gullible soul, that she was the descendant of the original grantees and therefore heiress to half of the state. Before he was exposed, Reavis managed to extract a lot of land from Arizona landowners. It is not a very exciting plot for a western, but Reavis is played by Vincent Price, and that makes it worthwhile—and believable.

There is another sense of history in *The Great Man's Lady* (Paramount, 1941), directed by William Wellman, which begins in 1941 with a town celebrat-

ing the birthday of its founder and namesake: the public square of Hoyt City is being graced with a statue of Ethan Hoyt, the heroic pioneer who carved the city out of the wilderness. Present at the ceremony to witness this celebration of Hoyt's great accomplishments is 109-year-old Hannah Sempler (Barbara Stanwyck), who, according to local gossip, is somehow related to Hoyt. She has steadfastly refused to tell her story—she has been offered as much as $100,000—but on this day the sympathy of a young woman reporter leads her to relate her story, the true story of the great man and the founding of the city. In a series of flashbacks, beginning in 1848, she relates how she eloped with Hoyt (Joel McCrea), suffered with him through the hardships of frontier life, and pushed him on to success. It is a tear-jerkingly sad tale, full of misunderstandings, jealousies, and secrets: believing her to be dead, he remarries, and rather than blemish his career, she sacrifices herself to obscurity.

The theme of self-sacrifice was not lost on wartime audiences. *The Great Man's Lady* was released as part of a double bill with *Our Russian Front*, a documentary narrated by John Huston about the heroic efforts of the Soviets against the Germans. During the forties, the Russians were heroic—and so was General George Armstrong Custer.

In 1940's *The Santa Fe Trail*, Errol Flynn played Jeb Stuart, Ronald Reagan played George A. Custer, and Olivia De Havilland played Kit Carson Holliday, the woman they fought for and over. In 1942's *They Died with Their Boots On* (Warner Brothers), directed by Raoul Walsh, Flynn assays the role of Custer, Olivia De Havilland wins his heart, Anthony Quinn is Crazy Horse, Arthur Kennedy is an evil man who sells guns to the Indians—even Sydney Greenstreet appears.

The first of a series of films starring Errol Flynn and directed by Raoul Walsh, *They Died with Their Boots On* tells the story of Custer from his career at West Point (he arrives dressed as a hussar and followed by a crowd of loyal hounds) through the Civil War (he is accidentally given a command and becomes a hero) to the Little Big Horn. Flynn makes a likeable Custer, and the film presents both Custer and the Indians in a sympathetic light—the Indians break their treaty only when a trading company invades their land. Flynn and Walsh made a number of war movies together, but the war in question was usually the Second World War, as in *Objective Burma* (1945).

The only western with a theme directly related to events in Europe is William Wellman's *The Ox-Bow Incident* (*Strange Incident* in Great Britain) (20th Century-Fox, 1943), which is based on a novel by Walter Van Tilburg Clark. Clark explained that he had written the novel in 1937 and 1938 when the world was getting increasingly worried about Hitler and the Nazis. He used the story of a lynching to tell a much broader story about mob violence. Lamar Trotti wrote the screenplay and produced the film.

The Ox-Bow Incident has no hero, for a hero would have had to go against the lynch mob and either prevent the hanging or die trying. The story is recounted by a cowboy (Henry Fonda) who, with his pal (Henry Morgan), witnesses the event. In an atmosphere of ominous darkness (much of the film was shot on indoor sets, giving it an eerie closeness, and most of the story takes place at night), three men—Dana Andrews, Anthony Quinn, and Francis Ford (John Ford's older brother)—are accused of killing a rancher and stealing his cattle. Led on by a righteous former Confederate officer, Major Tetley (Frank Conroy), a group of ordinary ranchers and townspeople hangs the three men, only to discover that the rancher is alive and did sell the cattle. The film leaves viewers—and the cowboy who narrates the story—with a sense of the weakness of society. The message, of course, is "it could happen here."

Audiences in 1943 were not eager for a grim tale with a sad ending. It was wartime (Henry Fonda volunteered for service in the Navy the day after he finished work on the film). The film was not a financial success. Its use of a western setting to relate a story about contemporary society has led to its being called the first antiwestern.

In 1948, director Wellman and producer Trotti made another western, *Yellow Sky* (20th Century-Fox). Trotti and W. R. Burnett wrote the screenplay, and the film has some of the dark mood of *The Ox-Bow Incident*. The story takes place in 1867. A group of gunmen—former soldiers in the late war—holds up a bank and is chased out into the desert by a troop of cavalry. After wandering across the salt flats for days, they stumble into a ghost town named Yellow Sky (the same town had seen service in at least two previous westerns: *In Old Arizona* and Tom Mix's 1925 *The Riders of the Purple Sage*). The only denizens of the town are an old man and his granddaughter. The town has water—and a hidden cache of gold. Gregory Peck, leader of the group, falls for the granddaughter (Anne Baxter) and eventually has to fight it out with his former friends. Gold makes men crazy.

No western—no other film—tells the story of "what gold does to men's souls" better than *The Treasure of the Sierra Madre* (Warner Brothers, 1947). John Huston directed the film and wrote the screenplay, based on a novel by B. Traven, a mysterious and elusive author. Traven promised to meet with Huston to discuss the film, but when Huston showed up at the appointed time, Traven was nowhere to be found. Finally, when Huston had about given up and was ready to leave, a small man appeared who claimed to represent Traven. Huston signed the man on and began filming.

Above: *Anthony Quinn and Dana
Andrews (on horseback) in* The Ox-Bow
Incident *(20th Century-Fox, 1943).*
Left *(left to right): John Russell,
Gregory Peck, Henry Morgan, Robert
Arthur, and James Barton in*
Yellow Sky *(20th Century-Fox, 1948).*

63

The Treasure of the Sierra Madre begins in February of 1925 in the coastal city of Tampico, Mexico ("some town to be broke in"). John Huston gave himself a role in the film, that of a wealthy tourist who is bothered by a persistent mendicant. The panhandler is Fred C. Dobbs (Humphrey Bogart). Giving Dobbs one final coin, Huston cautions, "But from now on, you have to make your way through life without my assistance."

Dobbs and another down-on-his-luck hobo (Tim Holt) team up with an old prospector (Walter Huston) who knows where there is gold. The fatherly old man warns the two men about what gold can do: "When the piles of gold begin to grow, that's when the trouble starts." The three men are honest and friendly, eager to help one another, as they begin to dig the gold. But soon, Bogart—whose face expresses much more than he says and who develops a strange glint in his eyes—asks, "When do we start dividing it up?" Moving by slow, eloquent paces, the story follows Bogart's decline into unreasoning mistrust ("Nobody puts anything over on Fred C. Dobbs") and greed, leading finally to his death.

The Treasure of the Sierra Madre was shot on location in the rugged Sierra Madre mountains. Walter Huston, who won an Academy Award as best supporting actor for his role as the old prospector, complained that his director-son had made him run up and down too many hills; John Huston won Oscars for best director and best screenplay, a unique father-and-son event in Academy Award history. The film was the debut of Alfonso Bedoya, who plays the Mexican bandit with the memorable line (repeated in *Blazing Saddles*, of course): "Badges? Badges? We don't need no stinking badges!"

And Traven? Huston believed that the strange little man claiming to represent Traven was the author himself. Perhaps he was. Many attempts have been made to identify the hermitlike writer. Most sources claim his real name is Berwick Traven Torsvan and that he was born in Chicago in 1890 of Swedish parents. However, in 1978, a team of researchers working for the BBC claimed to have identified him as Herman Albert Otto Maksymilian Feige, born in 1882 in the Polish city of Swiebodzin.

Lust for Gold (Columbia, 1949), directed by S. Sylvan Simon, tells the story of the search for the Lost Dutchman's Mine, a fabulous gold mine that, according to legend, is located in the Superstition Mountains east of Mesa, Arizona. The narrator of the story (William Prince) claims to be the grandson of the Jacob Walz for whom the $20 million treasure is named. In a series of flashbacks, the narrator tells the story of the mine and of the twenty-one men who died for it, beginning with a group of Mexican prospectors—the Peralta brothers—who find the gold, only to be killed by

Cochise for having trespassed on holy land. The longest flashback tells the story of the Dutchman himself (Glenn Ford) and his battles with those who would take away his mine. In its treatment of greed, *Lust for Gold* resembles *The Treasure of the Sierra Madre*, but it seems even grimmer, and it lacks the final optimism of *The Treasure of the Sierra Madre*: "The worst ain't so bad when it finally happens."

In 1942, *The Spoilers* was remade, having appeared first in 1914, then again in 1923 and 1930. This version, *The Spoilers* (Universal, 1942), directed by Ray Enright, was not the final one—it was remade in 1955 and may yet be remade again—but it may be the best: it stars John Wayne; Marlene Dietrich; Randolph Scott; Harry Carey; and William Farnum, the Farnum brother who had starred in the first version in 1914. The plot of the film—based on a novel by Rex Beach that is itself based on the life of Alexander McKenzie, a North Dakota politician who had crooked dealings in Alaska—changes very little from version to version and always includes a final fistfight of heroic proportions; in this version, it is between Wayne and Scott.

Another old favorite, *The Riders of the Purple Sage*, was remade in 1941. *The Riders of the Purple Sage* (20th Century-Fox), directed by James Tinling, stars George Montgomery as the avenging Jim Lassiter, searching for the man who wrecked his sister's life. The story is based on what is probably Zane Grey's most popular novel.

Western Union (20th Century-Fox, 1941), an epic in the tradition of *Pony Express*, *Wells Fargo*, and *Union Pacific*, may or may not be based on a novel by Zane Grey. He may have finished the book a few days before he died, or it may have been hurriedly put together by a ghost writer to cash in on the film's popularity. The film itself is justly popular: it stars Robert Young, Randolph Scott, and Dean Jagger. Scott plays an outlaw who falls in love with the sister (Virginia Gilmore) of an engineer (Jagger). Unfortunately, the sister also likes Robert Young, a Harvard graduate proving himself out West. Young and Scott are friendly enough until Young finds that Scott is still pals with some outlaws. And when the outlaws dress up as Indians and raid the telegraph company (something the Indians themselves habitually do in the film), things get rough. But the "singing wire" is strung along westward, and the film ends with a surprise twist.

Western Union was directed by Vienna-born Fritz Lang, the same monocled man who had directed *The Return of Frank James*. Samuel Fuller made his directorial debut with a sequel to that sequel: *I Shot Jesse James* (Screen Guild, 1949), a film that explains why Bob Ford shot Jesse and relates the rest of Ford's sad life. According to the story of the film, Ford (John Ireland) is in love with a woman (Barbara Britton) who insists he give up his career as an outlaw. When

amnesty is offered to anyone who brings in Jesse James alive or dead, Ford sees his chance and kills Jesse. Ford doesn't like what he has done, and neither does his girlfriend, but he doesn't give up hope of winning her love. She, however, now loves a lawman (Preston Foster), and when Frank James shows up to taunt Ford with this fact, Ford demands a showdown with Foster and is killed. A high point of the film comes when singer Robin Short sings a song about the "the dirty little coward" to Ford's face. The film looks forward to other confessional westerns of the fifties, such as *I Shot Billy the Kid*, *I Killed Geronimo*, and *I Killed Wild Bill Hickok*.

A decade after King Vidor's *Billy the Kid*, the story was retold, using the same book by Walter Noble Burns, *The Saga of Billy the Kid*. *Billy the Kid* (MGM, 1940), directed by David Miller, stars Robert Taylor as Billy and leaves out the matter of Pat Garrett altogether: Billy is an outlaw-fighting hero.

The story of the famed outlaw provided the excuse for one of the decade's most famous westerns, *The Outlaw* (United Artists, 1943), produced and directed (when he replaced Howard Hawks) by Howard Hughes. Billy is played by Jack Beutel; Pat Garrett, the lawman famous as the man who shot Billy the Kid, is played by Thomas Mitchell; Doc Holliday, who, of course, doesn't belong in this story at all—he goes with the Earps in Tombstone—is played by Walter Huston. The entire film was created for another character: Rio, played by Jane Russell. The film was first released in 1943, but was soon withdrawn, only to be rereleased three years later. Hughes had dared to exhibit the film without a seal of approval from the Hays Office. The film ends with the murderous Billy and the immoral Rio going off together, which was not the kind of morality the Hays Office liked to see condoned (although both *Stagecoach* and Vidor's *Billy the Kid* end the same way).

The film had other problems, too: Jane Russell's breasts, which Hughes worked into the film in remarkable ways (he even invented a special pneumatic bra to help give her heaving cleavage more depth). Censors were not pleased with all the romping done by Billy and Rio, and they were shocked by Miss Russell's anatomy. Although the film has merits as a western, including some exciting action scenes, its fame rests on Russell's bosom. As one judge, upholding the censorship of the film in Maryland, wrote, "Miss Russell's breasts hung over the picture like a summer thunderstorm spread out over a landscape. They were everywhere. They were there when she first came into the picture. They were there when she went out."

"Trash, trash, trash, trash, trash" is what Jennifer Jones says of herself in *Duel in the Sun* (Selznick Releasing Organization, 1946), after she has allowed Gregory Peck to seduce her. That is pretty much what the

Top: *Robert Young in* Western Union *(20th Century-Fox, 1941).*
Left: *Jane Russell in* The Outlaw *(United Artists, 1943).*

Catholic church thought of the film, calling it "morally offensive and spiritually depressing." Advertised as "the movie that brought sex to the western" and nicknamed "Lust in the Dust," *Duel in the Sun*, behind its heavy breathing, is a dramatic and compelling film, full of the tangibly sensuous moods that director King Vidor had first displayed in his *Billy the Kid* (1930).

The film had more than just censorship problems—although the story deals with Texas, it was shot in Arizona, a fact that didn't go unnoticed and led to much ill feeling between the two states.

The plot of *Duel in the Sun* concerns an evil cattle baron, Senator McCanlis (Lionel Barrymore); his wife (Lillian Gish), whom he has driven to drink; their two sons, one good, named Jesse (Joseph Cotten) and one bad, Lewt (Gregory Peck); and the beautiful, flirtatious half-breed girl, Pearl Chavez (Jennifer Jones), who comes to live with them after the deaths of her parents. The story of Senator McCanlis's battle against encroaching "civilization"—the railroad—is almost lost in the battle between Jesse, Lewt, and Sam Pierce (Charles Bickford) for Pearl. Lewt shoots both Pierce and Jesse, and Lewt and Pearl, in their climactic duel in the sun, shoot each other.

David O. Selznick (who married Jennifer Jones in 1949) produced the movie, and he went all out: the movie was in production longer and cost more ($6 million plus $2 million for promotion) than any picture up to that time. The publicity for the film was the most expensive and extensive Hollywood had ever seen. Ten thousand small parachutes with betting tickets for a horse were dropped over the Kentucky Derby. Other giveaways (each marked with an ad for the film) included light bulbs, paperweights, postcards, seed packages, pencils, stickers, crossword puzzles, lollipops, matchbooks, typewriters, blotters, money clips, gin-rummy pads, telephone pads, ashtrays, T-shirts, and buttons.

The film opened on May 7, 1947, "Duel Day," with suitable parades and fanfare, and it went on to make a healthy profit (by 1952, it had grossed $17 million). Its size and publicity made it popular with everyone. Even *Ripley's Believe It or Not* found something of interest: Jennifer Jones "wore out eighteen pairs of sandals and eight pairs of ballet slippers during the course of a year's shooting."

With so much sex in the West, Freud couldn't be far behind. He arrived in *Pursued* (Warner Brothers, 1947), directed by Raoul Walsh, a film that contemporary critics found "bewildering" and "almost absurd." They did not take well to a psychological mystery set in the West. Niven Busch, author of the screenplay for *The Westerner* and author of the novel on which the screenplay for *Duel in the Sun* was based, wrote the screenplay for *Pursued*—he wrote so many psychological screenplays that these years are fre-

quently called the period of the "burning Busch."

Pursued takes place in New Mexico around the turn of the century. The film begins with its hero, Jeb Rand (Robert Mitchum), about to be hanged by a lynch mob. Why? What has he done? And what is going on in all those flashbacks that constantly torment him? Mitchum, as always, seems vaguely somnolent and unconcerned, but the film has a dramatic, if confusing, plot, and the photography (by James Wong Howe) gives the film a dreamlike unreality.

Pursued is called the first psychological western. It certainly wasn't the last.

In 1945, Gary Cooper produced his first film, *Along Came Jones;* in 1946, John Wayne, never far behind Cooper, produced his first film, *Angel and the Badman*. Although neither film is dramatic or sensational, both are perfect examples of each star in his prime.

In *Along Came Jones* (RKO, 1945), directed by Stuart Heisler, Cooper plays a cowpuncher named Melody Jones, a kind-hearted, simple-minded fellow who lives up to his name: Cooper sings (or, rather, shyly mumbles) a song: "Old Joe Clark." Melody has a grumpy sidekick named George Fury (William Demarest). In order to get a pretty gal named Cherry (Loretta Young) out of a fix, Melody agrees to double for her boyfriend—who happens to be a vicious killer. So it is that Melody Jones passes for Monte Jarrad (Dan Duryea): their initials are the same and their physiques are similar, but their skills with a gun cannot be compared—Melody has trouble even holding a gun. Ultimately forced to face Monte, Melody's life is saved when Cherry shoots Monte right between the eyes.

Written and directed by James Edward Grant, *Angel and the Badman* (Republic, 1946) is a graceful film about a gunslinger named Quirt Evans (John Wayne) who is so attached to his weapon that he can't sleep without it. When Evans and his violent ways run into a family of very friendly Quakers, he—true to the William S. Hart tradition—is changed by the love of a virtuous woman, in this case the daughter, Penny (Gail Russell).

It takes a while for the pacifist ways of the Quakers to convert Evans. He is a hard man living in a world "where mayhem, theft, and murder are ordinary." When he goes blueberry picking with Penny, Evans explains that as a baby he was found along a cattle trail (a believable provenance for Wayne himself) and was raised by a cattleman who "threw a wide loop" (didn't pay much attention to whose cattle he was rounding up—a hint of the character Wayne was soon to play in *Red River*). Evans is under the constant watch of Marshal Wistful McClintock (Harry Carey), a sage and ornery old lawman who thinks Evans will never change his ways and believes the cowpoke is just using Penny. McClintock, like most of the characters

Top: *William Demarest (left) and Gary Cooper in* Along
Came Jones *(RKO, 1945). Above: John Wayne (left) and Stephen
Grant in* Angel and the Badman *(Republic, 1946).*

in this sweet western, has a humorous side, too: he complains about his horse, Jughead, whom he refers to as "a dollar-and-a-half brush jumper."

Evans has a score to settle with a certain Laredo Stevens (Bruce Cabot). He eventually goes into town to face Stevens, but he gives his gun to Penny—she has told him that she could never love him if he did anything to harm his soul (like killing another man). And so Evans faces Stevens armed only with his new-found faith. Stevens draws his gun—and is instantly shot dead by Marshal McClintock. As Evans goes off with Penny to begin his new life of peace, he declares, "From now on, I'm a farmer."

John Wayne's role in *Stagecoach* helped his career, but it did not make him John Ford's favorite actor. Ford chose Henry Fonda for his next two westerns, **Drums Along the Mohawk** (20th Century-Fox, 1939) and **My Darling Clementine** (20th Century-Fox, 1946).

The first film is a western only in the sense that it involves settlers fighting Indians. It takes place during the period of the Revolutionary War and gives Fonda the role of a heroic pioneer who, with his wife (Claudette Colbert), faces all the hardships of taming a raw land. *My Darling Clementine* is the third film based on Stuart N. Lake's biography of Wyatt Earp. As the title suggests, Ford took the story of the Earp brothers—or at least those portions he wanted—and molded it into his personal, lyrical view of the old West. A woman with the name Clementine, like a folksong come to life, plays an important role in the film, and Ford's version of the Earps, when compared to later versions—such as *Gunfight at the O.K. Corral* and *Doc*—seems like a gentle myth. In Ford's film, the gunfight at the O.K. Corral—the decisive moment toward which all versions of the Earp saga move—is not just an excuse for action. With Ford, the gunfight is the inevitable result of destiny, the Earp family against the Clanton family, order against chaos.

My Darling Clementine begins with the Earps driving a herd of cattle through Monument Valley. They stop near the "wide awake, wide open town" of Tombstone. Wyatt (Fonda) and two of his brothers, Virgil (Tim Holt) and Morgan (Ward Bond), go into town to get a shave, leaving behind the youngest Earp, James (Don Garner), to guard the herd. Wyatt's shave is disturbed by a drunken Indian shooting up the town. (This scene was repeated from the 1939 version of the story, *Frontier Marshal*. The role of the drunken Indian, called Indian Joe, was played by the same actor, Charles Stevens, in both films.) Fonda subdues the Indian, complaining, "What kind of town is this, selling liquor to Indians? Indian, get out and stay out!" It is not the kind of conduct toward Indians that makes a hero in contemporary westerns, but it makes Fonda the hero in Tombstone, and he is offered the job of

marshal. He turns it down, and the Earp brothers return to camp only to find their brother dead and the cattle stolen. So Wyatt returns to Tombstone and takes the job. It was the Clantons, of course, who killed James and rustled the cattle, and they receive their comeuppance at the O.K. Corral, but the film does not rush to its conclusion.

Like many Ford westerns, *My Darling Clementine* is about bringing civilization to the wilderness, changing the desert into a garden. When Clementine Carter (Cathy Downs) first arrives in Tombstone, she seems, like Mrs. Mallory in *Stagecoach*, like "an angel in the jungle," but she brings with her the civilizing forces of the East, and by the end of the film, Tombstone has become a civilized town and she has become its first schoolmarm.

The Earps and Doc Holliday (Victor Mature) bring law and order to the town. In a ritualistic scene common in Ford films, Wyatt visits the grave of his dead brother and promises him that someday Tombstone will be a place "where boys like you can grow up safe." The dedication of Tombstone's first church is celebrated with a dance (one of Ford's favorite rituals). Only the very skeleton of the church has been built, but the bell has already been installed in the bell tower, and beneath this symbol of the community even shy Wyatt joins in the dance.

There is a quiet, calm beauty about *My Darling Clementine*. The town is located in the middle of Monument Valley—step out any door and there are the mountains. The air—one of the first things Clementine remarks on when she arrives—is clean and clear. Ford makes the viewer sense the clear air, and he uses the angles of the town as frames for the action. When someone walks away down a sidewalk or a street, he or she disappears, at a geometrical vanishing point, into mist. In the saloon, characters walk away and disappear into a cloud of smoke. The cigar-smoking piano player, the fat and friendly bartenders, the card players, each intent on his hand, leaning in toward the stacked chips in the pot, all give the scenes the feeling of paintings. Even at its grimmest, Ford's West is picturesque. And humorous. Confused by his feelings for Clementine, Wyatt asks a bartender (J. Farrell McDonald), "Mac, you ever been in love?" "No," responds the barman, wiping the counter, "I've been a bartender all my life."

When the Earps and Doc Holliday go out to meet the Clantons (led by Walter Brennan as Old Man Clanton), it is dawn, and they turn up their collars in the chilly air. The gunfight—not a test of skills but a test of character—over, Wyatt rides away, saying, "I sure like that name. Clementine."

John Wayne became a star with his role in **Red River** (United Artists, 1948), directed by Howard

Hawks. It was the kind of role he would repeat many times, but never as sympathetically or as convincingly—the tough, hard-headed individualist who lives by his own laws. The character, Tom Dunson, becomes more than one man, however, eventually symbolizing the kind of men who opened the Chisholm Trail to begin the great cattle drives. Wayne presents a perfect version of the man—so absolutely essential to the history of the West—who in doing what is right for himself, what he thoroughly believes he has to do, does something good for the country.

No other western captures so vividly the sense of being outdoors. The elements of the plot, including the fording of a river (the river used is not Texas's Red River but the San Pedro River in Arizona), an Indian attack, and a cattle stampede, are melded into the on-going sense of what a trail drive must really have been like, with all its dust, humor, sudden and almost casual death, and dangerous stampedes. The yelling that begins the cattle drive has become a classic, echoed in numerous films and repeated in others (most notably and significantly in *The Last Picture Show*).

The film begins with Tom Dunson (Wayne) leaving a wagon train—and his girl—to go to some good grassland he has seen. He sets off with his pal (Walter Brennan), and they are soon joined by a lone boy named Matthew Garth (Montgomery Clift—played as a boy by Mickey Kuhn). Without missing a beat, the story of the film jumps ahead fourteen years, with Wayne convinced he can take his 10,000 head of cattle to Missouri. The cattle end up in Abilene, after Clift leads a mutiny against Dunson (*Red River* is frequently compared to *Mutiny on the Bounty*).

Based on a story by Borden Chase, "The Chisholm Trail," which first appeared in *The Saturday Evening Post*, *Red River* is the best portrait ever made of the western rancher-hero, the man whose own determination and stubbornness accomplish the impossible. The story is full of human touches, such as Clift rolling cigarettes for Wayne; a cowpoke, who wanted to buy his wife a pair of red shoes, killed in a stampede; a description of the strange feeling of being indoors after months driving cattle. "I built something, built it with my own hands," says Wayne as Dunson, but he ultimately has to admit he had help in the cattle drive, and he accepts Garth as a partner, drawing in the sand a picture of the new brand: a *D* for Dunson, a symbol like two *S's* to stand for the river, and a *G* for Garth.

Wayne was proud of his part in *Red River*. Howard Hawks, the director, was pleased, too, and he gave Wayne a gift to commemorate the film: a belt buckle with the Dunson brand on it. Wayne frequently wore the belt buckle in his later films (he also had a neckerchief given him by John Ford after *Stagecoach*, which shows up frequently).

The cast of *Red River* includes both Harry Carey

Henry Fonda (left) as Wyatt Earp and Victor Mature as Doc Holliday in My Darling Clementine *(20th Century-Fox, 1946).*

and Harry Carey, Jr. It was Harry Carey's last film—he died shortly after making it. It was also Clift's first movie, and it made him a star.

"Wherever they rode . . . that place became the United States." "They" are the troopers of the U.S. Cavalry, and John Ford based his cavalry trilogy—*Fort Apache, She Wore a Yellow Ribbon,* and *Rio Grande*—on their exploits. The three films are pictorially eloquent and full of exciting action. They are also intensely sentimental and full of slapstick humor.

The first of the three, *Fort Apache* (RKO, 1948), stars both John Wayne and Henry Fonda. Lieutenant Colonel Owen Thursday (Fonda) is sent from the East to take charge of Fort Apache. A by-the-book officer, rigid and unfriendly, Thursday is not pleased with his new command (it has meant a demotion for him) and is dismayed by the lack of discipline he finds among the troopers. They don't even wear proper uniforms. Thursday himself wears a regulation kepi with an attached cloth to guard his neck and shoulders from the hot sun. (Wayne, as Captain Kirby York, wears a slouch hat.) Thursday does not seek—or even accept—

the advice of the veteran Indian fighters, and each time he issues orders he ends them with a threatening, "Any questions?"

When he learns that the Indian chief Cochise is well-known in eastern newspapers, Thursday sees the opportunity for fame and sends York, who knows and is respected by Cochise, out to set up a parley. York arranges a meeting with Cochise (Miguel Inclan), and Thursday promises to come to talk about the Indians' grievances. Instead, he arrives at the scene with a cavalry troop and leads the men in a foolish charge that ends up in a Little Big Horn-style disaster. York and a small group that did not take part in the charge survive the battle.

The next scene takes place years later. York is now commander of the fort. We find him answering questions from newspapermen about the famous "Thursday's Charge." When one of the reporters recites a romanticized and thoroughly erroneous version of the charge, York says that it is "correct in every detail." Then, echoing Thursday, he asks, "Any questions?" and dons his hat—which is no longer his slouch hat; he now

John Wayne (left) and Montgomery Clift in Red River *(United Artists, 1948).*

wears a kepi with an attached desert cloth. York has taken on Thursday's catchphrase and his hat and is perpetuating a lie about Thursday's death.

Why? Perhaps, as in Ford's later film *The Man Who Shot Liberty Valance*, the idea is that "when the legend becomes fact, print the legend." Perhaps York is lying to protect the reputation of the cavalry—the nation needs and wants heroes, and although he was a bombastic fool, Thursday was courageous. The film offers no clues.

The period of the next film, *She Wore a Yellow Ribbon* (RKO, 1949), is 1876, just after Custer's defeat at Little Big Horn. John Wayne plays Captain Nathan Brittles, a veteran cavalryman, loved and respected by his men. Brittles's hitch is just about up—as the film begins, there are only six days more before his retirement. During this short time he is able to avert an Indian war and pass on some of his wisdom to those who will follow (his oft-repeated catchphrase is "Don't apologize. It's a sign of weakness"). Brittles ends the Indian uprising by stampeding the tribe's horses. Then, in what seems to be the end of the film, he rides away. But he is stopped and informed that he has been appointed chief of scouts.

In *Rio Grande* (Republic, 1950), John Wayne plays Lieutenant Colonel Kirby Yorke, a man with a very powerful sense of duty: as a Northern officer during the Civil War, he followed the orders of his commander, General Philip Sheridan (J. Carrol Naish), and burned down the plantation of his Southern-born wife (Maureen O'Hara). As the film begins, Yorke—who has not seen his wife and son for sixteen years—has been frustrated in his efforts to end Indian raids by an order prohibiting him to cross the Rio Grande into Mexico. The Indians raid the settlements in the United States and then escape back over the river to safety. To add to his problems, his son (Claude Jarman, Jr.) arrives as a new recruit, and his wife appears in an attempt to get the boy discharged. Then General Sheridan turns up and gives Yorke tacit permission to cross the border. Husband and wife court each other and are reunited, the son proves himself a worthy soldier, and the Indians are defeated.

The three films of Ford's cavalry trilogy have a lot in common. Each is a study in the loneliness and responsibility of leadership. The actors and the characters they play change little from film to film (Wayne's Kirby York in *Fort Apache* is similar in more than spelling to his Kirby Yorke in *Rio Grande*; Ben Johnson plays Sergeant Tyree in *She Wore a Yellow Ribbon* and Trooper Tyree in *Rio Grande*; Victor McLaglen plays a whiskey-loving sergeant in all three films). The music is similar in each, with frequent strains of "You're in the Army Now" mixed in with the folksongs. And, of course, the imposing vistas of Monument Valley appear in each.

The screenplays for all three films are based on stories by James Warner Bellah. Frank S. Nugent wrote the screenplays for the first two; James K. McGuinness wrote the screenplay for *Rio Grande*. (McGuinness served as the host for the first meetings of the Motion Picture Alliance for the Preservation of American Ideals, an anti-Communist organization the membership of which included John Wayne.)

The films also share a mood. When Thursday rides out of the fort with his troop of cavalry to his ill-fated meeting with Cochise, the wife of one of the officers, watching for her husband as the men ride away, says, "I can't see him. All I can see is the flags." Flags and patriotism figure largely in the films, and the character and importance of the cavalry and the men who lead it seem to extend beyond the borders of the old West.

Between *Fort Apache* and *She Wore a Yellow Ribbon*, Ford made a western that out-sentimentalizes the entire cavalry trilogy: *Three Godfathers* (MGM, 1948). Ford was familiar with the film, having made it before as *Marked Men* (Universal, 1919). He dedicated this version to Harry Carey (who had died in 1948, shortly after his role in *Red River*), calling him the "bright star of the early western sky."

Three Godfathers uses the Christmas story to tell a tale of self-sacrifice on the western frontier. The plot of the film involves three badmen—Robert Marmaduke Sangster Hightower (John Wayne), Pedro Roca Fuerte (Pedro Armendariz), and William Kearney, alias "the Abilene Kid" (Harry Carey, Jr.)—who hold up the bank in Welcome, Arizona. The Kid is wounded in the getaway, and a posse, led by Marshal Perley "Buck" Sweet (Ward Bond), takes off after them. Forced out into the desert, Bob, Pedro, and the Kid search for water. At a water hole, they find an abandoned wagon in which a woman is about to give birth. Pedro delivers the baby, and the mother dies, but not before making the three men promise to take care of her child. Taking their instructions from a Bible, they decide to take the child to the town of New Jerusalem. They follow a bright star in the western sky. Both the Kid and Pedro die along the way, but they return to Bob in hallucinations whenever his strength is about to give out. When he can go no farther, he finds a donkey. He makes his way to New Jerusalem, stumbling through the doors of its Last Chance Saloon on Christmas Eve. (He is given a one-year jail term—after which he will return to the town to raise his godson.)

Pasó por aquí

The cast for *Canyon Passage* (Universal, 1946), directed by Jacques Tourneur, includes Dana Andrews, Susan Hayward, Brian Donlevy, Hoagy Carmichael, Ward Bond, Andy Devine, and Lloyd Bridges. Carmichael plays a character named Hi Linnet, and he uses a mandolin (rather than a piano) to deliver four ballads. The film, based on a novel by Ernest Haycox, gives a realistic view of the pioneer days in Oregon, including a wonderful cabin-raising scene.

California (Paramount, 1947), directed by John Farrow, tells the early history of another state. Ray Milland made his western-film debut in *California*. He claimed that he did it out of fatherly pride: his son, Danny, was spending every Saturday at the movies cheering John Wayne, and Milland was getting jealous. The Welshman was not unfamiliar with horses, having spent four years in the King's Household Cavalry, and he enjoyed the experience—*California* was only the first of many westerns for Milland.

In *California*, Milland plays an army deserter who has become a guide leading a train of covered wagons to California. Barry Fitzgerald plays a gentle vine-grower from Ohio who wants to grow grapes for making wine in California—a noble aspiration. Barbara Stanwyck appears along the way as a lady of dubious virtue. The film covers the history of California from the gold strike in 1848 to its admission as the thirty-first state in 1850.

Ramrod (United Artists, 1947), directed by André de Toth, is based on a novel by Luke Short and stars Joel McCrea and Veronica Lake. McCrea plays the ramrod, or foreman, hired by Lake to contend with the local cattle king (Preston Foster), who wants to take away her ranch (to make matters worse, Lake's father wants her to marry the evil, land-grabbing Foster). McCrea eliminates Foster without much trouble, but he does not then go off into the sunset with Lake—instead, he goes back to his true love, the town seamstress (Arleen Whelan).

In *Blood on the Moon* (RKO, 1948), directed by Robert Wise, Robert Mitchum gets involved in a range war between cattlemen and homesteaders. Robert Preston is the villain, and the film includes a memorable fistfight between the two men.

Glenn Ford is the villain in *The Man from Colorado* (Columbia, 1948), directed by Henry Levin. The story deals with a sort of mental anguish with which postwar audiences were quite familiar—the damage that can be done by war. Owen Devereaux (Ford), former colonel and war hero, is appointed federal district judge in the town of Yellow Mountain. Del Stuart (William Holden), the town marshal, served as a captain under Devereaux during the war. Devereaux is slowly going insane—and he knows it. Something happened to him during the last days of the war, and since then he has been battling madness. In the first part of the film, he remains a sympathetic character because of his desperate battle to maintain his sanity, but then he goes mad, terrorizing the townspeople and his former soldiers. In the end he burns the town to the ground.

72

Above: *Glenn Ford in the final scene of* The Man from Colorado *(Columbia, 1948).* Opposite top: *Joel McCrea taking a loan from a bank in* Four Faces West *(United Artists, 1948).* Opposite bottom: *Barbara Bel Geddes nursing Robert Mitchum in* Blood on the Moon *(RKO, 1948).*

"Everything worthwhile in life is made possible through sacrifice" is the moral of one of the nicest westerns ever made, *Four Faces West* (*Passed This Way* in Great Britain) (United Artists, 1948), directed by Alfred E. Green. *Four Faces West* is an unusual western: it has no barroom brawl, no fistfights, no gunshots. The plot of the film involves a chase: Pat Garrett is after an outlaw (not Billy the Kid this time), but the more the lawman learns of the man he is chasing, the more he respects him. Indeed, the man on the run is a wonderful kind of hero and a truly unforgettable character.

Joel McCrea goes into a bank in Santa Maria, New Mexico, to "borrow"—he leaves an I.O.U.—$2,000. He wants the money to save his father's ranch, and he intends to pay it back (when he later comes into some money, he immediately sends it back to the bank). While McCrea is taking his little loan, the townspeople are listening to a speech from their new lawman, Pat Garrett (Charles Bickford). Garrett takes off after the bank robber, but he is not alone in the chase—the banker puts out a reward of $3,000 (more than was stolen), and others join the hunt.

Leaving his horse, McCrea boards a train and meets a nurse (played by his wife, Frances Dee) and a suspicious but friendly gambler (Joseph Calleia). When they have to leave the train and board a stagecoach, the gambler takes the two to visit Inscription Rock, a large rock on which "adventurers and scoundrels, brave men who leave their imprint" have carved their names and the words *pasó por aquí* ("He passed this way"). The words cut in the stone are the only traces of the many brave men who have come west to the new land. (Located 35 miles east of Zuñi Pueblo in New Mexico, Inscription Rock, or El Morro, has more than 500 inscriptions—the earliest dates to 1605.)

Continuing his flight alone, McCrea comes on a ranch where everyone is suffering from an outbreak of diphtheria. "I'm here to help you," says the outlaw, and he stops running to care for the sick. He uses all his bullets to make a smudge of sulphur for them and selflessly cares for the bedridden, eventually collapsing from exhaustion. He is there when Garrett, the nurse, and the gambler arrive. The lawman agrees to help influence the judge and jury if McCrea will turn himself in. It is the gambler who delivers the final judgment of McCrea: he is a "valiant gentleman."

The screenplay for *Four Faces West* is based on a story by Eugene Manlove Rhodes, a Nebraska-born writer who wrote eight novels and numerous short stories, including "Pasó por Aquí." The film was shot on location in New Mexico, where Rhodes lived and where Pat Garrett chased Billy the Kid. Rhodes had a keen sense of the West and a fondness for the brave, honest, and selfless individuals who settled it. *Four Faces West* captures that sense of heroic self-sacrifice, and it is not surprising that "Pasó por Aquí" is consid-

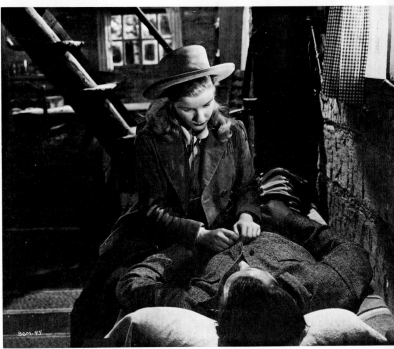

ered to be Rhodes's masterpiece. When he died, he was buried in the San Andres mountains of New Mexico near his ranch. The epitaph on his gravestone reads *Pasó por Aquí*.

Riding
Lonesome

1950–1959

"A lion in your lap"

The Second World War did what the first had failed to do: it joined the United States to the rest of the world. The responsibilities of world leadership included the tension of the Cold War. The Communists who invaded Korea in 1950 could be shot at; their comrades in the rest of the world had to be fought in another way. The Cold War called for a new kind of patriotism from Americans—in this bleak, ideological conflict, there was no glory, no idealism. Even fellow Americans were suspect. The nation's fear of Communism, evidenced in the trials of Alger Hiss and Julius and Ethel Rosenberg, was manipulated by Senator Joseph McCarthy to ruin the careers of countless Americans, particularly in the motion-picture business. McCarthy based most of his reckless accusations on information from unidentified informers, and many people were blacklisted without knowing it. They knew only that they suddenly could find no work.

The Second World War had also ended the Depression and brought about a period of great urban and industrial growth. Well-being brought with it anxiety and disillusionment. The search for a new national identity was mirrored in the search for individual identity in a complex and hostile world. It is not surprising that Americans sought escape in the old West. Westerns, whether on television or at the cinema, provided a world of traditional values in which issues were straightforward and there was still room for heroism and altruism.

While providing escape, westerns also served as an allegorical means of dealing with contemporary problems. Although blacks disappeared almost completely from westerns during the fifties (they had no traditional place in films about the old West, just as they had no established place in contemporary America), greater dignity was extended to Indians. Women were made more prominent and were frequently given leading roles. Sex—usually expressed in scenes of people bathing or removing articles of clothing—became more prevalent, as did graphic violence.

Like contemporary America, the old West on film became rife with neuroses, and in the "psychological" westerns of the decade, alienated individuals wrestled with personal problems. Anxiety and disillusionment hit the old West hard, and heroes and heroines accepted their duties with great reluctance. Being the hero was beginning to be such a lonely task that eventually no one would be willing to do it.

The 1950s saw the end of the traditional Hollywood studio system. Already challenged by foreign competition, the studios were further assailed by rising costs and diminishing profits. The close relationship studios had enjoyed with theaters—most theaters were either owned by a studio or were committed to one through binding contracts—was ended by a government antitrust suit. With the distribution of their product no longer assured, studios cut down their production of films, releasing directors and actors from contracts. The studio system was gradually replaced by independent filmmakers. The studios still distributed the films, but the films were made by individuals who assembled to create the "package." Actors began to get involved in the production and direction of their films, and the era of the glamorous "superstar" ended as actors, choosing their films carefully, created their own images without studio publicity departments. Hollywood was no longer even the center of film production because many filmmakers, faced with soaring domestic costs, went overseas to make their films.

The studios' major competition came from television, the brainchild of two Americanized Russians, Vladimir Zworykin and David Sarnoff. Television had an immediate effect on westerns, for westerns are what television producers chose to make. By the middle of the decade, television had killed off the B western entirely; by 1957, westerns dominated television; by 1959, eight out of the top ten programs were westerns. Among the most popular were "Gunsmoke," starring James Arness; "The Rifleman," starring Chuck Connors; and "Have Gun, Will Travel," starring Richard Boone. New westerns appeared constantly. Some, like "The Westerner," directed by Sam Peckinpah, disappeared after short runs; some seemed to go on forever. Television westerns were a good proving ground for young actors. Steve McQueen, fresh from his encounter with *The Blob* (1958), was given the role of bounty hunter Josh Randall on "Wanted—Dead or Alive." "Rawhide," an hour-long western that went on the air in 1959, included a character named Rowdy Yates. The part was given to a promising young actor named Clint Eastwood.

Filmmakers did not retaliate by making better movies. Instead, they decided to change the screen. Cinerama, with its three-part screen, was followed by VistaVision, Todd-AO, Technirama, Cinemascope, and Panavision—all attempts to change the experience of watching a movie by surrounding the audience with the screen.

Making the experience more exciting was the purpose of another innovation: 3-D (three-dimensional) movies. By wearing specially tinted Polaroid glasses, audiences were given the illusion of having things thrown right at them: the ads for the first 3-D movie, *Bwana Devil*, promised "a lion in your lap." The gimmick was short-lived—audiences didn't like having to wear the glasses—but many of the movies made in 1953, the height of 3-D, were originally released in 3-D. Westerns made in 3-D are easily recognizable: there is a constant flood of arrows, spears, rocks—anything

Preceding pages: Randolph Scott (right) guiding horse of captured outlaw James Best in Ride Lonesome (Columbia, 1959).

that flies—toward the viewer.

Before the decade ended, filmmakers tried AromaRama and Smell-O-Vision, but the best way to compete with television was to lure away its best directors and actors. Directors such as Sam Peckinpah and Arthur Penn came to film from television, and many actors who became popular on television—particularly on live television drama—found themselves offered movie roles. Many of these young actors brought with them another gift from the Russians: Method acting, based on the teachings of Constantin Stanislavski. Such actors as Paul Newman, Rod Steiger, Marlon Brando, Arthur Kennedy, and James Dean added a new style of "motivation" to the films of the fifties.

Riding lonesome

The 1950s also saw a new way of looking at films: the French *auteur* ("author") school of criticism, which holds that the director is the sole creative force behind a film. One of the leading exponents of the *auteur* school was André Bazin, editor of *Cahiers du Cinéma*, a French magazine devoted to film criticism. Taking their study of films very seriously, these French critics fell in love with a number of American directors of westerns, among them Howard Hawks, Nicholas Ray, Anthony Mann, and Budd Boetticher. They analyzed the films and claimed to discern in them the forms of each director's personal style. The *auteur* school has left its mark on film criticism, and it is common today to consider films as the personal statements of their directors. With the breakdown of the studio system—with directors and actors writing and producing their films—the issue is well taken, but many American critics are quick to point out that films are not made by one man, and each should be looked at as the product of a team. Certainly, in viewing westerns it is important to look beyond the director. Writers wrote the screenplays, and such authors as Niven Busch, Borden Chase, and Burt Kennedy have left their mark on westerns, in which the dialogue alone can make or break the film. Film editors spliced the film together, frame by frame, and many films owe their fame to editors—Elmo Williams's work on *High Noon*, for example. The musical score plays a crucial role in the mood of the film, and the works of Max Steiner and Dimitri Tiomkin—among many others—have enlivened many westerns. Being visual experiences, films are also judged by their cinematography, and such men as James Wong Howe, Lucien Ballard, and Vilmos Zsigmond have created true works of art.

Budd Boetticher, one of the directors singled out by the French *auteur* critics, loves bullfighting. A tall, strong man, he was trained as a *torero* by Lorenzo Garza, one of Mexico's greatest matadors. Compared to Ernest Hemingway because of his rough masculinity and his passion for both Mexico and bullfighting, Boetticher displays, in his best films, a novelist's interest in character, both the hero's and the villain's. He is best known for a series of seven low-budget westerns he made during the fifties, but these films have more in common than Boetticher's direction: Randolph Scott is the star in all of them; all but one were produced by Harry Joe Brown; and Burt Kennedy, who went on to direct his own films, wrote the screenplays for most of them.

The films all have poetic titles, exciting action, and, due in large part to the acting of Randolph Scott, a distinctive flavor. Scott is frequently compared to William S. Hart. He has the same angularly handsome—sometimes lonely, sometimes boyish—face; the same clear eyes; and the same quiet, self-effacing demeanor that makes him seem pale compared to the colorful villains. And Scott faces some extraordinary heavies in these films: Lee Marvin, Richard Boone, and James Coburn among them. The villain is frequently more interesting than the hero, and because the plots of most of the films are very similar—Scott is usually seeking revenge for the murder of his wife—the characters move within a specified area, like an arena, with the hero facing the villain in the same way the matador faces the bull. And, as at a bullfight, our eyes are on the bull. We wait to see what he will do, and part of us roots for him.

In *Seven Men from Now* (Warner Brothers, 1956), produced by John Wayne's Batjac Company, Scott plays a sheriff after the seven outlaws—including Lee Marvin—who killed his wife during the holdup of a Wells Fargo stagecoach. Scott is such a fast draw that we never see him go for his gun—the villain draws, and Scott's gun is already out and smoking.

Boetticher himself admitted that he had no idea of what the *T* in *The Tall T* (Columbia, 1957) stands for; advertisements for the film claimed it stood for "terror," but the suspense in the film is less frightening than intriguing, as Richard Boone and two companions hold Scott and a pair of newlyweds captive in a cave.

In *Decision at Sundown* (Columbia, 1957), Sundown is the name of the town Scott rides into, looking for the man who supposedly killed his wife (he has been searching for three years).

Scott makes the mistake of riding into Agry Town, a California border town controlled by the Agry brothers, in *Buchanan Rides Alone* (Columbia, 1958). His pockets are full of money he earned fighting in a Mexican revolution, and the Agrys, who include the town's judge, sheriff, and hotel keeper, are determined to relieve him of it.

Ride Lonesome (Columbia, 1959) finds Scott as a former sheriff turned bounty hunter named Ben Brigade. Brigade is out after a 19-year-old killer named

Billy John (James Best)—or is he out after Billy's brother? For his brother (Lee Van Cleef) hanged Brigade's wife as revenge for being sent to prison by Brigade. Brigade puts Billy on a horse with a noose around his neck and awaits his confrontation with the killer of his wife. (*Ride Lonesome* was James Coburn's first screen appearance.)

Westbound (Warner Brothers, 1959) takes place during the Civil War, with Scott as a captain in the Union Army setting up a stagecoach line to protect gold shipments to the North.

In *Comanche Station* (Columbia, 1960), the last of the series, Scott goes into Comanche territory to try to get back a white woman held prisoner by the Indians (his own wife was taken prisoner many years earlier). He rescues the woman (Nancy Gates), but her husband has put a reward on her head—$5,000, dead or alive—and Scott and the woman are joined by three eager, dangerous-looking men who are out after the money. Then the Comanches attack.

Boetticher was not the only director to make films with Randolph Scott. André de Toth also made a series of low-budget westerns with Scott—the screenplays were not as good as those for the Boetticher films, and the one-eyed Hungarian director did not exhibit Boetticher's fascination for character, but Scott is himself in the films, sometimes shining, sometimes fading away.

In *Man in the Saddle* (*The Outcast* in Great Britain) (Columbia, 1951), Scott's girlfriend (Joan Leslie) leaves him to marry a cattle baron (Alexander Knox). The wealthy rancher is jealous of Scott and decides to get rid of him. He hires a gunslinger (Richard Rober) to go after Scott, and Scott heads for the hills, taking with him a schoolteacher (Ellen Drew). These two are followed by yet another gunslinger (John Russell), who is interested in Drew. After all the battles, Drew and Scott are together, and Leslie is a wealthy widow.

The outlaws in *Carson City* (Warner Brothers, 1952) have a lot of style. They are called the Champagne Bandits because each time they hold up a stagecoach, they serve the passengers a scrumptious alfresco luncheon. The coaches are attractive targets because they are carrying gold and silver ore from the Comstock Lode. Scott is a railroad engineer trying to build a railroad from Carson City to Virginia City—the idea is to keep the precious ore away from the bandits. The leader of the gang, Big Jack Davis (Raymond Massey) does everything he can to foil the building of the rail line, and the residents of Carson City aren't keen on the idea, either—they don't want a boom town.

The Stranger Wore a Gun (Columbia, 1953) opens on a Mississippi riverboat. Scott plays Jeff Travis, a man with a past—he served for a short time as a spy for the Confederate guerilla leader Quantrill, quitting as soon as he realized that Quantrill was fighting for self-aggrandizement, not the cause of the South. When three men attack him—they know of his past—his life is saved by an unseen stranger. He jumps off the boat and later meets up with his savior in Prescott, Arizona. Mourrett (George MacReady) wants payment for his act—he wants Travis to take up the spying business again by going to work for a stageline and seeing to it that the stages fall into Mourrett's ambushes.

In *Riding Shotgun* (Warner Brothers, 1954), Scott plays a stagecoach guard who tries to alert a western town to the danger of a bandit raid. He is mistaken for an outlaw and charged with complicity with the gang. In order to prove his innocence, he has to fight the entire gang of outlaws.

In *The Bounty Hunter* (Warner Brothers, 1954), Scott is sent after a trio of train robbers by the Pinkerton Agency. His job is to track down the thieves, arrest them, and retrieve the $100,000 they've stolen. He finds the robbers in respectable positions in a small town—one (Howard Petrie) is the sheriff; one is the postmaster (Dub Taylor); and one is a dangerous woman (Marie Windsor).

Anthony Mann, another director embraced by the *auteur* school, was part of another fortuitous director-writer-actor team: five of Mann's westerns star James Stewart, and the screenplays for most of them were written by Borden Chase. Few directors made better use of color film and wide screens than Mann, and his westerns are justly famous for their beautiful expanses. But Mann does more with his panoramas than create atmosphere. Like Boetticher, Mann is concerned with character, and his wide-open spaces ultimately become a private, intimate world, within which his heroes rage against their fates. Mann's heroes do not want to be heroic: society has hurt them, and they usually refuse to do good for it until to do so either serves their purpose or they have no other choice. They are loners, cut off from other people by choice, and they perform their heroic acts only after battling with themselves. It is no wonder that Mann's last films, such as *El Cid* (1961), dealt with epic heroes. With Mann, the story is in the character himself, and his eventual courage is made more dramatic because it is so intensely personal.

Mann's first three westerns, all released in 1950, make use of themes that became common during the decade: *Devil's Doorway* is a sympathetic treatment of Indians; *The Furies* tells the story of a cattle baron; and *Winchester '73* was the first and best of a series of westerns about weapons.

Devil's Doorway (MGM, 1950), Mann's first western, stars Robert Taylor as Lance Poole (also known as Broken Lance), a Shoshone chief who served as a Union cavalryman during the Civil War and was awarded the Congressional Medal of Honor for his courage. He returns to his people and their beautiful homeland in Wyoming, an area guarded by the Devil's Doorway (reminiscent of another Wyoming valley, in another movie, guarded by Heaven's Gate). Poole is eager to become a rancher, but he finds that under the Homestead Act Indians cannot own land. Although he has fought bravely for his country—risked his life—the law makes him a ward of the government and prohibits him from owning land. A crooked and bigoted attorney (Louis Calhern) connives to cheat the Indians of their land, and when Poole and a few followers try to fight back, the cavalry is called in. There is no lack of irony

when Poole, dressed in his bemedaled uniform, faces the cavalry. Mortally wounded, he salutes the cavalry commander before falling dead.

The screenplay for *The Furies* (Paramount, 1950) was based on a novel by Niven Busch and, like Busch's earlier *Duel in the Sun*, *The Furies* is about a tyrannical cattle baron who has family difficulties, in this case a stubborn daughter (Barbara Stanwyck) who has no intention of sharing either her father's affections or his land. The gutsy old rancher (Walter Huston, in his last performance) has a New Mexico ranch, The Furies, that is so empirelike that he prints his own money when he finds himself short of cash. When Huston

Barbara Stanwyck and Walter Huston as father and daughter with some homemade money in The Furies *(Paramount, 1950).*

brings Judith Anderson to the ranch and allows that he intends to marry her, Stanwyck throws scissors at Anderson's face as an expression of her disapproval. The rancher, who in his time was not above killing to acquire land, admires his daughter's pluck and lets her have her way.

Winchester '73 (Universal, 1950), the screenplay for which was written by Borden Chase and Robert L. Richards based on a story by Stuart N. Lake, begins in Dodge City on July 4, 1876. As part of the centennial celebration, there is a shooting contest—the prize is a special presentation model Winchester '73. ("The gun that won the West," the Winchester 1873 was a repeating rifle of great power and accuracy.) Overseeing the proceedings is a sweet, wryly humorous Wyatt Earp (Will Geer). James Stewart rides into town seeking the man who killed his father. The man (Dan Duryea) is there, and the two of them compete for the gun. Stewart wins, but Duryea steals the gun and leaves town. The rifle goes through many hands—including those of Rock Hudson as an Indian chief and Tony Curtis as a cavalry trooper—before Duryea gets it back again and Stewart catches up with him. Their final shootout is one of the most exciting ever filmed, the two men blasting away at each other amid barren, craggy rocks, the bullets ricocheting wildly.

James Stewart began a new trend with *Winchester '73* by becoming a partner with Universal: he didn't get a salary, sharing in the film's earnings instead. The idea caught on—William Holden made his fortune by trading a salary for a percentage of the box-office returns for *The Bridge on the River Kwai* (1957).

Winchester '73 was the first of the series of westerns Mann made with James Stewart. In *Bend of the River (Where the River Bends* in Great Britain) (Universal, 1952), Stewart plays a man with a troubled past (he fought as a raider in the Kansas-Missouri border war) who is leading a wagon train of farmers to Oregon. He has taken the job not because he believes in it, but because the farmers make good biscuits. Without hesitation and without pausing to make inquiries, he stops a lynching because "I just don't like hangings." The man about to be hanged (Arthur Kennedy) becomes his friend, and the two of them share a good-natured, sophisticated friendship—based on their professional expertise—that sets them apart from the farmers. They are both wanderers, men who live outside society, going where they please. Stewart explains to one of the farmers that if he points his wagon at the North Star each night, he will know the direction of travel the next morning. "Yes," Kennedy adds, "I pick out a different star each night."

The destination of the wagon train is Portland and the Columbia River, where a riverboat, relocated from the Mississsippi River (including Stepin Fetchit among its crew), carries the farmers and their fruit trees upriver to "a new country where they can make things grow." Stewart and Kennedy eventually clash over supplies destined for the settlers. With the discovery of gold nearby, Portland has become a boom town, and Kennedy wants to sell the supplies, at inflated prices, to miners. Stewart, alone and inwardly raging at the evil machinations of his fellow man, is determined to see that the farmers get what they need, and the two end with a dramatic fistfight in a bubbling stream.

Greed and Stewart's self-control figure largely in *The Naked Spur* (MGM, 1953), in which Stewart again plays a man with a bitter past—his wife left him and sold their ranch while he was away at war. He has become a bounty hunter, and he sets off to track down Robert Ryan, a murderous outlaw, so that he can collect the $5,000 reward and start a ranch. He is joined in his efforts by an aging prospector (Millard Mitchell) and a dangerous man recently kicked out of the army (Ralph Meeker). They capture Ryan and his female companion (Janet Leigh). The outlaws, like the villains in so many westerns of the fifties, know human nature, particularly its less pleasant aspects. Ryan taunts the three greedy opportunists, setting them against one another by arousing their suspicions. Infuriated, Stewart comes very near to losing his self-control and is tormented by nightmares. Leigh manages to attract the affections of both Stewart and Meeker, further dividing the captors. Added to these problems are threatening Indians. The film ends with a three-way shootout among Stewart, Ryan, and Meeker above a rushing torrent.

Stewart's portrayal of lonely, alienated characters reaches its peak in *The Far Country* (Universal, 1955), in which he plays a man who, because he was once hurt in a love affair, does not want to be responsible for anyone—he wants no human involvement at all. The film begins with Stewart and his sidekick (Walter Brennan) taking a herd of cattle to Alaska. In Skagway, they lose their cattle to an evil sheriff (John McIntire) when Stewart—accidentally this time—busts up a hanging. He manages to steal back his cattle and get them to Dawson, where he sells them to the highest bidder, which means to the corrupt group that wants to take over the area. He and Brennan buy a claim, and Stewart pays no attention to the claim-jumping tactics of the villains until Brennan is killed. Only then, after having refused all along to help the good citizens, does he fight.

The title of *The Man from Laramie* (Columbia, 1955) is misleading: as Stewart explains, "I can't rightly say any place is my home. I belong where I am." As Will Lockhart, Stewart is both an army officer performing a mission (out of uniform) and a man in search of revenge. Someone has been selling repeating rifles to the Apaches, and his duty as an officer is to find out

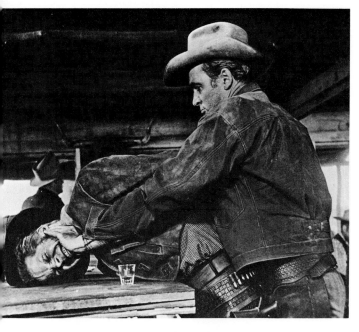

who. His brother was killed by one of those guns at a place called Dutch Creek, and finding the gun dealers is therefore a personal matter.

The Man from Laramie is also about a feud between two ranch owners, Kate Canaday (Aline MacMahon) and Lec Waggoman (Donald Crisp). There is a further dispute between Waggoman's son, Dave (Alex Nichol), and his foreman, Vic Hansbro (Arthur Kennedy), for inheritance of the ranch. Old Mr. Waggoman, growing blind ("I own one hundred thousand acres and I can't see ten of them") and soon to retire, has been having dreams of someone coming to kill his son. He fears that Lockhart is that someone. He is wrong.

The son—thoroughly spoiled and rotten to the core (he makes people say "please" before he will do anything)—and the foreman are the ones who have been selling the rifles, and it ends up being the foreman who kills the son. The son, not having learned anything from his father, was foolish enough to believe that the Indians, in return for the rifles, would help in the range war—they would use the guns only against the Canaday ranch. The foreman wanted the money.

His mission accomplished, Stewart rides off back to Laramie. Canaday and Waggoman, who were once engaged, are again united, ending the range war.

The Last Frontier (The Savage Wilderness) (Columbia, 1955) concerns a fort, manned by one hundred rookie soldiers, that has to hold out against Indians until the spring, when help can arrive from Fort Laramie. The commander of the fort is Colonel Frank Marston (Robert Preston), a vicious and barely sane officer who has earned the nickname "Butcher of Shiloh." He is eager to get out of the fort: as one character says, "He's got to get out and kill Indians." The Indians, mistreated by corrupt agents and the colonel, are eager to meet him. There are a few sane people, including an old fur trapper, who laments, "Civilization is creeping up on us, lads"; Victor Mature, the star of the film, in the role of an army scout; and the colonel's wife (Anne Bancroft), who is understandably drawn to Mature.

The Tin Star (Paramount, 1957), like *The Naked Spur*, involves a man who, because of some personal hurt, has become a bounty hunter. As the bounty hunter, Henry Fonda plays a bitter but wise ex-sheriff who comes into a town to collect his reward for shooting a wanted outlaw. He ends up having to stay in the town, waiting for the reward check to arrive, and he takes it upon himself to educate the young, bumbling, and unsure sheriff (Anthony Perkins). He teaches the

Top: *James Stewart (right) and Dan Duryea in* Winchester '73 (Universal, 1950). Center: *Ralph Meeker being bitten by Janet Leigh in* The Naked Spur (MGM, 1953). Left: *Anne Bancroft resisting the advances of* Victor Mature in The Last Frontier (Columbia, 1955).

81

youthful lawman all he knows, such as "study men—a gun's only a tool," a bit of advice repeated in a different situation in *Nevada Smith*. It is a learning experience for both the green sheriff and the bounty hunter. Fonda's role in the film led to his role as Simon Fry in "The Deputy" on television.

Although it stars Gary Cooper, Mann's penultimate western, *Man of the West* (United Artists, 1958), is not well loved. When it was first released, critics complained about its violence and Julie London's striptease (both of which seem tame by today's standards), but perhaps viewers simply found it difficult to believe mild-mannered Cooper—who was at that time 57—in the role of a former hoodlum.

The film begins with Cooper, in standard heroic fashion, riding alone across rugged terrain. He goes into a town to wait for a train and jumps back, frightened, when the train pulls into the station. It is to be his first train ride, and his comment on the train is, "That's the ugliest thing I ever saw in my life."

"You never saw my ex-wife," points out Arthur O'Connell, who is also waiting to board the train. Cooper (as Link Jones) is on his way to Fort Worth to hire a schoolteacher for his small town. He has been entrusted with the savings of the community, which he has in a bag—along with his gun, the first hint of his past. O'Connell (as Sam Beasley) introduces him to a potential schoolmarm, Julie London (as Billie Ellis).

The train stops to take on wood, and all able-bodied men are asked to help. So it is that Link Jones is picking up sticks when the train is held up. As another indication of his former life, Jones slaps his bare (ungunned) thigh when he hears the gunfire. The train robbers make off with all the passengers' valuables, including his bag with the money.

Jones, Beasley, and Ellis set off on foot to reach civilization, but Jones leads them instead to an old shack, explaining, "I used to live here once."

"When you were a boy?" asks Ellis.

"I don't know what I was," responds Jones. In fact, the shack is the hideout of a notorious gang led by Dock Tobbin (Lee J. Cobb), and it happens that Jones was once Tobbin's right-hand man—together they used to rob banks and commit murder. The vicious gang members force Ellis into a striptease, which Jones is able to stop only by asserting that he has returned to rejoin the gang. Now that he has got his best gunman back in the fold, Tobbin decides to knock over a bank. But Tobbin's information is badly dated, and there is no longer a bank in the town. The town is nearly deserted, and its empty streets become the scene of a gun battle between Jones and the gang members. Jones then confronts Tobbin, declaring, "You've outlived your time." Tobbin dies, Jones finds the missing money, and he and Ellis set off together. But it is an odd ending: Cooper is going home to his wife ("I know

there's no hope for *us*," says Ellis), and Ellis may or may not become the town's schoolmarm.

Mann's last western was a remake of *Cimarron* (MGM, 1960), starring Glenn Ford. Although nowhere near the equal of the 1931 film, *Cimarron* indicates the direction—toward the epic—that Mann was taking. His next two films were *El Cid* (1961) and *The Fall of the Roman Empire* (1964). He died in 1967.

Blood brothers

From dime novels to Wild West shows and through nearly fifty years of western movies, Indians had played their part, whether as ominous red shadows on the horizon or as noble red men facing their tragic fate. In such films as Ince's *The Heart of an Indian* (1913) and Seitz's *The Vanishing American* (1927), Indians received sympathetic treatment; in Ford's *Fort Apache* (1948), Cochise (played by Miguel Inclan) was presented as an honorable man, willing to listen to reason; and in Mann's *Devil's Doorway*, it was clear that the villain was the underhanded lawyer, not the courageous Indian. But in the majority of westerns, Indians performed less enviable roles—they tumbled from ponies as fast as Winchesters could be cocked, they threw tomahawks with alarming accuracy, and, signaling to each other with cunning birdcalls, they crept up on unwary pioneers.

The role of Indians in western movies was changed forever by *Broken Arrow* (20th Century-Fox, 1950), directed by Delmer Daves, which moved the red men from their position as distant targets to the foreground, where they were discovered to be just like white men—maybe even a little better.

Broken Arrow achieved this image reversal by casting a popular actor, Jeff Chandler, as Cochise, and by making it clear that conflicts between Indians and whites are the result of misunderstandings and the malfeasance of scoundrels. Except for a few hotheads, both sides prefer peace.

Based on *Blood Brother*, a novel by Elliott Arnold, *Broken Arrow* relates the story of Tom Jeffords (James Stewart in his first western since *Destry Rides Again*) and his efforts to establish peace between the whites and the Apaches. Jeffords studies the ways of the Indians, learns to speak the Apache dialect, marries an Indian woman (Debra Paget), and befriends Cochise. The two men struggle to maintain the peace between their two peoples, and when Jeffords's wife is murdered by white men, it is Cochise who consoles him.

To make the film as realistic as possible, it was shot on location in Arizona, near the White River Reservation, home of many of the descendants of Cochise. Nearly four hundred Apaches were given parts in the movie, and the producer, Julian Blaustein, was very careful with the details in the film, relying on the In-

dians themselves to provide the dances, music, and war paint. In a further effort to make the film's portrayal of Indians accurate, the speech of the Indians was delivered—in English—in poetic phrases that were supposed to approximate true Indian language.

Broken Arrow was very popular and was followed by a horde of films about Indians. Chandler reprised his role as Cochise in *Battle at Apache Pass* (Universal, 1952), directed by George Sherman, the story of which takes place before the arrival of Tom Jeffords.

Using Chandler in the role of Cochise led the way for other big, male stars—such as Burt Lancaster and Charlton Heston—to play Indians. Heston, whose imposing physical presence and commanding expression made him a favorite actor for biblical epics such as *The Ten Commandments* and for historical spectaculars such as *Ben Hur* and *El Cid*, made an equally impressive Indian—or half-Indian, as was frequently the case. In *The Savage* (Paramount, 1952), directed

by George Marshall, Heston plays a character named Warbonnet, a white man who, following the massacre of his family by Crow Indians, has been brought up by the Sioux. Warbonnet's crisis occurs when he must choose between the Indians and the whites when a war brews between them. In *Arrowhead* (Paramount, 1953), directed by Charles Marquis Warren and based on W. R. Burnett's novel *Adobe Walls*, Heston plays a white man who was raised by the Apaches. However, in this film the experience has not made him love the Indians; rather, he has learned to loathe them, and he can't comprehend how anyone could think of making peace—according to Heston, they must be destroyed. Heston's opposite number is his former blood brother, an Indian named Torriano (Jack Palance) who has been educated at a white man's school in the East. Brian Keith, in the role of a naive cavalry commander, believes the Apaches have agreed to go to a Florida reservation. He does not understand their treachery, and

Jeff Chandler as Cochise (left) passes a gourd to James Stewart as Tom Jeffords in Broken Arrow *(20th Century-Fox, 1950). Jay Silverheels (right) looks on.*

the film ends with a vicious hand-to-hand battle between Heston and Palance.

Florida was, in fact, the location of a reservation for Apaches, and when Geronimo finally surrendered, in 1886, that is where he was sent. Not all the Apaches agreed to go, and *Apache* (United Artists, 1954), directed by Robert Aldrich, tells the story of one such warrior, Massai, played by Burt Lancaster. (Geronimo is played by Monte Blue in his last film after a long career that began with a bit part in *The Birth of a Nation*.)

The musical score for *Apache* (by David Raksin) adds a sense of wildness to the film by using the recorder as its central instrument. Lancaster himself seems half-wild and acts bewildered when, having escaped from the train taking him to the Florida reservation, he confronts the white man's world as he wanders through the crowded streets of New Orleans, staring at a player piano, women in bustles, and a man getting a shave (a similar scene was used in *Broken Arrow*, when Debra Paget, as the Indian maiden, is shocked to see Stewart shave). He is finally "civilized" by the love of a woman and the birth of a child. He even learns to plant corn.

There was plenty of room in Florida for the Apaches because the Indians who had lived there, the Seminoles, had long before been relocated to Oklahoma. One of the so-called Five Civilized Tribes—along with the Cherokee, Creek, Choctaw, and Chickasaw—the Seminoles fought the U.S. government, on

and off, from 1816 to 1843 in the most costly Indian war in U.S. history. Aside from wanting to move the Seminoles to the Indian territories beyond the Mississippi, the government disliked them because they gave refuge to runaway slaves, thereby undermining the institution of slavery. The Indians didn't go without a fight, and the Seminole Wars provide the background for a number of films. In *Distant Drums* (Warner Brothers, 1951), Gary Cooper plays a veteran swamp fighter named Quincy Wyatt who is sent into the Everglades to put down an uprising and destroy a fort being used by gunrunners to supply the Seminoles with weapons. Having destroyed the fort, the small group of soldiers has to contend with the dangers of the swamps and guerilla fighting with the Indians. The screenplay for *Distant Drums* was written by Niven Busch, but the film was directed by Raoul Walsh and has a score by Max Steiner, and it resembles more than anything else Walsh's *Objective Burma*, a Second World War story of Asian jungle fighting.

Budd Boetticher directed *Seminole* (Universal, 1953), which stars Rock Hudson as an army officer fighting the Seminoles, and in 1955 there appeared *Seminole Uprising* (Columbia), directed by Earl Bellamy and starring George Montgomery.

Below: *Burt Lancaster as Massai in* Apache *(United Artists, 1954). Opposite: John Wayne as Ethan Edwards in* The Searchers *(Warner Brothers, 1956).*

"We'll find them as sure as the turning of the earth."

The Searchers

One of the most popular plots for early dime novels was the capture of whites by Indians and their subsequent rescue by the hero. The tale is made even more urgently exciting if the captured whites are females, for white women in a tepee face "a fate worse than death." In westerns, white men who are captured by Indians frequently wind up being chiefs, but white women become squaws, are cruelly abused, and grow old before their time. If left too long with the Indians, they don't want to return to the white world—they cannot stand the shame and would prefer death.

The Charge at Feather River (Warner Brothers, 1953), directed by Gordon Douglas, tells the story of cavalrymen sent to rescue two white sisters (Vera Miles and Helen Westcott) held captive by a Cheyenne tribe for several years. The rescue effort is actually a diversion—it is hoped that while dealing with the intruders the Indians won't notice a railroad being built across their land—and the soldiers chosen are the dregs—the drunks, loafers, and nincompoops—the "Guardhouse Brigade." Because anonymity is essential to their success, they are decked out in mufti. They are also supplied with repeating carbines and given, as their commander, Guy Madison. Madison does his best to train the misfits in guerilla warfare, and he manages to instill in them a little pride.

Off they go, and it doesn't take long for them to rescue the two girls, but one of them—Miles—has become an Indian princess and is slated to marry an important chief named Thunder Hawk. Not only does she not want to return to white society, she does her best to sabotage the rescue attempt. The other girl (Westcott) doesn't want to go back, either, but that is because she is afraid of how she will be treated. The sisters' problems are neatly solved: Miles is killed and Westcott and Madison fall in love.

The film, with spots of comedy and a score that seems better suited to a Latin romance, has the ambience of a horror film, but that is because 1953 was the year of 3-D, and few conflicts fill the air with as many missiles as a cavalry-Indian battle. In *The Charge at Feather River*, the air is loaded with arrows, tomahawks, fists, bodies—of men and horses—rocks, knives, spears, and sabers. In one scene, a sergeant (Frank Lovejoy), confronted with a rattlesnake while sneaking up on the redskins, uses the one silent weapon available to him—he turns and spits at the reptile, his spittle hurtling out of the screen directly into the audience's lap.

Chased by the Cheyenne under Thunder Hawk, the soldiers make their last stand at Colorado's Feather River. Wave after wave of Indian assailants is thrown back by the smoking repeaters. Finally, in a hand-to-hand knife fight, Madison kills the chief. The Indians retreat, and all seems peaceful, but lest his men put down their guard, Madison warns them, "They'll

charge again as soon as they pick a new chief." The Indians are not granted the time to select a new leader, for the cavalry arrives to rescue the beleaguered group.

Trooper Hook (United Artists, 1957), directed by Charles Marquis Warren, relates the story of a white woman (Barbara Stanwyck) who is rescued from the Apaches and sent—along with the son she has borne a chief—to join her white husband. Sergeant Hook (Joel McCrea) has to defend her both from pursuing Apaches (the child's father wants him back) and the prejudice of other whites. There is a good deal of tension, but it comes nowhere near the frightening atmosphere of a similar film, *The Stalking Moon* (1968).

In *The Last Wagon* (20th Century-Fox, 1956), directed by Delmer Daves, Richard Widmark plays Comanche Todd, a white man, son of a missionary, who has been brought up by the Comanches and has learned their ways. The story takes place in 1873 in the Arizona Territory and begins with Comanche Todd fighting the four Harper brothers, the subhuman louts who raped and killed his Indian wife, killed his two sons, and left him for dead. He kills three of them and is captured by the fourth, who delights in describing how he plans to hang Todd—a special method that takes more than half an hour. The evil Harper, dragging Todd through the dirt behind his horse and refusing to feed him or give him water, comes upon a wagon train. The good pioneers do not respond well to Harper's un-Christian barbarities (he even eats before they finish saying grace), and eventually Todd gets his chance to kill Harper with an ax. This prompts one of the kids with the wagon train—played by Tommy ("Lassie") Rettig—to exclaim, "Gosh, I bet Comanches are about the best battle-ax throwers there are!" Having been reared by Indians, Todd's senses are keenly developed, such that when he is befriended by one of the girls, he remarks, "You sure smell good." (John Wayne gives another version of Indian olfactory prowess in *Hondo*, when he explains to Geraldine Page, "I'm part Indian, and I can smell you when I'm downwind of you.")

When the adults of the wagon train are all slaughtered by Indians, Todd takes over custody of the six surviving children (who were off taking a midnight dip during the attack) and gets them safely to civilization, where a judge excuses Todd for the murders of the four Harper brothers because he has saved the lives of the six kids.

When Richard Widmark, as Comanche Todd, assumes command of the group of youngsters in *The Last Wagon*, he says to the kids, "Maybe you could think some like an Indian if you tried." To "think like an Indian" means to learn to live off the land, to be resourceful, to walk quietly. In the comfortable tradition of *Broken Arrow*, the mind of the Indian is not so very alien, and it can be understood and even appreciated; Indians are like white people, differing only in the ways

in which they have adapted to the land.

In another film about Comanches, *The Searchers* (Warner Brothers, 1956), directed by John Ford, to think like an Indian involves shooting out the eyes of the dead so that they will be blind in the next world. It is Ethan Edwards who "blinds" the dead, and it is Ethan Edwards who stands both as John Ford's greatest character and John Wayne's greatest role. The embodiment of the standard Ford theme of civilization versus wilderness, Ethan Edwards is torn apart and has no home. He is a perfect example of the western hero—the strong, self-guided loner—but he is vaguely mysterious, and there is something dark mixed into his character.

The Searchers begins with Ethan Edwards returning after the Civil War to the Texas ranch he owns with his brother, Aaron (Walter Coy). But he has not come straight home: it is 1868, the war has been over for nearly three years, and Ethan's whereabouts during that period are never explained ("Don't believe in no surrender" is his only comment). While he is away, the ranch is attacked by Comanches led by Chief Scar (Henry Brandon). The Indians kill everyone except two girls, Debbie (played, as a child, by Lana Wood) and Lucy (Pippa Scott). Edwards and Martin Pawley (Jeffrey Hunter) set off to get back the two girls. They find Lucy—dead—but it takes them five years to track down Debbie (played by older sister Natalie Wood). Ethan's determination to find the girl ("We'll find them as sure as the turning of the earth") becomes an obsession. When they finally find Debbie, she has become an Indian, one of Scar's wives. Ethan wants to kill her—he believes she has been destroyed. It is Pawley who saves her.

Nothing is done in *The Searchers* to mitigate the brutality of the Indians, and the character of Ethan Edwards on his five-year search is that of a man obsessed with hatred and savagery. Based on a novel by Alan Le May (the screenplay was written by Frank S. Nugent), *The Searchers* is perhaps Ford's most compelling film, one of the greatest westerns ever made. Ford used the new wide-screen process called Vista-Vision, and the film's epic scope combined with Ford's usual human touches—the breezes that pull women's skirts, barking dogs, uneven floorboards, the doorways that frame arrivals and departures, and the pride in being a "Texican"—give the film a powerful emotional force.

Being taken captive is not the only way for a white to join the Indians, and in one of the decade's most popular films, *Run of the Arrow* (RKO, 1956), written and directed by Samuel Fuller, a white man not only wants to join the Indians—he is willing to face a fearful entrance exam.

The advertisements for *Run of the Arrow* claimed the film was "the first motion picture to portray American Indians with authentic realism." The film is actually more symbolic than realistic. It begins on Palm Sunday, April 9, 1865, the last day of the Civil War. A Confederate sharpshooter named O'Meara (Rod Steiger) fires the last bullet of the war: it almost kills Lieutenant Driscoll of the U.S. Cavalry (Ralph Meeker), but Driscoll survives and O'Meara retrieves the bullet. His friends make the bullet into a kind of souvenir—they even have it engraved: "To Private O'Meara, Sixth Virginia Volunteers, who shot this last bullet in the war—and missed." For O'Meara the war is not over. Most of his family was killed during the war—his father fell at Chickamauga—and he decides to remain a Rebel. "I am a Rebel because I want to be, not because I have to be," he says. He goes west to join the Indians in their fight against the U.S. government and meets a very talkative Sioux scout (Jay C. Flippen) who, in a very short time, manages to teach O'Meara to speak Sioux. The two are captured by a gang of whiskey-drinking Sioux (the old scout complains that today's youths are all insolent rebels) who decide to hang the scout and skin O'Meara alive. At the last minute, the scout declares, "We're faster than the run of the arrow," and the two captives are allowed to try to outrun pursuing arrow-shooting Indians, something no one has ever succeeded in doing. The scout dies of a heart attack, but O'Meara has the good fortune to collapse near a friendly squaw (Sarita Montiel) out collecting firewood. She takes O'Meara to her tribe, which is ruled by Blue Buffalo, a wise chief who allows O'Meara to live—and stay with the tribe. The U.S. Cavalry appears, and since O'Meara speaks both Sioux and English, he is chosen to act as guide for a group looking for a site for a new fort. The group of cavalrymen is led by Brian Keith and includes Driscoll, the man O'Meara nearly killed. Keith, a kind man, tries to talk O'Meara out of his hatred. "Lee's surrender was not the end of the South—it was the birth of the United States," says Keith, and he uses the example of Philip Nolan (the character from "The Man Without a Country," by Edward Everett Hale) to show O'Meara that a man needs allegiance to a nation. Keith is killed, and Driscoll takes over and decides to build the fort on Indian land. The Indians, led by Blue Buffalo, attack and kill most of the soldiers. They begin to skin Driscoll alive, but O'Meara puts him out of his misery—by shooting him with the bullet he has been saving since the end of the Civil War. O'Meara realizes that he really is a white man and an American. As his squaw says to him, "You were born an American, and what you were born you will die." Just so that no one will miss the import of the film, it ends with the statement, "The end of this story can only be written by you."

Amid the bloody battle scenes (and they are gruesome; almost every arrow is flaming) and the dense morality of *Run of the Arrow*, one Indian stands out—

Blue Buffalo, played by Charles Bronson. One of fifteen children born in Pennsylvania to a Lithuanian coal miner, Bronson had had roles in a number of films by the time he did *Run of the Arrow*. He acted under variations of his original name, Bunchinsky, using Buchinski or Buchinsky, until 1954, when he changed his name to Bronson as a response to McCarthyism—he feared Buchinsky sounded too Russian. The first film he made using the name Bronson was a western called *Drum Beat*.

In **Drum Beat** (Warner Brothers, 1954), directed by Delmer Daves, Bronson plays Captain Jack, the historical leader of the Modoc Indians in their war (1872–1873) with the U.S. government. The hero of the film is Alan Ladd, who plays a frontiersman sent by President Grant to negotiate a peace treaty with the Modocs. The president wants it done without the use of violent force, but that proves impossible, for Captain Jack is a fearsome Indian. *Drum Beat* did not make Bronson a star. He had not yet earned his French nickname, *le sacre monstré*—"the sacred monster."

Both *Across the Wide Missouri* and *The Big Sky* are about Kentucky fur trappers exploring the territory of the Blackfoot Indians during the early 1830s. Both films are based on popular novels. Bernard De Voto won a Pulitzer Prize for *Across the Wide Missouri* (1947); *The Big Sky* (1947) is the first of a trilogy of historical novels by A. B. Guthrie. The other two books, *The Way West* (1949) and *These Thousand Hills* (1956), were also made into films.

Of the two films, **Across the Wide Missouri** (MGM, 1951), directed by William A. Wellman, feels the most like a historical novel, probably because all the Indian dialogue is spoken in Indian and then translated into pidgin English by Adolphe Menjou, in the role of a French-Canadian. Great care was taken to make the Indian spoken—both Blackfoot and Nez Percé dialects are used—accurate, but the laborious translations, however realistic, slow down the conversations.

Clark Gable stars in *Across the Wide Missouri* as a rugged mountain man named Flint Mitchell, who leads an expedition in search of beaver pelts. To facilitate his dealings with the Indians, he marries an Indian (played by Mexican actress Maria Elena Marques). Their marriage of convenience leads to love, they have a son, and when she is killed (Indian wives of white men led short lives in most films), he takes their son and wanders off into the wilderness.

The film's supporting actors include Ricardo Montalban, who, like Charles Bronson, was cast as an Indian in many films, and Alan Napier, who plays a kilted Scotsman—accompanied by a manservant—out West for the hunting.

The notion of using an Indian woman to ease relations with the Blackfoot was used in *The Big Sky*

(RKO, 1952), directed by Howard Hawks. Grinning—even when one of his fingers is sliced off—Kirk Douglas and his band save the life of a Blackfoot princess and then tote her along on their journey, by keelboat, up the uncharted Missouri River. The film is full of lusty humor, and Arthur Hunnicutt shines in the sort of role he made famous—grizzled old Uncle Zeb.

Contemporary reviewers compared *Across the Wide Missouri* to *Broken Arrow* and felt *The Big Sky* was more epic—they likened it to *The Iron Horse* and *The Covered Wagon*.

Kirk Douglas made his debut as a film producer in **The Indian Fighter** (United Artists, 1955), directed by André de Toth, a film about covered wagons set in Oregon in 1870. Douglas plays Johnny Hawks, a tough scout sent out from Fort Laramie to lead settlers through Sioux territory. He leads the wagon train out of its way so that he can visit his girlfriend (Elsa Martinelli). Douglas's real-life ex-wife (Diana Douglas) has a role in the film—that of a widow who tries to wed the wild scout. The villains of the film are Lon Chaney, Jr., and Walter Matthau.

In **Wagonmaster** (RKO, 1950), directed by John Ford, the wagon train comes to resemble the stagecoach in *Stagecoach*—it is the uneasy home to a crowd of disparate people thrown together on a journey. A group of Mormons led by Elder Jonathan Wiggs (Ward Bond), a disciple of Brigham Young, hires two horse traders (Ben Johnson and Harry Carey, Jr.) to lead them to Utah. Along the way they are joined by a group of traveling actors and a family of outlaws (the Cleggs). The film led to the television series "Wagon Train," starring Ward Bond.

In **Westward the Women** (MGM, 1951), directed by William A. Wellman, Robert Taylor and John McIntire set out to lead a wagon train of mail-order brides 2,000 miles, from Chicago to California.

Thunder in the Sun (Paramount, 1959), directed by Russell Rouse, deals with a wagon train of French Basques who are toting grapevines to California—it is their admirable intention to make wine. (Most Basques out West raised sheep.) The guide for this trip, Jeff Chandler, is distracted by one of the women, Susan Hayward, and the wagon train is attacked by Indians. But the Basques—who wear berets—defeat the redskins by using fancy guerilla tactics.

Television stars could fight Indians as well as anyone else, and **Yellowstone Kelly** (Warner Brothers,

Top: *Kirk Douglas (center, with musket) in* The Big Sky *(RKO, 1952).* Right: *The last lap in the journey is about to begin in* Westward the Women *(MGM, 1951).*

1959), directed by Gordon Douglas, stars three men who were well-known from television. Yellowstone Kelly, the Indian-wise trapper, is played by Clint Walker, star of "Cheyenne"; John Russell, from "Lawman," appears as an Indian chief; and Edward "Kookie" Byrnes, more at home at "77 Sunset Strip," plays a tenderfoot.

There are cows, cowboys, and Indians in Argentina, and Argentine-born director Hugo Fregonese made westerns (such as *Savage Pampas*) both in his native country and in Hollywood. *Apache Drums* (Universal, 1951) differs little from most of the Indian-attack westerns of the period, but it increases the tension by using, instead of a tribe of screeching Indians, a small, grimly determined band. The film begins with a gambler (Stephen McNally) thrown out of the town of Spanish Boot by its righteous mayor, who is also the local blacksmith (Willard Parker). On his way to the next town, the gambler encounters the remains of a group of dance-hall girls, who were also run out of town. The gambler returns to Spanish Boot, but no one will believe his warnings of an impending Indian raid until an empty stagecoach, studded with arrows, bounces into town. Everyone in the town takes refuge in the church, and the Indians attack. The besieged townspeople are eventually rescued, as per tradition, by the arrival of the cavalry.

Tradition was served with a remake, in 1955, of *The Vanishing American* (Republic). Directed by Joseph Kane, this version of the venerable film veers from the original plot and tells the story of land squabbles in New Mexico in which white men and Navajo join forces to battle evil, land-grabbing whites—who, in turn, have as allies Apache renegades.

The arms race

Mann's celebration of a rifle in *Winchester '73* set off a series of films about guns. With a declared "arms race" between the United States and the Soviet Union, the concern for finding a better weapon—and keeping it out of enemy hands—was as contemporary then as it is today.

Colt .45 (Thundercloud) (Warner Brothers, 1950), directed by Edwin L. Marin, tells the sad tale of a gun salesman (Randolph Scott) who goes out West with a pair of demonstration models of the new pistol. While showing the guns to the sheriff of a small town, a bandit (Zachary Scott) gets his hands on them, kills the sheriff, and makes off with the prized pistols. Scott is at first held as an accomplice, but when he gets free he takes off after the villain to retrieve the hardware. The movie served as the basis for the television series "Colt .45," starring Wayde Preston as Chris Colt.

Springfield Rifle (Warner Brothers, 1952), directed by André de Toth, is not really about a gun—the rifle

is of some importance, but the story of the film concerns the birth, during the Civil War, of the Army Intelligence Department (a true Cold War tale). It is 1864, and the Union Army is preparing for a spring offensive, but it cannot obtain horses because the Confederacy has established an efficient spy network (including a "mole") and is stealing the horses. The solution is counterespionage, but the Union Army brass balks at the suggestion—it would be undignified. Major Lex Kearney (Gary Cooper) finally convinces them, and he infiltrates the raiders. He even has the leader of the Rebels killed—a nasty bit of spy work—so that he can take command. The rifle appears as the special weapon used to round up the Confederate horse thieves.

The Springfield rifle plays a larger role in *The Gun that Won the West* (Columbia, 1955), directed by William Castle. It was the Winchester that was called "the gun that won the West," but that hardly matters. In this film General John Pope's men are given the new weapon to help keep down the Sioux in the Dakota Territory.

The original title of *Fort Dobbs* (Warner Brothers, 1958), directed by Gordon Douglas, was *Fifteen Bullets from Fort Dobbs*, a reference to the repeating rifles that someone is selling to the Indians. It takes the film forty-five minutes to get to the fort of the title, but the trip is exciting, with Clint Walker (this was his first film, but he was well-known from his television series, "Cheyenne") leading Virginia Mayo and her son (Richard Eyer) to safety.

There were no Gatling guns during the Civil War (the gun was not approved as army ordnance until 1866), but that fact has not deterred filmmakers. *The Siege at Red River* (20th Century-Fox, 1954), directed by Rudolph Mate, is about Southern spies (Van Johnson and Milburn Stone) who steal a Gatling gun from Union forces and take it on a long journey. Then Richard Boone gets his hands on the gun and sells it to an Indian.

Action oaters

Six men, carrying $60,000 in gold, are attacked by Apaches. Five of the men are slaughtered; the sixth—along with the gold—disappears. The son of one of the men sets out to investigate. He hopes his father is one of the dead men and not, as he fears, the survivor who made off with the gold. (He doesn't like his father.) As he travels along, he comes into conflicts with other men. When, for the umpteenth time, someone takes a shot at him, he expresses his exasperation: "Oh, no, not again!"

The film is *Backlash* (Universal, 1956), directed by

John Sturges, and its similarity to other westerns might prompt the viewer to echo the hero's lament—"Oh, no, not another western about . . . " Revenge? Father and son? Cavalry versus Indians? Homesteaders versus cattlemen? Outlaws versus lawmen? *Backlash* has no message to deliver. It is a simple western, one of the many that are sometimes referred to as "action oaters," and its scenes easily meld with similar scenes from countless other westerns: the indistinguishable towns; the smoky saloons with their little glasses of redeye laid out along the bar; the fisticuffs and the horse chases; the final gunfight won by the hero.

The screenplay for *Backlash* was based on a novel by Frank Gruber, a prolific writer of western stories who is frequently quoted as having said that there were only seven western plots: the story of the railroad; the ranch story; the cattle-empire story—which is just the ranch story on a bigger scale; the revenge story; the cavalry-versus-Indians story; the outlaw story; and the marshal, or "law and order," story. There is a certain amount of cynicism behind this short list, and Gruber was far from the best writer of westerns—this list may reflect his own limitations. Unlike dime novels, not all westerns are written according to formulas, but many of them do fit into categories, such as those outlined by Gruber. With the possession of land such an important feature of the West, it is not surprising that the "ranch story" and the "cattle-empire story" were often used.

The cattle-empire story is really no one single story, and the vast expanses of land available in which to establish mini-empires become a sort of outer space in which mutant forms flourish. The basic story is about possession of land—and maintaining it from generation to generation—but from printing their own money (*The Furies*) to leading their own armies (*Forty Guns*), cattle emperors—and empresses—are alike only in their hardheadedness. The one thing many cattle-empire stories have in common is Barbara Stanwyck (who owns land so well that she did it on television in "The Big Valley").

The title of *Cattle Queen of Montana* (RKO, 1954), directed by Allan Dwan, is straightforward enough. Barbara Stanwyck and her father drive a herd of 2,500 cattle from Texas to Montana. The bad elements in an Indian tribe (led by Anthony Caruso) stampede the herd, killing her father, and most of the remaining steers are rustled by white men (led by Gene Evans). Lance Fuller plays a university-educated son of a chief who wins out over the Caruso faction in the tribe, and Evans is brought to justice by a government undercover man played by Ronald Reagan. Thus, Stanwyck gets back her herd and also wins a husband with whom she can continue the dynasty.

Ride the Man Down (Republic, 1952), directed by Joseph Kane (who directed many Gene Autry films),

Donna Reed and Richard Widmark in Backlash *(Universal, 1956).*

tells another tale of inheritance. When the powerful owner of a 700,000-acre ranch dies, his daughter (Ella Raines) has to fight off land-grabbing neighbors; she is aided by the foreman (Rod Cameron). It is clear in the film that Raines deserves the land not just by right of ownership but because she has inherited her father's pioneer spirit.

Inheriting land and the necessary spirit to control it provides a powerful theme, particularly when the story concerns families blessed with more than one son. There are usually two sons: one is bad—he has inherited only the rough qualities of his empire-building father; one is good—he is aware of the wrongs his father has committed. Faced with encroaching "civilization" (usually small ranchers), the patriarch turns to his rambunctious son, who seems to have the requisite pluck to hold the empire together. The gentle son, espousing peaceful coexistence, has to wait. Sometimes the familial squabbles begin when the father remarries; sometimes racial concerns insinuate themselves, as when one son (the good one) is attracted to

the "wrong" woman—an Indian, of course.

Director Edward Dmytryk, who was born in Grand Forks, British Columbia, of Ukranian parents, had a great deal of success with *The Caine Mutiny* (1954), and Fox asked him to direct a western—his first. *Broken Lance* (20th Century-Fox, 1954) tells the story of a domineering cattle baron (Spencer Tracy), his four sons (Richard Widmark, Hugh O'Brian, Earl Holliman, and Robert Wagner), and his Comanche wife (Katy Jurado). Only the youngest son, Wagner, is a son of Jurado, and the other three dislike both their stepmother and their half-brother. Tracy rules his mutinous household and his cattle empire with his own sense of justice. Civilization is moving in—miners, this time—and he ruthlessly sets out to stop it. Most of the film is told in flashback by Wagner, who goes to prison to protect his father. The film is a remake of *House of Strangers* (1949), which starred Edward G. Robinson.

The Halliday Brand (United Artists, 1957), directed by Joseph H. Lewis, is a more traditional version of the father-son story: the sheriff-rancher father

(Ward Bond) has two sons—the good one is Joseph Cotten and the bad one is Bill Williams—and one daughter (Betsy Blair). Fiercely proud of his family name—he calls it the Halliday brand—Bond wants to keep it untainted, going so far as to refuse protection from a lynch mob for the half-breed his daughter loves.

"What do you want to do, son, wind up using the gunman's sidewalk? That's the middle of the street. It's where they all die, sooner or later." So says a wise lawman to wild Tab Hunter in *Gunman's Walk* (Columbia, 1958), directed by Phil Karlson, a heavily psychological western written by Frank Nugent based on a story by Ric Hardman. Van Heflin is the father with two sons: Tab Hunter is the bad one; James Darren is the good one. Heflin, an old-time rancher who feels hemmed in by the towns and fences growing around him, is a breeder of horses and is very much concerned with bloodlines. Hunter, who emulates the violent side of his father, hates all things of mixed blood; Darren wants to marry a squaw.

From Hell to Texas (*The Hell-Bent Kid*) (*Manhunt* in Great Britain) (20th Century-Fox, 1958), directed by Henry Hathaway, provides a harrowing account of what happens when a rancher (R. G. Armstrong) loses his sons. Don Murray plays a peaceable, wandering cowboy named Tod Lohman who has the misfortune of accidentally killing one of a wealthy rancher's three sons. The second son dies in a horse stampede. Chased by the rancher's men, Lohman saves himself when he saves the life of the last son (Dennis Hopper).

A wealthy rancher with a missing son is the target of a con man in *Branded* (Paramount, 1950), directed by Rudolph Mate. Alan Ladd pretends to be the long-lost son of Charles Bickford—Ladd wants to inherit the spread. But when he falls in love with his "sister" (Mona Freeman), Ladd decides to find the real son, who was kidnapped by a Mexican bandit (Joseph Calleia) twenty-five years before.

In the tradition of *Duel in the Sun*, ranch stories provide rich opportunities for sexual intrigues. It isn't just the sweat and leather. If a man is in charge of the ranch, his wife is usually peeking out from behind the curtains at all the men; if a woman is in charge, things get more complicated—she doesn't need to timidly peek, and where a male uses violence to get his way, a female can use sex.

In *The Violent Men* (Columbia, 1954), directed by Rudolph Mate, Barbara Stanwyck plays the wife of cattle baron Edward G. Robinson. Robinson, who carved his empire out of the wilderness and fought Indians with his bare hands, is a cripple, confined to a wheelchair. Stanwyck is having an affair with his brother, played by Brian Keith, and although Robinson doesn't know about their dalliance, his daughter (Dianne Foster) does. The real trouble begins with the arrival of Glenn Ford, a very peaceable rancher—he has become a pacifist after service as a cavalryman during the Civil War. Robinson cannot abide the small ranchers who are moving into "his" valley, and his henchmen, in true gangster fashion, burn ranches, stampede horses, and murder ranch hands. Ford eventually resorts to violence and uses the guerilla tactics he learned during the war to put an end to the conflict.

Robinson was not the only former gangster operating out West. James Cagney (also wounded—he has a bullet in his back that pains him) plays Jeremy Rodock, a cruel horse-ranch owner in *Tribute to a Bad Man* (MGM, 1956), directed by Robert Wise. Cagney hangs a lot of horse thieves, shocking a young Pennsylvanian (Don Dubbins) and the rancher's own wife (Irene Papas).

Jubal (Columbia, 1956), directed by Delmer Daves, is a sad film about loneliness and the search for a home. Glenn Ford plays the errant cowboy Jubal Troop (the film is based on Paul Wellman's novel *Jubal Troop*) who has the good fortune of encountering a friendly rancher named Shep (Ernest Borgnine). Shep's wife (Felicia Farr, in her screen debut) doesn't love him and has been having an affair with one of his hands, Pinky (Rod Steiger), but when she sees Jubal she redirects her extramarital affections.

As Shep, Borgnine plays a big-hearted but coarse man who claims there are only three things in life worth fighting for: "a woman, a full belly, and a roof over your head." As the lonely Jubal, Ford plays a man forever wandering in search of a home. He believes he has finally found it on Shep's ranch and explains, "Shep gave me a reason for living." But when Shep makes Jubal his foreman, Pinky sets out to get rid of Jubal.

The year before *Jubal*, Borgnine had won an Academy Award for his lead role in *Marty* (1955). *Marty* itself was a significant film because it was based on a teleplay (Steiger had first made a name for himself playing the title role on television)—proof that filmmakers were beginning to see television as a source of more than competition.

Jubal was the film debut of Valerie French, who appears as a member of a religious group of "rawhiders," people traveling in search of a "real home" (rawhiders appear in a less sympathetic light in *Will Penny*). Riding with the rawhiders is Charles Bronson, shining in a pleasantly nonvillainous role. The cast of *Jubal* also includes Jack Elam, the former accountant who had begun his movie career in 1950's *The Sundowners*—he had agreed to help finance the film in return for a part and had gone on to become one of Hollywood's most popular heavies. His protruding eyes helped make him appear thoroughly evil—his left eye is in fact sightless, the result of a childhood fight.

Having a woman in charge of a cattle empire doesn't mean peace for the neighborhood. Female land

owners exhibit the same proclivities as their male counterparts. Sometimes, they are even more vicious.

Man Without a Star (Universal, 1955), directed by King Vidor, has nothing to do with badgeless lawmen. It is a noisy film about a cowboy (Kirk Douglas) who stumbles into the territory of a cattle baroness (Jeanne Crain) who is exploiting the open range and impoverishing the small landowners. Douglas has a visceral hatred of barbed wire and a fascination for indoor plumbing. He even sings—no one stops him—a song called "And the Moon Grew Brighter and Brighter." His battle with Crain and her men is less loud. This film was remade in 1969 with the title *A Man Called Gannon.*

The original title of *Forty Guns* (20th Century-Fox, 1957) was *Woman with the Whip*, and, indeed, Barbara Stanwyck uses a whip to rule her private army of forty mounted gunslingers—she calls them dragoons. They go everywhere with her. Mounted on a white horse, she leads her dark-horsed men on patrols of the countryside. She even has a dining room big enough and a table long enough to seat them all at supper. She sits at the head of the table. "She's a high-ridin' woman with a whip," as the film's song says,

and, as the boss of Cochise County, Arizona, she doesn't respond well when Barry Sullivan and Gene Barry, lawmen brothers, try to bring law to the town. They are a very Earp-like pair, with dark suits and the knack of coldcocking their quarry.

Written, produced, and directed by Samuel Fuller, *Forty Guns* is a favorite with certain critics, who claim to see sexual designs in some of the scenes—double rows of mounted men dividing to allow passage of a wagon; lines of men riding between canyon walls. There is more sexual innuendo than meets the eye. As one of the lawmen brothers says of a local female gunsmith: "She's built like a forty-forty. I'd like to stay around long enough to clean her rifle." Stanwyck's whip is not the only element of sadism in the film, which has more than enough vicious violence. It also has at least one full-screen close-up of an eye. The film is said to have inspired Sergio Leone.

The Civil War divided families, setting brother against brother. The end of the war did not stop disputes among brothers, however. *Horizons West* (Universal, 1952) begins with three brothers, former Confederate soldiers, returning home to Texas. Two of

James Cagney and Irene Papas in Tribute to a Bad Man *(MGM, 1956).*

Kirk Douglas in Man Without a Star *(Universal, 1955).*

them are happy to be back on their father's ranch—the third has dreams of bigger things and starts rustling cattle and killing people preparatory to starting his own cattle empire. The bad brother is Robert Ryan; Rock Hudson and James Arness are the good brothers; the father is John McIntire. Although Budd Boetticher directed it, *Horizons West* does not stand out from other cattle-empire tales.

Nor does *Three Violent People* (Paramount, 1956), directed by Rudolph Mate (who also directed *The Violent Men*). The film begins with an enormous donnybrook between southerners and carpetbaggers and the lament, "It happens a dozen times a day." Charlton Heston is the star, and even though he doesn't take part in the initial fisticuffs (a bartender says to him, "You sure have mellowed down a lot"), he manages to get knocked cold before the film is three minutes old. Heston has a brother (Tom Tryon), and although the two sons are without a father and Tryon is missing one arm, they fight each other quite well. The plot is about postwar government officials stealing land away from ranchers in Texas.

Rod Serling, famous for his television series "The Twilight Zone," wrote the screenplay for *Saddle the Wind* (MGM, 1958), directed by Robert Parrish. The title of the film was originally going to be *Three Guns*, but it was changed to cash in on the title song, which (as in *Man of the West*, also released in 1958) is sung by Julie London. Robert Taylor stars as a former gunslinger (he rode with Quantrill) who buys a ranch and wants to lead a peaceful life. Local problems between farmers and ranchers and intimate problems with his brother (John Cassavetes)—who straps on a gun and goes after the reputation of "fastest draw"—upset all of his plans.

Gregory Peck wanted to produce films, so he formed a company, called it Anthony Productions (named after one of his sons), and got together with director William Wyler. The result was *The Big Country* (United Artists, 1958), a film with a remarkable cast—Peck, Jean Simmons, Burl Ives, Carroll Baker, Charlton Heston—and beautiful, wide-screen panoramas of prairies and mountains. Peck plays a merchant sea captain from the East (he unnerves his western hosts by finding his way unerringly across the prairie using only a compass) who comes West to marry a girl (Carroll Baker) whom he met while she was attending an eastern finishing school. This sea captain, with his own code of ethics, gets involved in a dispute over water rights. (The next film Peck produced was not a western: *Pork Chop Hill*, in 1959.)

"Isn't Texas green?"

"Well, no, not altogether. . . . It's almost a different country."

Texas is more than a different country. It is "a state of mind," and *Giant* (Warner Brothers, 1956), directed by George Stevens, presents that state of mind in such a harsh way that Texans were not pleased with the film (it was shot in Arizona, anyway). Like *Cimarron*, *Giant* is based on an epic tale by Edna Ferber. It was the ninth of her works to be made into a movie, but it was the only one she watched being filmed. The story chronicles thirty years of one Texas family's life, from 1923 to 1953, from cattle Texas to oil-rig Texas.

Rock Hudson, owner of the 595,000-acre Reata Ranch, weds Elizabeth Taylor in Maryland and takes her back to the ongoing dust storm that is Texas. They pass through a gate stuck in the middle of nowhere to an enormous Victorian mansion that rises straight up out of the perfectly flat, dry land. (The mansion was built at the Warner Brothers studio in Los Angeles and then shipped in pieces on flatcars to the site.) The rest of the story, a soap-opera-like tale of jealousies and power struggles, is made fascinating by James Dean as Jett Rink (J. R.), who kicks dust, grumbles to himself—half hoping someone will hear—and laments his role. He inherits land that no one wants—until it is discovered to have oil. And then he becomes Mr. Texas, with all the eyes of Texas upon him.

Giant was Dean's third and last film (the other two are *East of Eden*, 1955, and *Rebel Without a Cause*, 1955). He died in a car crash two weeks after finishing his part.

George Stevens is one of the few directors who started out as a cameraman; he began his career as a cameraman in silent movies, photographing numerous Laurel and Hardy comedies. *Giant* is the third and last film in Stevens's so-called American Dream Trilogy, the first two being *A Place in the Sun* (1951) and *Shane* (1953).

Not all westerns promote landowning. *These Thousand Hills* (20th Century-Fox, 1959), directed by Richard Fleischer, presents the case for the little man, the honest, hard-working cowboy. Lat Evans (Don Murray) gets himself a ranch and exchanges his dance-hall girl for a banker's niece. He even decides to run for public office, and that's when his troubles start.

Regardless of its title, *Rancho Notorious* (RKO, 1952), directed by Fritz Lang, does not fit in with Gruber's ranch stories. The title song ("The Legend of Chuck-a-Luck") says it is a tale of "hate, murder, and revenge," and just about everyone in the moody film gets killed. The film begins with the rape and murder of a woman. Her boyfriend (Arthur Kennedy) takes off seeking revenge and eventually learns that the man he is after is probably hiding at Chuck-a-Luck, a secret hideout for outlaws located near the Mexican border.

Marlene Dietrich—who won the money to buy the place playing a game called Chuck-a-Luck—is the proprietress. Her house rule is "peace and quiet and no talk about the past." The film should have been called *Chuck-a-Luck*.

The various relationships among the characters in westerns frequently make the films hard to locate on Gruber's list. One of director Don Siegel's first films, *The Duel at Silver Creek* (Universal, 1952), involves some overlapping in its revenge theme and some humor in the names of its characters. Lightning Tyrone (Stephen McNally) is the fast-draw lawman in Silver City. He is out after a bunch of claim jumpers who killed his pal. The Silver Kid (Audie Murphy) rides into town looking for the same gang—they killed his father. Lightning makes the Kid his deputy. Aside from the claim jumpers (Gerald Mohr and Lee Marvin), the two lawmen have to face Rat Face Blake (James Anderson) and Johnny Sombrero (Eugene Iglesias).

Audie Murphy shows up again in *Night Passage* (Universal, 1957), directed by James Neilson. He is a member of a gang that steals a payroll from a railroad company. His brother (James Stewart), who works for the railroad, loses his job because of the heist but is rehired and sent out to get the money back. His dispute with his brother doesn't keep Stewart from singing a few tunes.

In *The Naked Dawn* (Universal, 1955), directed by Edgar G. Ulmer, Arthur Kennedy plays a Mexican bandit who robs a freight train and has to hire a young farmer (Eugene Iglesias) to help him collect the money. The farmer's wife (Betta St. John) falls for Kennedy and plans to run off with him; the farmer falls for the money and plans to kill Kennedy. Then the lawmen catch up with them.

Gun the Man Down (Arizona Mission) (United Artists, 1956), directed by Andrew V. McLaglen, stars James Arness. In this film he plays an outlaw out for revenge—his pals and his girl (Angie Dickinson) left him behind when he was wounded during a bank holdup. He catches up with them in a town near the border.

One of the best westerns about revenge, *The Bravados* (20th Century-Fox, 1958), directed by Henry King, begins with Gregory Peck riding into the town of Rio Arriba to watch the hanging of four killers (Stephen Boyd, Lee Van Cleef, Albert Salmi, and Henry Silva). He believes the four men are the men who raped and murdered his wife. The townspeople of Rio Arriba, eagerly awaiting the arrival of a hangman named Simms, are interested in seeing the men hang, too, and when—aided by the hangman—the four men escape, a posse is formed to chase them. Peck joins the posse, saying, "I'm going to find them if it's the last thing I do." He rides ahead of the posse and kills two of the

men, one at a time, when they fall back to shoot him. Peck has to cross the border into Mexico for the last two. He kills one of them, but when he catches up to the last man, he discovers that he was wrong—they had nothing to do with the death of his wife; it was a neighbor who killed her. *The Bravados* has more scenes inside churches, more singing choirboys, and more religious discussions than most westerns. The men Peck killed were innocent of the crime he killed them for but were guilty of other crimes. That fact does little to console him, and the film ends with Peck asking the townspeople of Rio Arriba to remember him in their prayers.

Ben Piazza and George C. Scott made their screen debuts in *The Hanging Tree* (Warner Brothers, 1959), directed by Delmer Daves. The film stars Gary Cooper as Doc Joe Frail, an embittered man—he discovered his wife was having an affair and killed the man; his wife killed herself; and he burned down their house— who is drinking himself to death in Skull Creek, a remote mining town in Montana. (The screenplay for the film is based on a story by a Montana author, Dorothy

M. Johnson; Cooper, the star of the film, was born in Montana; and the film is set in Montana—it was filmed in Washington State.) When a young Swiss girl (Maria Schell) suffers blindness as the result of exposure following an Indian attack on a stagecoach, Doc Frail cures her. And when Scott—in the role of a religious fanatic—organizes a lynch mob and is about to hang Frail, she saves the doctor's life.

The Hanging Tree was one of Cooper's last westerns. He made a guest appearance in *Alias Jesse James* (United Artists, 1959), a Bob Hope comedy-western directed by Norman McLeod. That same year Cooper made his last western, *They Came to Cordura* (Columbia, 1959), directed by Robert Rossen, in which he plays an army officer accused of cowardice who is given the task of selecting soldiers for the Medal of Honor. The action takes place in Mexico in 1916, during the punitive expedition led by General Pershing against Pancho Villa.

By 1960, Cooper was gravely ill—he was dying of cancer. His illness was kept a secret, and although in terrible pain, he agreed to narrate a television documentary called "The Real West," in which he separated the truth about the old West from the fictionalized film accounts. He was awarded a third Oscar in 1961, but he did not appear at the ceremony—James Stewart accepted the award on his behalf. Cooper's sickness was no longer a secret. When he died, May 14, 1961, the world mourned his passing.

Cooper may well have been the last "altruistic" hero, the last recognizable good guy. When he died, he took with him a tradition that went back to the earliest westerns: the man who eventually does what is right. His sincerity was based on more than his good looks—he was a man of the West, and he knew what the western experience had really meant to Americans. He was born in Helena, Montana, in 1901—just two years before the birth of western movies. As a boy, he grew up listening to old-timers—men who had taken part in the real West. He remembered hearing one say, "It's big and purty now, all right—and I helped build it. But, by damn, wouldn't it be fun to tear it down and start all over again!"

"You haven't gotten tough. You've just gotten miserable."

Cowboy

The year 1952 saw two movies about the rodeo circuit. *The Lusty Men* (RKO, 1952), directed by Nicholas Ray, is perhaps the first western about rodeo—it is certainly one of the best. Horace McCoy (who later wrote *They Shoot Horses, Don't They?*) collaborated on the screenplay. The film stars Robert Mitchum as a rodeo champion who has been forced to retire because of injuries. Having squandered his winnings on women and gambling, he goes back home to Oklahoma, where he meets a young cowboy (Arthur Kennedy) and his wife (Susan Hayward). He agrees to teach Kennedy his rodeo skills in return for half the take. Kennedy does well and is quickly raking in money and spending it on wine and women instead of putting it away for a ranch. (As Mitchum warns him, "Either you beat the money or the money beats you.") Mitchum gets himself killed in an effort to set Kennedy straight.

Budd Boetticher's *Bronco Buster* (Universal, 1952), based on a story by Peter B. Kyne (Horace McCoy again collaborated on the screenplay), tells a very similar tale of the rodeo circuit: a rodeo champ (John Lund) teaches a promising newcomer (Scott Brady). Success turns Brady into an egomaniacal brute—he even goes after Lund's girl (Joyce Holden), the daughter of a rodeo clown (Chill Wills). Brady's bullriding gets Wills killed and, in a typical Boetticher scene, Brady and Lund hold their own bullriding contest in a darkened arena. The film includes scenes of real rodeo performers, such as Casey Tibbs.

The theme of a former star teaching a youth the

ropes of rodeo was repeated in *When the Legends Die* (1972).

A year before he died, Frank Harris published *My Reminiscences as a Cowboy*, an autobiographical account of his experiences on the cattle trails in 1871. Since much of Harris's writing is considered spurious at best—he enjoyed creating scandalous accounts of his contemporaries—his reminiscences are undoubtedly exaggerated. They provide the material from which Edmund H. North wrote the screenplay for *Cowboy* (Columbia, 1958). Directed by Delmer Daves, *Cowboy* stars Glenn Ford (Daves and Ford also made *Jubal* and *3:10 to Yuma* together) as a tough cattleman named Reese and Jack Lemmon as Frank Harris. The film begins with Harris working as a clerk in a Chicago hotel. When Reese arrives, having just completed a cattle drive, Harris manages to join up with him and takes part in the next drive. The film seeks to represent a deglamorized version of the workaday world of cowpunchers. Harris's ideals are offended by the cowboys' casual treatment of death ("cattle count, not men") and brutality. He and Reese battle it out through the cattle drive, Reese silently impressed by Harris's pluck and Harris embittered by the experience (at one point Reese tells him, "You haven't gotten tough. You've just gotten miserable"). Through a cattle stampede, an Indian attack, and fistfights, Harris grows to appreciate the cowboy's life, and Reese softens up. The film ends with the two men taking baths in the Chicago hotel, joyously shooting cockroaches off the wall.

"You're not like the book! You're not him!"

The Left-Handed Gun

The authors of dime novels and penny dreadfuls and journalists writing for such publications as the *National Police Gazette* began glorifying the exploits of Billy the Kid long before he was killed. Billy did nothing to correct these exaggerated accounts and may even have killed a few men in an attempt to live up to his public image. The events of his life—his friendships with John Tunstall and John Chisum; his involvement in the Lincoln County War; his capture and subsequent escape; his murder by Pat Garrett—have been used in many westerns. The sequence of events rarely changes, but the character of Billy is never the same. Sometimes he is portrayed as a hero; sometimes he is a punk killer; sometimes he is just a misunderstood teenager.

In *I Shot Billy the Kid* (Lippert, 1950), directed by William Berke, Garrett (Robert Lowery) tells the story of Billy (Donald Barry) and explains why he killed him. The film claims to be factual—a remarkable claim, considering that except for the basic outline of his career, scholars agree on very little about Billy—his real name is still the subject of dispute. They cannot even

James Stewart (left) and his "brother," Audie Murphy, in Night Passage *(Universal, 1957).*

agree on whether or not he was left-handed.

It is clear from the title which hand Gore Vidal opted for when he wrote his television play about Billy. Arthur Penn, who directed the film version of the play, *The Left-Handed Gun* (Warner Brothers, 1958), said that the controversy over whether or not Billy was left-handed was not important—he believed that spiritually and psychologically Billy was left-handed. The film presents Billy the Kid as a "kid," a juvenile delinquent who loves dancing, listening to loud music, and playing pranks. Like most teenagers, part of his body is always in movement, and he is full of an energetic righteousness that blinds him to the consequences of his actions. Paul Newman plays Billy in the film, and his Method acting leads to wild, uncontrolled body movements: when Billy nods his head in assent, his chin strikes his chest. Newman's acting combines with the pointedly religious symbolism in the film to make a potent mixture that is not to everyone's liking.

Another controversy about Billy the Kid is whether or not he was literate. In *The Left-Handed Gun* he is learning to read. His fatherly benefactor, Mr. Tunstall, teaches him how to decipher "the black marks" on the page. When Mr. Tunstall is gunned down, Billy begins shooting people, and everything he does is reported in newspapers "from the East." By the end of the film, books are being written about his life. In one of the books, he is described as "a figure of glory," and when the newspapers declare him dead, Billy duplicates the Mexican *Pascua* (Easter) rite of rebirth from fire. Billy is followed by an eastern drummer who is a true believer until he realizes that Billy is not the true glory—he is only human. "You're not like the book!" yells the drummer. "You're not him!" In true Judas fashion, the drummer turns Billy in to the law. Billy dies, a victim of his own publicity.

Were the James brothers, Jesse and Frank, villains or victims? In the tradition of *Jesse James* (1939), *The Great Missouri Raid* (Paramount, 1950), directed by Gordon Douglas, depicts the James Brothers—MacDonald Carey as Jesse and Wendell Corey as Frank—as essentially honest men driven to outlawry by circumstances, in this case a vindictive northerner (Ward Bond) who becomes a detective for a bankers' association and hunts them down. In another tradition—one that goes back to *When the Daltons Rode* (1940) and continued past *Butch Cassidy and the Sundance Kid* (1969)—the outlaws are pursued by agents who emerge, mounted on leaping horses with guns blazing, from railroad cars.

Films have made heroes of the James brothers, and to many of their contemporaries, particularly in Missouri, they were heroic figures, local Robin Hoods. But to most of the country, they were outlaws, men who robbed banks and shot people. When the James boys and their gang (including the Younger brothers) rode into the small town of Northfield, Minnesota, they got a big surprise: the townspeople were waiting for them. In the ensuing battle, the James gang was shot to pieces—they weren't heroes to the people whose money they stole.

The True Story of Jesse James (*The James Brothers* in Great Britain) (20th Century-Fox, 1957), directed by Nicholas Ray, begins in the middle of the Northfield raid and, in a series of flashbacks that leads back up to the raid, tells the story of the James brothers—this time presented as typical fifties teenagers, with Robert Wagner as Jesse and Jeffrey Hunter as Frank. The film is "true" only to the myth of Jesse James created by film—indeed, *The True Story of Jesse James* uses the same screenplay by Nunnally Johnson that was used in the 1939 *Jesse James*.

The True Story of Jesse James was the fourteenth film version of the Jesse James story; the twenty-fifth film about Jesse was *The Great Northfield Minnesota Raid* (1972). And in 1980 Jesse and his gang, dressed as always in their long dusters, ride into Northfield in *The Long Riders*. And once again they are surprised when the locals open fire.

Poor John Wesley Hardin! The greatest killer of the old West, who far outshot the likes of Billy the Kid and Jesse James, has remained unknown, even though Bob Dylan wrote a song about him (and misspelled his name as "Harding"). The story of his life reads like a western novel: at 15 he killed his first man, probably in self-defense, and as his prowess with a gun grew he had to deal with persistent punks trying to challenge his reputation. Sent to prison, he taught himself the law. His life ended when a small-time lawman shot him in the back in the Acme Bar in El Paso.

The Lawless Breed (Universal, 1952), directed by Raoul Walsh, stars Rock Hudson as John Wesley Hardin. The film dances around the facts of Hardin's life and ends with him allowing himself to be shot to prove to his son that life with a gun is wrong. Hardin himself would have found the film amusing.

Law and Order (Universal, 1953), directed by Nathan Juran, is a remake of the 1932 film about the Earp-like Frame Johnson. In this film, Johnson (Ronald Reagan) cleans up Tombstone and then tries to retire his guns. He moves to another town, but he finds that again he has to assume the job of marshal.

Were the Earps upstanding lawmen or were they thieves, pimps, con men, and killers? Stuart N. Lake and Walter Noble Burns both wrote books that make the Earps out to be heroic figures, but the facts are open to interpretation.

Leon Uris, author of such best-selling novels as *Exodus* and *QB2*, wrote the screenplay for *Gunfight at the O.K. Corral* (Paramount, 1957), directed by John Sturges. This rendition of the famous shootout—which took place in Tombstone, Arizona, on October 26,

Revenge and the sweet sound of a cappella *singing: Gregory Peck in* The Bravados *(20th Century-Fox, 1958).*

1881—is every bit as fictionalized as the other film versions, such as Ford's *My Darling Clementine*. The film is probably the biggest and loudest presentation of the Earp legend, and, with Burt Lancaster as Wyatt and Kirk Douglas as Doc Holliday, it has a lot of virile action. It also continues the fifties theme of the lone gunfighter, in this case Wyatt, who says at one point, "All gunfighters are lonely. They live alone and they die without a dime, a woman, or a friend." The film's version of the gunfight is lengthy and even bursts out of the corral into the streets of Tombstone. Like *High Noon*, the film has a ballad written by Dimitri Tiomkin and Ned Washington—it is sung by Frankie Laine at the beginning and end of the film. Like *My Darling Clementine*, its cast includes John Ireland. In Ford's film he plays Billy Clanton; in *Gunfight at the O.K. Corral* he plays a character named John Ringo.

The real John Ringo (the character on whom Jimmie Ringo in *The Gunfighter* is based) was not at the O.K. Corral at all. He was in Tombstone at the time of the gunfight, however, and legend has it that he—alone—invited Wyatt and his two brothers to "step out into the street." All three refused. Although he did not die at the O.K. Corral, he did not outlive it by much—he was shot down a few months later by John O'Rourke, alias Johnny-behind-the-deuce.

Stuart N. Lake, the man whose biography of Wyatt Earp was used as the basis for numerous films, served as the technical adviser for *Wichita* (Allied Artists, 1955), directed by Jacques Tourneur. This film presents Wyatt (Joel McCrea) in his early days (around 1874) taming a wild cow town in spite of objections from the local businessmen who are making a lot of money off the troublemaking cowpokes.

McCrea plays another famed lawman, Bat Masterson, in *Gunfight at Dodge City* (United Artists, 1959), directed by Joseph M. Newman. Bat Masterson really did serve as a lawman in Dodge City, and, like Wyatt Earp, he had brothers. In this film, Masterson, seeking revenge for the murder of his brother, becomes sheriff and has to shoot it out with Don Haggerty. Viewers of the film were troubled by McCrea's outfit—he wears a Stetson and carries a sixgun instead of wearing a bowler and carrying a cane, as did Gene Barry in the role of Bat Masterson on the television series (which had begun in 1957). The producers of the film hastened to inform people that both outfits were authentic. In fact, Bat Masterson went through numerous changes of hats: he began his career as a buffalo hunter, became a scout, a gambler, a lawman—and ended his days as sports editor for *The New York Morning Telegraph*. (He died in 1921.)

McCrea made this film at the same time that Randolph Scott made *Comanche Station*: both men then retired from films before being teamed, for the first time, in *Ride the High Country* (1962).

The war in the West

From prewar Kansas to postwar California, the Civil War and its aftermath provide the background for countless westerns. Although films about particular battles may not qualify as westerns, films about raids, spies, or events in the West—films that usually involve mounted men and sixshooters instead of lines of uniformed soldiers—have become accepted members of the genre.

Jesse James learned his violent ways while riding with Quantrill along the Kansas-Missouri border, but that area was the scene of vicious battles even before the war. At issue was how Kansas would be admitted to the Union—with or without slavery—and the conflict was fought by the so-called Border Ruffians, pro-slavery raiders, and the abolitionist Jayhawkers. *The Jayhawkers* (Paramount, 1959), directed by Melvin Frank, tells the story of two men, one of them (Jeff Chandler) a leader of the Jayhawkers—he dreams of building an empire, of becoming a Napoleon of the plains—and the other a wily farmer (Fess Parker) spurred on by private vengeance.

On a rainy Saturday in April of 1862, James J. Andrews, a Union spy, and a group of nineteen volunteers took part in a daring raid behind Confederate lines. Their object was to burn railroad bridges along the Georgia railway in the hope of cutting off Rebel supplies. They commandeered a train and took off on what has become known as the great locomotive chase. The Walt Disney-produced version of these events, *The Great Locomotive Chase (Andrews' Raiders)* (Buena Vista, 1956), directed by Francis D. Lyon, stars Fess Parker as Andrews.

The Raid (20th Century-Fox, 1954), directed by Hugo Fregonese, relates another actual incident from the Civil War. Confederate prisoners escape from a Union prison camp near the Canadian border and, posing as civilians, plan to burn and pillage a small town in Vermont. It is 1864, and they hope to create a diversion to draw Union troops away from the front. However, their leader (Van Heflin) is eventually torn between his sense of duty and his affection for a Union war widow (Anne Bancroft).

The Horse Soldiers (United Artists, 1959), directed by John Ford, tells the story of yet another actual raid: the film is based on a raid led by Colonel Benjamin H. Grierson, a former Illinois music teacher who was sent by U.S. Grant with a force of 1,700 mounted men on a raid tearing up railroad tracks and checking enemy troop strength around Vicksburg. The colonel's name is changed in the film to Marlowe, and the role is played by John Wayne (a man difficult to imagine as a music instructor). The Union cavalry in *The Horse Soldiers* is not the happy family it is in Ford's films about the West, and the Civil War is portrayed as futile, with no winners—just a lot of wounded.

A Confederate raid into southern Indiana provides a few dramatic moments in *Friendly Persuasion* (Allied Artists, 1956), directed by William Wyler. A wholesome comedy—a true "family picture"—*Friendly Persuasion* tells the story of a family of pacifist Quakers who are faced with problems of conscience when the Rebels begin burning down nearby farms. The head of the family is Gary Cooper, his wife is Dorothy McGuire, and it is their eldest son, Anthony Perkins, who finally decides that he has to fight. In between the "thees" and "thous," most of the film deals with the father's fondness for fast horses and his wife's concern with the evils of music. When the Confederate troops arrive, Cooper's advice to his anguished son is, "Man's life ain't worth a hill of beans unless he lives up to his own conscience."

That sort of advice was not always helpful during the fifties. The screenplay for *Friendly Persuasion* was written by Michael Wilson (based on the best-seller by Jessamyn West). Wilson was given no screen credit, because he had pleaded the Fifth Amendment when he was summoned, in 1951, as a witness before the House Un-American Activities Committee. When the screenplay was nominated for an Academy Award, it was rejected for the same reason.

The screenplay for another western made in 1956 did win the Academy Award. Robert Rich won the award for best writer (motion picture story) for the screenplay for *The Brave One* (IND, 1956), directed by Irving Rapper. Rich did not come forward to pick up his Oscar; indeed, he could not be found. For nineteen years the Oscar remained unclaimed. In 1975, the producers of the film sent the Academy of Motion Pictures an affidavit explaining that "Robert Rich" was actually Dalton Trumbo. Trumbo had been blacklisted—he was one of the Hollywood Ten—and had written the screenplay under the pseudonym.

To many people the Communist threat was very real, and they believed that it was essential for all Americans to join in the battle. The theme of Americans putting aside their differences to confront a common enemy—a red menace—is reflected in the many films about "galvanized Yankees," Confederate prisoners of war who were released from prison to fight Indians out West under the Union flag. Numerous films during the fifties and sixties (Sam Peckinpah's *Major Dundee* may be the best example) concentrated on the irony of Confederate soldiers fighting alongside Union soldiers.

Two Flags West (20th Century-Fox, 1950), directed by Robert Wise, is an early version of that theme, and it uses a number of stereotyped roles—the Yankee officer is a by-the-book, foolish disciplinarian; the Southern officer is flashy, open, and likeable. The starchy Yankee commander is Jeff Chandler; Joseph Cotten is the suave Rebel officer, always on the lookout for an opportunity for him and his men to escape. The Rebels are sent West to fight the Kiowas, who took advantage of the Civil War to try to get back their land. (Kit Carson, Bat Masterson, and 300 other volunteers fought the Kiowas at Adobe Walls, in the Texas Panhandle, in 1864.) Chandler kills the son of an Indian chief, the Indians surround the fort, and Cotten gives up his chance to escape to go to their aid. But the fort is saved only when Chandler turns himself over to the Kiowas.

In *Escape from Fort Bravo* (MGM, 1953), directed by John Sturges, William Holden is the cold Northerner and John Forsythe is the warm, polite Southerner. The two officers vie for the affection of Eleanor Parker at Fort Bravo, a Union cavalry post in Arizona, in 1863. The fort is being used to house Confederate prisoners of war, and when they escape, Holden takes off in pursuit and comes upon them just before the Indians do. Most of the men, both Union and Confederate, are killed off by the Indians before they are saved by the arrival of the cavalry.

Only the Valiant (Warner Brothers, 1951), directed by Gordon Douglas and based on a novel by another director, Charles Marquis Warren, tells the story of another tense situation in the cavalry. Gregory Peck plays a cavalry captain who, because of a misunderstanding, is believed by the men to be a coward. To prove himself, he chooses those troopers who hate him the most—who are eager to see him dead—for a crucial mission. With his small band of spiteful soldiers, Peck has to hold a narrow mountain pass against the Apaches.

Day of the Outlaw (United Artists, 1959), directed by André de Toth, concerns a small town in the Wyoming mountains—its population numbers twenty-four men and four women—that is seized by a gang of renegades who have held up a Union Army paymaster's wagon. Their leader, a certain Captain Jack (Burl Ives), keeps his rabble from terrorizing the townspeople (they want to "have a little fun" with the women) and shows himself to be a decent man. Robert Ryan, one of the men in the town, is in love with one of the few women (Tina Louise); the fact that she is married is no problem—he plans to kill her husband. Ryan ends up leading the gang out of town.

Gun Fury (Columbia, 1953), like *Friendly Persuasion*, is about pacifism and how it doesn't always work. Based on the novel *Ten Against Caesar*, by K. R. G. Granger—the screenplay was written by Roy Huggins, who also directed, and Irving Wallace—the film deals with a former Yankee (Rock Hudson) who is weary of violence. When his fiancée (Donna Reed) is kidnapped by an outlaw gang led by an embittered Southerner (Philip Carey), Hudson finds himself obliged to do battle with the gang.

Copper Canyon (Paramount, 1950), directed by John Farrow, takes place in Nevada (the film was shot in Arizona) just after the Civil War. Former Rebs have gone there to work in the copper mines, but the local smelters are former Yanks, and they refuse to smelt the Rebel ore. Then a stageshow marksman (Ray Milland) appears in town. Although he denies it, the Rebs recognize him as their beloved Colonel Desmond, former officer in the Confederate Army who has escaped from a Yankee prison. The film has a comic aspect, with tobacco-chewing mules, cigar-smoking women, and a garrish stageshow. Hedy Lamarr is the heroine; the heavy is MacDonald Carey. Milland puts an end to the dispute by leading his men in one last charge.

The wonderful country

Very few westerns deal with our neighbor to the north, Canada, but Mexico—with its revolutionary turmoil and appealing lifestyle—has become, in westerns, almost an extension of the American Southwest. When, around the turn of the century, civilization closed down the options north of the border, more and more Americans—escaping the law or searching for a place in which to continue "living by their guns"—crossed the border into Mexico where they found a home in the chaos of the Mexican Revolution. Westerns rarely seek to clarify the issues involved, and such names as Madero and Diaz, Huerta and Carranza, Villa and Zapata, are dropped to supply a vague excuse for the action.

Viva Zapata! (20th Century-Fox, 1952) tells the story of the Mexican revolutionary leader Emiliano Zapata, whose army fought against the various regimes of Madero, Huerta, and Carranza, and whose movement, *zapatismo*, exemplified the Mexican agrarian movement. Zapata's rallying cry was "Land and liberty!"—it seems fitting that the screenplay for the film was written by John Steinbeck. The film was directed by Elia Kazan, founding member of the Actors Studio and a major exponent of Method acting. The film stars Marlon Brando, who a year earlier had made his fame in Kazan's film version of *A Streetcar Named Desire*. But it was Anthony Quinn, in the role of Zapata's brother, who won an Academy Award—his first.

Quinn's own life was touched by the revolution. His father was an Irish-American adventurer and his mother was Mexican. As an infant, he had been smuggled out of Mexico during the revolution. His acting career had gotten a boost when he played the lead role in the Broadway play *A Streetcar Named Desire*. He made a convincing Mexican, and in *Ride, Vaquero* (MGM, 1953), directed by John Farrow, he plays a Mexican bandit named Jose Esqueda who terrorizes the border country and comes into conflict with a settler (Howard Keel) and his wife (Ava Gardner).

"I tell not the fall of Alamo. . . . not one escaped to tell the fall of Alamo."
—Walt Whitman, *Leaves of Grass*

It is not surprising, considering his passion for both Mexico and bullfighting, that Budd Boetticher chose to direct a film about the Alamo. The premise of *The Man from the Alamo* (Universal, 1953) is that one man did escape to tell the fall of Alamo. (Boetticher claimed the story was factual and that the one man who escaped was Jewish.) The man in the film is Glenn Ford. He is branded a deserting coward by most people because they do not know the reason for his survival—the men inside the Alamo drew lots to choose one man to escape and warn their families about the danger. The families are all wiped out by renegades disguised as Mexican soldiers, and Ford has to join the gang in order to expose the villains.

Ford was slated to star in Boetticher's next film, but he got hurt in a fall and the part was given to Van Heflin, who had just finished his role in *Shane*. The title of the film, *Wings of the Hawk* (Universal, 1953), is a reference to the falcon on the flag of Mexico, and the story of the film takes place in 1911, during Pancho Villa's insurrection. Heflin plays "Irish" Gallagher, an American engineer whose gold mine is appropriated by the Mexican provisional governor (George Dolenz). Heflin joins the revolutionary forces (which include Julia Adams) and ends up destroying his own mine. The film was Abbe Lane's debut.

Villa, Zapata, and their twentieth-century revolution are not the only source of western-style action in Mexico's history. After liberal leader Benito Juarez won the War of Reform (1858–1861), the defeated conservatives sought foreign aid—and got more than they had bargained for. France decided to establish an empire in Mexico and sent a Hapsburg prince, Maximilian, to take charge (the United States would have tried to prevent this, but the Civil War presented more urgent problems). With the arrival of Maximilian and his French troops in 1864, Juarez had a new foe. In 1865, with the end of the American Civil War, the Mexican conflict seemed appealing to restless American gunfighters and adventurers. Many of them rode across the river into Mexico, offering their services as mercenaries to the highest bidder. *Vera Cruz* (United Artists, 1954)—a very popular western and an important film in the history of westerns—tells the story of two such men.

Gary Cooper and Burt Lancaster are the stars of *Vera Cruz*: Cooper plays Ben Trane, a Louisiana plantation owner who has lost his fortune fighting for the Confederacy during the Civil War; Lancaster is Joe Erin, a colorful leader of a gang of desperadoes. The two soldiers of fortune are hired by the Emperor Maximilian to escort a countess (Denise Darcel) through territory held by Juaristas. The trip is actually a cover

Opposite top: Hedy Lamarr and MacDonald Carey in Copper Canyon *(Paramount, 1950). Opposite bottom: Marlon Brando (right) as Zapata in* Viva Zapata! *(20th Century-Fox, 1952).*

for a shipment of gold being sent to the emperor's troops. Cooper's sympathy is won by an idealistic peasant girl named Nina (Sarita Montiel), and he and Lancaster end up battling over possession of the gold.

Directed by Robert Aldrich, whose films are noted for their violence, *Vera Cruz* is the granddaddy of the "spaghetti"—Italian-made—westerns of the sixties. The two double-crossing heroes have no moral scruples or political interests, their marksmanship never fails, and for them killing is a natural reflex. They are *ronin* (wandering samurai), the progenitors of Sergio Leone's bounty killers. They differ from Leone's characters by having likeable personalities and—in the case of Cooper—approachable hearts. *Vera Cruz* is full of vicious and sadistic violence and plenty of action. Its stuntmen had a field day: the film boasts 175 falls—from horses, rooftops, church spires, and trees.

Mexico, gold, and American soldiers of fortune provide the story of *Garden of Evil* (20th Century-Fox, 1954), directed by Henry Hathaway. Gary Cooper plays Hooker, a former sheriff from Texas; Richard Widmark plays Fiske, a cardsharp with the requisite philosophical bent; Cameron Mitchell plays Daly, a cowardly killer. All three, en route to the goldfields of California, are stranded in a Mexican fishing village. They are hired by a certain Leah Fuller (Susan Hayward) to rescue her husband from the cave-in of a gold mine. The mine is located in an area that the Indians call the Garden of Evil, and to get there they will have to travel through territory full of bandits and hostile Indians. The men aren't keen on risking their lives to save the woman's husband, but there is the promise of gold, so they agree. Their guide for the journey is Victor Emanuel Mendoza, in the role of a Mexican tough—the group doesn't get very far before it is discovered that he is marking the trail. That is only the beginning of their worries, and it is a tough round-trip journey (reviewers noted that Hayward wears only one outfit throughout the film). One of the film's most pleasant scenes takes place in a cafe in the fishing village, where Rita Moreno sings two songs: "La Negra Noche," by Emilio D. Uranga, and "Aquí," by Ken Darby and Lionel Newman.

Budd Boetticher's *The Man from the Alamo* was not the only film about the Alamo during the fifties. The real story of the Alamo is the battle itself, the heroic thirteen-day siege that marked the beginning of the Texas Revolution, the conflict during which the United States took Texas from Mexico. The men who defended the Alamo against the massed troops of Santa Anna have become legends (many were legends during their own lifetime): William B. Travis, James Bowie, and Davy Crockett. The famous names and the famous battle have provided the story for many westerns, notably John Wayne's *The Alamo* (1960), in which Wayne chose for himself the role of Crockett.

The Last Command (Republic, 1955), directed by Frank Lloyd, tells the story of the Alamo battle from the viewpoint of Jim Bowie (Sterling Hayden), the man famous for his big knife. The role of the trailblazing frontiersman Davy Crockett was taken by Arthur Hunnicutt; Richard Carlson plays Travis.

The First Texan (Allied Artists, 1956), directed by Byron Haskin, stars Joel McCrea as Sam Houston. Houston didn't die within the walls of the Alamo. He is the Texan who exacted revenge by defeating Santa Anna's forces (and capturing Santa Anna) at the battle of San Jacinto, six weeks after the fall of the Alamo.

Following the Texas fight for independence, the Rio Grande became the dividing line between two countries, and *The Wonderful Country* (United Artists, 1959) is about a man split between the two. The film was directed by Robert Parrish; its screenplay was written by Robert Ardrey, author of *African Genesis* and *The Territorial Imperative*. Ardrey based his screenplay on a novel by Tom Lea, and Lea himself appears in the film as a barber named Peebles.

The Wonderful Country tells the moody, almost sad tale of a man (Robert Mitchum, who also produced the film) who, at the age of 13, kills a man to avenge his father's death and flees to Mexico ("the wonderful country"). There he becomes a pistolero in the employ of a local dictator. Sent across the river to buy weapons, he falls and breaks a leg, gets involved with Julie London, the wife of a cavalry officer, and because of a shootout, has to go on the lam. Back in Mexico, he refuses to carry out an assassination and finds himself truly divided. There is a price on his head in the United States, and his Mexican associates are after him. He never really finds a home and is forever an outsider. The name of his horse is Lagrimas ("tears").

Some of the supporting characters in the film are delightful, including Leroy "Satchel" Paige as Sergeant Tobe Sutton.

"Help me off with this boot."
The Tall Men

Elvis Presley made his screen debut in a western, *Love Me Tender* (20th Century-Fox, 1956), directed by Robert D. Webb. The king of rock plays the youngest of four brothers in the post-Civil War South. His three older brothers (led by Richard Egan) have run-ins with the authorities over a stolen Union payroll, but the action leaves plenty of time for Elvis to sing a few songs, including the title hit. He does a modified twist while he strums his guitar, and he even takes requests from family members.

Another top-of-the-charts hit provided the basis for *The Legend of Tom Dooley* (Columbia, 1959), directed by Ted Post. The film stars Michael Landon; the Kingston Trio provides the music.

More than a decade ahead of its time—Vera Cruz (United Artists, 1954), with Burt Lancaster (left) and Gary Cooper as two American soldiers of fortune in Mexico.

Clark Gable in The King and Four Queens *(United Artists, 1956)*.

Elvis's were not the only hips swinging through the old West. In a western with an ominous title—*River of No Return* (20th Century-Fox, 1954)—Marilyn Monroe, clad for much of the film in a wet T-shirt, sings and sashays around the Canadian Rockies during the gold rush days of the 1870s. She teams up with Robert Mitchum and Tommy Rettig (as Mitchum's son) on a raft ride down a dangerous river. They have to contend with warring Indians and a jealous Rory Calhoun, but it is not a frightening film—even though it was directed by Otto Preminger.

Clark Gable made a number of serious westerns (such as *Across the Wide Missouri*) and a number of not-so-serious westerns, including two directed by Raoul Walsh: *The Tall Men* and *The King and Four Queens*.

The Tall Men (20th Century-Fox, 1955) begins in Montana in 1866. As Gable and his brother (Cameron Mitchell) ride into a small town, they pass a man hanged from a tree. "Looks like we're getting close to civilization," remarks Gable. The two brothers join with Robert Ryan on a cattle drive and pick up Jane Russell along the way. She's a good cook. "You sure give a honey-and-molasses flavor to this rabbit," says Gable. "That's not honey and molasses," responds Russell, "That's girl."

As the only girl around the tall men, Russell plays the field. She starts with Gable. "Help me off with this boot," she asks, extending her leg to him. When she realizes he is not an overly ambitious man—he wants to settle down to a simple life in a small Texas town called Prairie Dog Creek—she asks Ryan to help remove her boots. He has bigger dreams—he plans to own the state of Montana—but in the end it is Gable who earns the chore of kneeling in front of Russell to wrestle with her tight footwear.

In *The King and Four Queens* (United Artists, 1956), Gable rides into a ghost town inhabited by the mother of four bandits and the bandits' supposed widows. Are the bandits dead? Did they really hide a cache of gold somewhere on the premises? Gable against the four gals wouldn't be a fair fight, but the mother (Jo Van Fleet) evens up the sides.

Raoul Walsh also directed a British-made comedy western starring Kenneth More and Jayne Mansfield. *The Sheriff of Fractured Jaw* (20th Century-Fox, 1959) is about an English gunsmith—decked out in bowler, spats, and cane—who goes out West and uses Indians as allies to tame a town. ("They aren't savages," he explains to Mansfield. "They're relatives.") Mansfield does more than look good—she sings (the songs were dubbed by Connie Francis). The exteriors for the film were shot in Spain (something that was soon to become standard); the interiors were shot in London.

The introduction of sheep to cattle country was no laughing matter: cattlemen believed the sheep polluted the waterholes and ruined the grazing land by cropping the grass too close. There was also a racial aspect to the dispute, for many of the sheepmen were Basques and Mexicans. *The Sheepman* (MGM, 1958), directed by George Marshall, gives a comic version of the feud between the cattlemen and the sheepmen. The sheepman in question is Glenn Ford, who arrives in town with a freight train full of sheep. He says he likes them better than cattle because "they are easier to kick—woolier, you know." His conflict with the local cattle baron (Leslie Nielsen) and his romance with the baron's girl (Shirley MacLaine) provide the material for one of the funniest westerns ever made.

"Bang, bang, you're dead, Kane."
High Noon

The story, the film, is about to begin. A man alone, on horseback, rides across open country. He is the hero, by definition a man apart, separated from the mass of men by his character and his special skills. As he rides into town he passes the blacksmith at his forge, the owner of the general store sweeping off his sidewalk, the banker out for a stroll. The lone rider dismounts, tethers his horse, and strides over to the saloon. He pushes open the batwing doors and pauses for a moment, silently taking in the scene. Conversation stops as the men crowded at the bar turn to examine the tall stranger. The piano player, thumping on the keys, is the last to notice the change in atmosphere. Surprised by the silence, he stops playing, stops chewing his cigar, and turns to face the newcomer. All eyes are now on him. They are not looking at his face, however. They are staring at the gun in a dark holster strapped low on his leg. The lone man is a gunfighter.

Where did he come from, this hero? The men in the bar don't know, and historians, film critics, and sociologists can only guess. He is composed of violence and gentility, folklore and history. He is America's White Knight or wandering samurai, but unlike those traditional, well-armed heroes, he refuses to reside in the past, and he changes his tradition in response to changes in society. Rather than having a heritage, he seems to grow into his roots with every new generation. When a weary gunman in a seventies western laments the passing of "the good old days," he is not necessarily referring to any time in history—he is talking about the days of William S. Hart and Tom Mix, Randolph Scott and Joel McCrea, the days when a man could make a living doing nothing but wearing a gun.

Until 1950, the gunfighter's life was enviable. He rode into town and into someone else's problems; he put an end to the problems, using his gun, and then either rode back out again or settled down with the prettiest girl, having found something better than life in the saddle. (He has to either leave town or settle down and hang up his guns—if he did not, he might become a dictator. A hero's powers are useful in a crisis; they are dangerous and undemocratic when there is nothing for the hero to fight.) When Jimmy Ringo (Gregory Peck) rides into Cayenne in *The Gunfighter* (20th Century-Fox, 1950), he brings with him his own problems: a past he can't shake and a dream of the future he can't realize. He is a famed gunman, and everywhere he goes there is some punk eager to make a name for himself by putting a bullet in Jimmy Ringo. Ringo wants to quit the life of the gunfighter, get back together with his wife and son—whom he hasn't seen for eight years—and "find a little ranch and settle down." As he says, "I'm thirty-five years old, and I don't even have a good watch."

Directed by Henry King (who had just finished another film with Peck, *Twelve O'Clock High*), the film begins with Ringo riding alone across rough terrain. He stops at a town, goes into the saloon, and before he can finish his drink is forced to kill a young tough. The kid's three brothers want revenge, and they follow Ringo when he leaves. Just outside the town, he gets the drop on them, takes their guns and runs off their horses, and tells them to walk back to town. Instead, they follow him on foot. Ringo knows that he has only a limited amount of time to visit with his wife—the time it will take the three brothers to get to town—and when he gets to Cayenne, he goes into the saloon and stays there, with a few brief forays within the town, for the length of the film.

The marshal of Cayenne, Mark Street (Millard Mitchell), is an old pal of Ringo's—they used to ride together in the same outlaw gang, but the marshal gave up the gunslinger's life when a little girl was killed in a shootout. He doesn't even wear a gun anymore, and he wants Ringo to leave town—his presence there has already brought on a school holiday, with all the local boys gathered outside the saloon. Ringo agrees to go as soon as he sees his wife (Jean Parker). When he meets with her, he asks her if she will go with him to California. When she says no, he asks, "What about South America?" She finally agrees to meet with him in a year's time, but he hasn't bargained on the three brothers finding horses, and they are not the only enemies he has in the town. There is another young punk.

The gunfighter had always been separate from society—his skill with a gun excused him from busting sod or poking cows—but with *The Gunfighter*, the separation was becoming permanent; the gunslinger was evolving into an alienated hero. *The Gunfighter* was followed by a flurry of films about gunmen trying to hang up their sixshooters, the most famous of which is *Shane*. But it is Jimmy Ringo's loneliness that marks the film as an important milestone. Gunfighters were not the only lonely men of the West. Being a lawman could be just as lonely. In a decade famous for its "con-

The last moments of Jimmy Ringo in The Gunfighter
*(20th Century-Fox, 1950). Left to right: Helen
Westcott, Gregory Peck, and Millard Mitchell.*

formity," the western became a critical tool for examining the role of the individual against society. The citizens of the dusty frontier towns began to resemble the complacent, selfish citizens of America during the fifties. And the heroes that rode into town—whatever their mission in the film—were in search of that lost American ideal of individual freedom. Senator Joseph McCarthy made the theme even more dramatic.

The Gunfighter is also important for its limitations of time and place. Ringo has only a short, measured amount of time to spend in Cayenne—the time it will take the three brothers to reach town—and he frequently glances at clocks. Most of the film takes place in the saloon. These elements—borrowed from classical tragedy—were used again and again in westerns of the fifties. By trading the wide-open vistas of Monument Valley for the narrow streets of a town or the four walls of a room, the tension is increased, and there is more room for the incessant chatter that typifies the psychological films of the decade.

Almost all of the action in *Rawhide (Desperate Siege)* (20th Century-Fox, 1951), directed by Henry Hathaway, takes place inside a stagecoach relay station and is confined to a twenty-four-hour period. Tyrone Power is a station attendant at the Rawhide station and Susan Hayward is a passenger with a small child who has to spend the night at the station. They are all held hostage by a group of outlaws (led by Hugh Marlowe and including Jack Elam in one of his most maniacal roles) that takes over the station. The outlaws—who assume that Power and Hayward are husband and wife—are waiting to hold up the gold-laden eastbound stage due the next morning. The prisoners try to escape and warn the coming stage, and there are some tense moments when the westbound stage pulls in and they have to pretend that there is nothing wrong. (Hathaway used the limited-time format in another film in 1951: *14 Hours*.)

"For, behold, the day cometh, that shall burn as an oven; and all the proud, yea, and all that do wickedly, shall be stubble."
—Malachi, 4:1

The search for the "wicked" in Hollywood had been going on since 1947, when the House Un-American Activities Committee (HUAC) had begun its investigations. By 1951, things were getting hot for writer Carl Foreman, and he wrote the screenplay for *High Noon* while under subpoena from HUAC to testify about his alleged Communist affiliations. Foreman had no intention of being a "friendly" witness—he was not going to name names—and he believed that *High Noon* would be his last film, his farewell to Hollywood. The allegorical power of *High Noon* has diminished as the memory of McCarthyism has faded, and it no longer seems important that "Hadleyville," the town in the film, stands for Hollywood. For more than thirty years the film has been alternately praised and scorned, but *High Noon* remains one of the most important westerns ever made, and the image of Gary Cooper standing alone in the empty streets of Hadleyville has become a national symbol of commitment and courage.

High Noon (United Artists, 1952) runs for 85 minutes, and the length of the film corresponds exactly to "real time": the story begins around 10:40 in the morning and ends shortly after noon. It is a Sunday, the wedding day for Will and Amy Kane (Gary Cooper and Grace Kelly). The marshal is hanging up his guns and taking off his badge to marry a peace-loving Quaker—he is going to start a new life. But as the newlyweds are saying their farewells, word comes that Frank Miller (Ian MacDonald), a vicious outlaw Kane sent to jail, has been released and is arriving on the noon train. Three of Miller's friends are already waiting for him at the station. It is clear that Miller intends to exact revenge.

Kane and his bride are rushed out of town, but Kane decides that he cannot run away. His wife abandons him when he resolves to fight, and he goes through the town looking for help. His friends all find reasons for not supporting him. Some, such as the local judge (Otto Kruger), refuse to help him out of cowardice. Some, such as Kane's deputy (Lloyd Bridges), refuse for personal reasons—the deputy resents not having been chosen to replace Kane and is jealous of Kane's former relationship with a local woman (Katy Jurado). The men in the saloon refuse to help him, and it is hinted that they think things were better—more lively and lucrative—when Miller was around. When he goes into the church, disturbing the day's reading, Chapter 4 of Malachi, he is allowed to speak—"I need all the special deputies I can get," he pleads—but the God-fearing folk have their own reasons for refusing to help him. It is clear to them that the trouble would disappear if Kane left town. They think a gunfight in the streets would be bad for the town's reputation. Why not just wait until the new marshal arrives Monday morning?

The one-eyed town drunk offers to help, but Kane turns him down, giving him money for a drink. One other man promises to stand by Kane, but he backs out when he realizes he is the only volunteer. He explains that he would like to help, but he is a family man. Kane is alone.

Much of the fame of *High Noon* rests on Cooper's acting. His face expresses with moving clarity the anguish and fear of Will Kane (some of Cooper's pained looks were the result of a recent ulcer operation). His bride has forsaken him, his former friends have turned their backs on him. Not only has he been refused help, he has been scorned for asking. As he walks alone through the streets, kids run by him, shouting, "Bang, bang, you're dead, Kane," and the sound of busy ham-

Gary Cooper as Marshal Kane in High Noon (United Artists, 1952).
The only sound he hears as he walks alone through the empty streets
of Hadleyville is the undertaker hammering together his coffin.

mering rings from the coffin-maker's shop. As the hour of judgment approaches, Kane collapses in his office. In lonely despair, he writes out his will, the scratching of the pen and the ticking of the clock the only sounds until the silence is shattered by the whistle of the arriving train.

There is something gruesomely civilized about *High Noon*. The killer is not riding in from the hills—he is coming on a train, and the train will arrive on schedule. Every room Kane enters has a clock to remind him of the passing minutes, and except for a brief scene in the beginning of the film, all of the action takes place in the town, with its storefronts and closed doors. It is one thing to be alone in open country, quite another to be alone in the streets of a town, with other people there but unseen. The townspeople, in true civilized manner, are divided into those in the saloon and those at church. Most of all, there is the "division of labor" that makes dealing with outlaws the responsibility of the lawman. Miller and his henchmen are after only Kane—there is no immediate threat to the rest of the townspeople.

The train pulls into the station, Miller joins his men, and Kane has to battle all four of them. No one in the town changes his mind and rushes to Kane's defense. Only his wife—joined to him by one of the few bonds civilization has left us—helps him. And when it is over, Kane throws his badge in the dirt and rides away with his wife, disgusted with the town.

Directed by Fred Zinnemann—it was his only western—*High Noon* won four Academy Awards: best actor (Gary Cooper); best editing (Elmo Williams and Harry Gerstad); best score (Dimitri Tiomkin); and best song ("Do Not Forsake Me, Oh, My Darling," music by Tiomkin with words by Ned Washington—the song was sung by Tex Ritter). The film was the screen debut of Lee Van Cleef, in the role of one of Miller's men.

Like Kane, Foreman could find no "special deputies" to save him. He was blacklisted. United Artists didn't even want to put his name on the credits—they were afraid of picketing. Foreman left the United States and went to live in England, where he helped create such films as *The Bridge on the River Kwai* and *The Guns of Navarone*. He returned to the United States after twenty-three years.

"That's just what I need—to get advice from a guy who never saw *Shane*."
—Arthur Fonzerelli, "Happy Days"

Shane (Paramount, 1953) is more than a western: it is a perfectly fashioned morality play. George Stevens, the director, felt that after more than fifty years of motion pictures, it was time for the western legend to be redefined in its true terms. *Shane* does that—eloquently restates the fundamentals of the western fable—but it adds lessons about violence and heroism.

The film reassures us that the good man always comes out on top, that right can have violence on its side, and that heroes can't have the comforts of ordinary men.

Stevens also wanted to show audiences the horrors of violence. As he said, "We used gunplay only as a last resort of extreme violence. . . . There's no shooting in *Shane* except to define a gunshot, which for our purposes is a holocaust." When Shane shows young Joey how to shoot, the sound of his gun being fired is like a cannon shot. To emphasize the terrible power of gunshots, Stevens had the two main victims—Elisha Cook, Jr., and Jack Palance—rigged so that they could be jerked backward when shot. Cook flies back to splatter in the mud; Palance is thrown back into tables and chairs. Stevens achieved the effect of violence—so much that it thrilled and delighted both audiences and filmmakers. Gentle, poetic *Shane* marks the beginning of graphic violence in westerns. As Sam Peckinpah has been quoted as saying, "When Jack Palance shot Elisha Cook, Jr., in *Shane*, things started to change."

The screenplay for *Shane* was written by A. B. Guthrie, author of *The Big Sky*, based on the short novel by Jack Schaeffer.

The plot of the film has the simplicity of a childhood fable: Out of the beautiful mountains rides Shane—that is all he has for a name—breathing loneliness and searching for a peaceful home. He is taken on as a hand by the Starrett family and becomes involved in their fight against a powerful cattleman and his henchmen. Although he had hoped to put away his gun, Shane is inevitably forced to strap it back on and do battle with the cattleman's hired killer. Having defeated the villain, Shane rides away, back into the mountains.

The film acts out the simple fable, exposing its more subtle meanings. To Joe Starrett (Van Heflin), the rancher, Shane (Alan Ladd) is a strong companion, a friend; to young Joey (Brandon De Wilde), Shane is a dream come true; to Mrs. Starrett (Jean Arthur), Shane is a disturbing challenge to her love for her husband. Shane has the power to take whatever he wants—Joey's admiration or Mrs. Starrett's love—but he is benevolent and self-sacrificing, a human god. (Ladd's slight stature—he was five foot five—makes him seem positively angelic.)

Although it is never stated, the story of *Shane* is based on the Johnson County War, the archetypal cattlemen-versus-homesteaders conflict that serves as the background for *The Virginian* and *Heaven's Gate*. When the cattlemen finally resolved to rid themselves of the ranchers, they hired professional gunmen. In *Shane*, that role is played by Jack Palance. Like Charles Bronson, Palance (born Walter Jack Palahnuik) is the son of a Pennsylvania coal miner. His taut and expressive face is the result of severe burns suffered when the bomber he was piloting during the Second World War

The heroic determination of Gary Cooper in High Noon.

crashed. He makes a frightening hired killer—named Wilson—but not all of his fearsomeness is the result of acting. He was nervous around horses and had difficulty mounting and dismounting. With great effort—and a grimly determined expression—he accomplished a perfect dismount, and Stevens used it for scenes of both his dismounting and, run in reverse, mounting.

Having used his gun, dispatched Wilson, and betrayed his past, Shane has to leave. Civilization, in the form of Starrett families with their good cooking and their Independence Day celebrations, is taking over the West, leaving no room for cattle barons or lone gunfighters. Shane's sorrow is that he cannot stay, cannot enjoy the new home he has found, and thousands of viewers, including the immortal "Fonz," have shed tears as Shane, resigned to his fate, rides away. The last scenes of the film, in which the wounded Shane explains to the distraught Joey why he has to leave ("There's no living with a killing") were not easy to film. It was a moving moment for everyone involved, except Brandon De Wilde. Every time Ladd spoke his lines of farewell, Wilde crossed his eyes and stuck out his tongue. Finally, Ladd called to the boy's father,

"Make that kid stop or I'll beat him over the head with a brick." De Wilde behaved, and as Shane rides away toward the distant, icy-blue mountains, he calls out after him. The dream is over.

When it was first released, **Hondo** (Warner Brothers, 1953), directed by John Farrow, became the butt of a Hollywood joke: "Ain't it a *Shane* about Wayne?" It isn't, but the beginning of *Hondo* does resemble the beginning of *Shane:* out of the desert walks Hondo Lane (Wayne), carrying his saddle and his Winchester, his dog, Sam, following behind. Like Shane, he is first spotted by the boy of the house, Johnny (Lee Aaker), and like Shane he does the chores, chopping wood and shoeing horses. The similarities end there, and Wayne's characterization of Hondo Lane has joined the Ringo Kid (*Stagecoach*), Ethan Edwards (*The Searchers*), and Rooster Cogburn (*True Grit*) as one of Wayne's best.

Hondo Lane, a dispatch rider for the U.S. Cavalry in Arizona around 1874, comes upon an isolated ranch. The man of the house, Ed Lowe (Leo Gordon), has fled out of fear of an Apache attack. Angie Lowe (Geraldine Page) and her son, Johnny, have stayed behind.

Top: *Joey (Brandon De Wilde) and Shane (Alan Ladd) in* Shane *(Paramount, 1953). Opposite: A tense moment in* Silver Lode *(RKO, 1954), starring Lizabeth Scott and John Payne.*

She is determined to protect her home. That kind of spirit in a woman always wins over a Wayne character, and Hondo Lane is drawn to her because she reminds him of his dead Indian wife. He tells her, "I'm part Indian, and I can smell you when I'm downwind of you. I could find you in the dark, Mrs. Lowe." Hondo leaves Mrs. Lowe and her son and rides into town. While he is gone, the Apaches do indeed attack, but their chief, Vittorio (Michael Pate), is so impressed by Johnny's courage in defending his mother that he adopts the boy as a blood brother. Believing her husband dead, he brings over a selection of braves for her to pick a new husband (she manages to put off the choice).

In town, Hondo gets into an argument with a stranger, and when he leaves town the stranger ambushes him. Hondo kills him and discovers that he has killed Ed Lowe. The conflict with the Indians becomes more pressing when Vittorio is killed ("Everybody gets dead. It was his turn," says Hondo). The film ends with Hondo, Mrs. Lowe, and her son going away to Hondo's ranch in California.

The image of Wayne striding along alone, carrying his saddle and his Winchester, the cuffs of his jeans rolled up, and a look of amused determination on his face—a reflection of a similar scene in *Stagecoach*—may be his best portrait. (Wayne liked it, too, and fell in love with the hat he wore in the film—he called it his *Hondo* hat and tried to get it into other films.) *Hondo* is about lying and telling the truth, about Indians and their way of life. It is also about John Wayne: Wayne always dominated the films he was in, and he was at his best in films that, like *Hondo,* used his character to tell the story.

Silver Lode (RKO, 1954) continued the theme initiated by *High Noon* of the weakness of society (a review in *The Village Voice* called *Silver Lode* "an astonishing anti-McCarthyism western"). The events of the film, which take place in the town of Silver Lode, are confined to the period of one day. It is Independence Day, and John Payne and Lizabeth Scott are about to be married when Dan Duryea arrives in town, claiming to be a marshal sent to arrest Payne. Duryea is lying, but he manages to convince the townspeople of Payne's guilt, and Payne has to shoot up most of Silver Lode to prove his innocence.

Silver Lode was directed by Allan Dwan, who began his career in motion pictures in 1909 writing scenarios for the Essanay Company—Broncho Billy's outfit. The year after *Silver Lode,* he directed John Payne in another western, *Tennessee's Partner* (RKO, 1955), based on the story by Bret Harte. Payne plays Tennessee, and his partner is named Cowpoke. Cowpoke was played by Ronald Reagan, and Rhonda Fleming played "the Duchess," proprietress of a "marriage market," where girls who can cook are on display in search of potential customers.

Johnny Guitar (Republic, 1954), directed by Nicholas Ray, has been called an anti-McCarthyism western, a lesbian western, a metaphysical western, a Marxist western, a neurotic western, and not a western at all. A particular favorite of French critics and Europeans in general—who delight in what they see as its political implications—the film has become a cult classic in America. It is loved by many people who don't like westerns, including architecture students (director Nicholas Ray was a friend of Frank Lloyd Wright's and designed his sets in accordance with Wright's theories).

Whatever its message and whatever its appeal, *Johnny Guitar* is different from all other westerns. Anti-McCarthyism may come closest to describing the film—it is certainly about paranoia and the manipulation of a weak society by a powerful leader—but its sexual concerns, memorable dialogue, and heavily symbolic scenes make it unique.

There are two male leads in *Johnny Guitar*—Sterling Hayden as Johnny Guitar and Scott Brady as the Dancin' Kid—but they provide only the chorus line. The story is about the conflict, based on sexual jealousy and greed, between Vienna (Joan Crawford) and Emma Small (Mercedes McCambridge). Emma is jealous of Vienna's relationship with the Dancin' Kid: she expresses her jealousy in hatred for both of them, and she accuses them of being criminals. "They both cast the same shadow," she says of Vienna and the Kid. Vienna's explanation of Emma's rage is simple: "He makes her feel like a woman, and that frightens her." Emma wants the land Vienna's saloon is on—the railroad is on its way through, and the land will soon be very valuable. To get rid of Vienna, Emma convinces the townspeople that Vienna is evil, that she is "not one of them." She even blames Vienna for the railroad, which will bring in thousands of poor "squatters" to force out Emma and the other landowners. When the Dancin' Kid's gang holds up the local bank, Emma tries to implicate Vienna. She can't prove that Vienna had anything to do with the robbery, but she extracts a "confession" from one of the outlaws, telling him, "Just tell us Vienna was one of your bunch, and we won't hurt you . . . you'll go free." Emma's personal crusade almost gets Vienna lynched, and the film ends in a gun duel not between the two male leads, but between Emma and Vienna.

A Man Alone (Republic, 1955) was directed by "R. Milland"—Ray Milland, who also plays the lead. The title of the film went through several changes that reflect the plot: Wes Steele (Milland), a notorious gunman (the film was originally called *The Gunman*) becomes prisoner in a house (the title was changed from *The Gunman* to *The Hostage*) and ends up no longer a man alone (the final title).

The film begins with the lone gunslinger, Milland,

Joan Crawford as Vienna and Sterling Hayden as Johnny Guitar in Johnny Guitar *(Republic, 1954).*

emerging from blowing sand to come upon the scene of a stagecoach holdup. He reaches over to caress the hair of a dead woman—the first indication that he is a gentle man. He rides into the nearby town and is immediately confronted by a local deputy, who makes the mistake of pulling a gun on him. The deputy shot, Milland runs away through the dark town, at one point hiding out in the bank, where he overhears a discussion of the recent holdup. The town's leading citizen, its banker (Raymond Burr), is the leader of the outlaws (bankers had been villains in westerns since the Depression; the reaction to McCarthyism made all upright citizens suspect). Milland eventually hides out in the cellar of a house. A benevolent and resourceful man, he feeds canned peaches to a kitten and investigates the contents of a hope chest. The house turns out to be that of the local sheriff; it is quarantined because the sheriff has yellow fever. A large part of the film takes place in the cellar, where Milland and the sheriff's daughter (Mary Murphy), owner of the hope chest, engage in some intense conversations, each exposing personal secrets and both deciding that running away from life's problems is not the answer. Even the sheriff (Ward Bond) has something he wants to talk about. He is in the pay of the villainous Burr, but only so that his daughter will have the advantages that money can buy—something he was never able to give his wife. Their problems out in the open, Milland emerges from the house to fight Burr and his henchmen.

Bad Day at Black Rock (MGM, 1955), directed by John Sturges, pits a hero in the traditional mold against a society directly borrowed from both *The Ox-Bow Incident* and *High Noon.*

For the first time in four years, a Santa Fe streamliner stops at the little southwestern town of Black Rock, and a lone man gets off. The stranger, whose left arm is crippled, is not welcomed by the town's thirty-seven inhabitants. John J. Macreedy (Spencer Tracy) has come to Black Rock to deliver a medal to the father of the man who saved his life at Salerno. His questions about the father, a Japanese-American farmer, elicit only hostility from the townspeople, led by Reno Smith (Robert Ryan). They try to get rid of the stranger, but although he doesn't wear a gun, Macreedy has lethal skills—he knows martial arts—and he eventually uncovers the truth: one night, driven by "patriotic" zeal fueled by vicious jealousy, a gang of men burned down the farmer's house and shot him.

Bad Day at Black Rock is a modern film—the villain is dispatched with a Molotov cocktail—and its concern for the mistreatment of Japanese-Americans during the Second World War takes it beyond the confines of the old West. But its setting and its lone hero—on what turns out to be a mission of vengeance—qualify it as a western, and its townspeople—weak men led to violence by a twisted egomaniac—are recogniz-

able: we met them in *Johnny Guitar* and *Silver Lode.*

Not all the people in western towns were proficient at gunplay. Not everyone had to fight his way West—the pioneers, yes, but those who followed may never have seen an Indian or heard a gunshot. The hero (Fred MacMurray) of *At Gunpoint* (Republic, 1955), directed by Alfred L. Werker, is such a man. The owner of a general store, he can't remember ever firing a gun before, but when an outlaw gang rides into town and robs the bank, he manages to kill one of them. He becomes the local hero, the pride of his fellow citizens—until the outlaws return for revenge. The townspeople then turn against him. They want him to leave town to purge the trouble. He refuses to run away, and his decision to stand his ground eventually shames the other citizens into helping him—precisely what didn't happen in the film's progenitor, *High Noon.*

When, on the outskirts of Hadleyville, Will Kane turns his buckboard around and heads back to town, he explains that he is going back because he has to—he knows he cannot run away. Running away never works in westerns—the past must be faced, even when it may mean death.

In *Tension at Table Rock* (RKO, 1956), directed by Charles Marquis Warren, a gunman (Richard Egan) is unjustly accused of killing a friend—the leader of a gang of outlaws—without giving him a chance to draw. The event is even celebrated in a popular ballad. To escape the song and the scorn he encounters everywhere, he takes a job at a remote stagecoach depot, but he cannot run away from his past, and Table Rock is the name of the town where he finally makes his stand, helping a cowardly sheriff.

Flat Rock, the town in *The Proud Ones* (20th Century-Fox, 1956), directed by Robert D. Webb, is a quiet Kansas frontier town until the first trail herd arrives from Texas. Flat Rock becomes a boom town, and its marshal (Robert Ryan) finds that the past he wants to forget shows up with the cattle in the form of two men who would like to see him dead: a youth (Jeffrey Hunter) who believes the marshal killed his father in an unfair fight, and a gambler (Robert Middleton) who has already forced the marshal to flee one town.

The youth becomes the marshal's deputy—it is the only job he can find—and is eventually won over to the marshal's side. The marshal explains to him that his father was armed, drew first, and was a killer hired by the gambler. The gambler again hires killers, two of them, and the deputy helps the marshal face them.

The title of *Star in the Dust* (Universal, 1956), directed by Charles Haas, is a reference to the last scene of *High Noon,* but the film resembles *High Noon* only in that it deals with a sheriff beset by a hostile community, and the story of the film is told all in one day.

John Agar is the sheriff in a town torn by a dispute

Opposite top: *Ray Milland in* A Man Alone *(Republic, 1955).*
Opposite bottom: Tension at Table Rock *(RKO 1956).*

between the ranchers and the farmers. Richard Boone, a gunman in the employ of the ranchers, kills three farmers and—sentenced to hang at sundown—is put in jail. The cattlemen, led by Leif Erickson, who is also the town banker, intend to break Boone out of jail; the farmers plan to lynch the prisoner first. To complicate the plot, the sheriff is in love with the banker's daughter (Mamie Van Doren).

Red Concho, feared and famous gunfighter, is boss of the town of Cripple Creek. His skinny little brother, Johnny, thrives on Red's reputation and becomes the local bullying braggart. Then Red is gunned down, mean outlaws take over the town, and Johnny reveals himself to be a groveling coward. When one of the wicked newcomers calls to him, "Are you gonna lay on that steel, or are you gonna crawl?" Johnny crawls. Then he runs away. When the girl who has fled to join him says she wants to marry him—and has $300—he says, "Congratulations, you just bought yourself a three-hundred-dollar rat." And straight from the Rat Pack, for Johnny Concho is Frank Sinatra, and although he starts out a mean bully, he learns his lesson, and when he stands up to the villains and allows himself to be shot, the rest of the townspeople, inspired by his courage, finally shoot down the badmen. *Johnny Concho* (United Artists, 1956), directed by Don McGuire, was Sinatra's first serious western (*The Kissing Bandit* of 1948 was a musical).

In *The Fastest Gun Alive* (MGM, 1956), directed by Russell Rouse, Glenn Ford plays a peaceable shopkeeper in the small town of Cross Creek who just happens to be the fastest gun alive. He has a strong distaste for violent gunplay, having seen his lawman father shot down, and he tries to hide his skill. Only his wife (Jeanne Crain) knows his secret. He gets drunk one night and shows off his prowess. It isn't long before a rival (Broderick Crawford) appears and threatens to tear down the town if Ford doesn't face him in a title match. Ford's portrayal of the fastest gun was reprised eleven years later in *The Last Challenge* (MGM, 1967), directed by Richard Thorpe, in which he plays the fastest gun in the West, now a town marshal who enjoys the leisurely life until a young gunslinger (Chad Everett) arrives to challenge his reputation.

The Lonely Man (Paramount, 1957), directed by Henry Levin, is a quiet western about an aging outlaw (Jack Palance) who wants to retire and win back the affection of his son (Anthony Perkins), whom he hasn't seen in seventeen years. He doesn't have much time, however, because he is going blind and his former gang members are after him. His son is not eager to renew their relationship—he believes his father deserted his mother and is responsible for her death.

There are elements of both *High Noon* and *Shane* in *3:10 to Yuma* (Columbia, 1957), directed by Delmer Daves. The hero of the film is ostensibly Van Heflin, the rancher who, like Will Kane, stubbornly does what he feels he has to do even when everyone deserts him. But the character played by Glenn Ford, the outlaw Ben Wade, resembles Shane: he is the most powerful character in the film, a wandering gunman with an appealing character, and he decides the outcome, allowing himself to be taken to prison when he could easily have escaped.

While looking for stray cattle, Heflin and his sons come upon Ford and his gang holding up a stagecoach. "Aren't you going to do something?" asks one of his sons. Heflin can do nothing. He cannot stop the holdup, just as he can't provide for his family. He is a man beaten down by events. His cattle have been dying from a drought, but he is afraid to ask for a bank loan. When his wife (Felicia Farr) insists about the loan, he says, "I suppose I could try. . . . In six months we'll be happy, won't we?" Neither he nor his wife is convinced, but he sets off for town to see about the loan.

While Heflin is worrying about his grim future, Ford and his gang ride into the nearby town of Bisbee. Ford wants to report the holdup—he is a very compassionate outlaw. A posse takes off to see about the stage, and Ford's men leave him behind in the saloon. A charming character, he is soon having an affair with the barmaid (Leora Dana). He lingers too long and is captured by the posse. Because he is the best shot, Heflin is chosen to take Ford to Contention City to await the train for Yuma, site of the state penitentiary. Heflin agrees to do it only when the owner of the stageline offers him $200, which happens to be the amount he needs to save his ranch.

On the way to Contention City, they stop for dinner at Heflin's ranch, and in a scene reminiscent of *Shane*, Ford's presence disturbs both Heflin's sons and his wife. Although he is manacled, Ford is in control, and he promises Heflin's fearful wife that he will get her husband back home safely.

They arrive in Contention City early in the morning and take a room in a hotel to wait for the 3:10 train. It isn't long before Ford's men know they're there and surround the town. Some of the local men volunteer to help, but they desert as soon as they realize what they're up against. Only the town drunk stays.

Most of the film takes place in the small hotel room where Ford tries to talk Heflin out of trying to get him on the train. Ford's arguments are cogent—he has understood Heflin's predicament, seen his wife and sons. He offers him money—up to $7,000—but Heflin, although he wavers in his resolve, gradually becomes more determined. The outlaws catch the drunk, shoot him, and hang him in the hotel lobby. The owner of the stageline declares that there is no longer any reason

Preceding pages: *Jack Palance in* The Lonely Man *(Paramount, 1957).*

to go through with the plan to meet the train—he says he'll pay Heflin the money anyway. Heflin's wife arrives and tries to talk him out of it. And then there is the sound of thunder—a storm is brewing, which means rain and an end to the drought. All of Heflin's reasons for risking his life are gone, but he remains determined to get Ford on the train to take him to Yuma. He explains that the town drunk was willing to give his life and that he wants to do it so that his boys "can remember how their old man walked Ben Wade to the station."

The walk to the station is nerve-racking. Ford's men are everywhere, trying to get a clear shot at Heflin. Ford and Heflin reach the train as it is about to pull out of the station. If Ford merely dropped to his knees or moved aside, his men could easily shoot Heflin, but instead Ford jumps on the train, saving Heflin's life and offering as explanation, "I've broken out of Yuma before." The train rolls along as rain begins to fall. Heflin has performed his heroic mission, but it was all Ford's doing. He has fulfilled his promise to Heflin's wife and has restored Heflin's dignity.

A similar story is told in *The Ride Back* (United Artists, 1957), directed by Allen H. Miner, in which another likeable outlaw passes up an opportunity to escape out of sympathy for his captor. William Conrad—who also produced the film—plays a lawman sent across the border into Mexico to bring back a suspected murderer. The outlaw (Anthony Quinn) is a happy, self-satisfied character—he has a particular fondness for children—who enjoys life. His captor, Conrad, is a lonely man, tormented by anxieties. He sees himself as a failure—the compassionate outlaw keeps him from failing again.

Kirk Douglas made his western debut in *Along the Great Divide* (Warner Brothers, 1951), directed by Raoul Walsh. U.S. Marshal Ken Merrick (Douglas) rescues Pop Keith (Walter Brennan) from a lynching. Keith is accused of rustling cattle and of killing one of a rancher's two sons. The likeable old codger wryly admits to a little rustling but denies any part in the murder. Merrick resolves to take him to distant Santa Loma for a proper trial, and to avoid the rancher's henchmen he decides to take the desert route. Merrick, Pop Keith, Keith's daughter (Virginia Mayo), and two deputies take part in the journey. To pass the time, Pop Keith begins singing, and his discordant croaking elicits from Merrick the comment, "Mister, they're trying you for the wrong crime." But when Pop Keith sings "Down in the Valley," the lawman's response is different: the song drives him crazy—it was his father's favorite, and it reminds him of his guilt over his father's death. Eager to escape, Pop Keith keeps singing in an effort to distract Merrick ("Something's gotta give," says Keith). His daughter—even though she and the lawman are drawn to each other—sometimes provides

the chorus. Merrick has to deal with Keith's singing, a sandstorm, the lack of water, sleeplessness, and attacks by the pursuing gang. He finally falls asleep, but Pop Keith does not run away; rather, he saves the lawman's life. In Santa Loma, a jury finds Pop guilty, but the lawman saves his life.

For the purposes of the film, tough, one-eyed Raoul Walsh taught Douglas how to roll cigarettes. The actor never got the hang of doing it one-handed.

In *Last Train from Gun Hill* (Paramount, 1959), directed by John Sturges, Douglas plays a marshal who has to go into a town and arrest the young hoodlum who raped and killed his half-breed wife (played by Israeli actress Ziva Rodann). As in *High Noon* and *3:10 to Yuma*, the drama hinges on the schedule of the local trains: the lawman gets the boy and then holds him in a hotel room, waiting for the last train from Gun Hill to Pauley. The boy happens to be the son of a friend (Anthony Quinn) of the lawman's, a tough patriarch who ends his sentences with "man" and has had to raise the boy alone: "It ain't easy to raise a boy without a mother, man," he says. The boy has no regrets: "It ain't my fault you married a damn squaw" is his only apology. As in *3:10 to Yuma*, the high point of the film is the trip to the train station.

Douglas's determination to arrest the boy—even when he has to fight both an old friend and most of the town's inhabitants—is made more powerful by the addition of revenge—it was *his* wife who was raped and murdered (although he says, "My wife or somebody else's, makes no difference"). *The Hangman* (Paramount, 1959), directed by Michael Curtiz, tells the story of a deputy marshal named MacKenzie Bovard (Robert Taylor), a lonely man who does his job because he believes that "the human race is full of rats." Known as "the toughest lawman in the territory," Bovard is ruthless and uses and abuses people in the search for a certain "rat," a wanted criminal (actually innocent) named Johnny Butterfield (Jack Lord). Bovard tries to bribe the outlaw's old girlfriend (Tina Louise) into helping him locate the criminal. When he finally finds Butterfield, he is living under a new name—Johnny Bishop—in a town called North Creek. The outlaw has become a well-respected member of the community, and he has a loving wife. Against the open hostility of the townspeople and the purposeful lack of cooperation from the local deputy (Fess Parker), Bovard puts the outlaw in jail. The outlaw's friends break him out, and Bovard gets the fleeing man in his gunsights. But he shoots in the air: he has learned something about justice and the human race, and he turns in his badge and takes off to begin a new life in California—along with Tina Louise.

John Wayne didn't like *High Noon*. In an interview in *Playboy* (May, 1971), he said *High Noon* was "the most un-American thing I've ever seen in my whole life. . . . I'll never regret having helped run Foreman out of the country." Howard Hawks agreed with Wayne. Both men thought the premise of *High Noon* was ridiculous. They believed that no marshal would have expected townspeople to help fight outlaws, and no citizens of the old West, tough conquerors of the frontier, would have refused if asked. They also disliked *3:10 to Yuma*. They didn't like its treatment of heroism, and they thought the outlaw's taunting of his farmer-captor could have been easily handled. Hawks and Wayne—as director and star—presented their case in *Rio Bravo* (Warner Brothers, 1959), a film in which a sheriff and a few pals hold off a gang of outlaws. John Wayne as Sheriff John T. Chance never asks for help from the townspeople and even turns it down when it is offered. He is a professional, and he doesn't want any amateurs getting in the way. As he says, "If they're really good, I'll take them. If not, I'll just have to take care of them."

Sheriff Chance captures a killer named Joe Burdett (Claude Akins) and puts him in jail in the small town of Rio Bravo. The town and the jail are soon besieged by the killer's brother, Nathan Burdett (John Russell), a wealthy rancher with a host of henchmen. The sheriff is aided by his toothless deputy, Stumpy (Walter Brennan, on leave from "The Real McCoys"); a former deputy named Dude (Dean Martin), who has been on a two-year binge as the result of a failed romance but manages to sober up to help his old boss; and Colorado Ryan (Ricky Nelson, well-known for both his singing— ads for the film called him "the rockin' baby-faced kid"—and his role in "Ozzie and Harriet"). The cast also includes one of Hawks's "discoveries." He was fond of using unknown actresses and claimed to have discovered Lauren Bacall and Carole Lombard and to have started the careers of Frances Farmer, Rita Hayworth, Joanne Dru, and Joan Collins. In *Rio Bravo*, he added 26-year-old Angie Dickinson to this list, giving her the role of Feathers, the shapely dancehall girl.

When the jailed Burdett begins to taunt his captors, Stumpy (in a reply to *3:10 to Yuma*) assures him that come what may he'll be the first to die. The situation doesn't keep Dude and Colorado from singing, and the long (141 minutes) film is remarkably suspenseless. It ends in a big shootout, with the lawmen using dynamite to break up the Burdett forces.

Hawks and Wayne liked the format of *Rio Bravo* so much that they repeated it in two more movies: *El Dorado* and *Rio Lobo*. The three films form a trilogy and have more in common than their plot elements— John Wayne (who wears his *Red River* belt buckle in all three) is the star, and the screenplays for all three were written by Leigh Brackett (she wrote the screenplay for *Rio Bravo* with Jules Furthman based on a story by B. H. McCampbell, Hawks's daughter). The

three films are favorites with French *auteur* critics, who attribute their shared style to Hawks's direction. All three are about groups of men who are united in their professionalism and their group loyalty.

Like *Rio Bravo*, *El Dorado* (Paramount, 1967) is about the siege of a jailhouse. Robert Mitchum, in Dean Martin's alcoholic role, plays Sheriff J. P. Harrah. Mitchum, who claims that his drooping eyelids are the result of chronic insomnia and a boxing injury that caused astigmatism in both eyes, makes a convincing drunk. He is helped by an old pal named Cole Thornton (John Wayne), an aging gunfighter carrying around a bullet lodged against his spine. They are joined by a dapper (he wears a flat-topped derby), knife-throwing (he carries a sawed-off shotgun in a holster but can't hit a thing with it) youth named Mississippi (James Caan). Mississippi, in what must be an oblique explanation of the title, frequently quotes lines from Edgar Allan Poe's poem "Eldorado," the tale of a knight who grows old and tired in search of Eldorado. The aged jailer is played by Arthur Hunnicutt; the prisoner in the cell is Edward Asner; the group has to hold out until a federal marshal can reach them; they're surrounded by the feisty members of the MacDonald family. It is a great film for Arthur Hunnicutt's fans, and the primary colors of the neckerchiefs Wayne wears around his size-18 neck are dazzling.

Rio Lobo (NGP, 1970) was Howard Hawks's forty-fourth and final film; it was John Wayne's 144th film and his fifth with Hawks. The film begins during the Civil War. A group of Confederate soldiers steals a gold shipment from a Union Army train—the canny Rebs use hornets and greased tracks to pull off the heist. The Union Army officer responsible for the gold, Captain Cord McNally (Wayne), goes off after the thieves and is captured by them. Knocked off his horse into a stream, he sprawls, unconscious. "Hmm," mumbles the Confederate soldier trying to drag him out of the water, "he's heavier than a baby whale." (Wayne was getting to be sincerely fat.) An amicable rapport is established between the Rebel captors and Captain McNally. He wants to know who in his outfit has been giving out the information about the gold shipments. The two leading Rebels, Tuscarora (Chris Mitchum) and Lieutenant Pierre Cordona (Jorge Rivero), won't tell him, but after the war the three men meet again, and the former Rebs explain that there were two men involved. In Rio Lobo, the three pals get involved in a dispute over land rights, which leads to the taking of prisoners. Conveniently, the two Union traitors are among the villains. McNally and his friends end up with one of the villains in jail—they have to hold him until the cavalry can arrive. The role of the jailer is taken by a man named Phillips (Jack Elam), and true to the tradition of *Rio Bravo*, Phillips assures the prisoner, "Don't worry, you'll be the first to die" if something happens.

Sheriff J. P. Harrah (Robert Mitchum) marches a prisoner (Edward Asner) off to jail in El Dorado *(Paramount, 1967).*

Top: *Felicia Farr and Glenn Ford in* 3:10 to Yuma
(Columbia, 1957). Above: Production shot from
Warlock *(20th Century-Fox, 1959).*

When he is offered help, McNally, echoing a similar line in *Rio Bravo*, responds, "They won't be much help unless they're *real* good." When Phillips starts blasting away with a shotgun at some distant villains, McNally chides him, "Scatter-gun's useless." "Don't mind if I shoot, do you?" responds Phillips. "It makes me feel good."

Hawks was not the only director making films about professional gunmen. In *Man with the Gun* (*The Trouble Shooter* in Great Britain) (United Artists, 1955), directed by Richard Wilson, Clint Tollinger (Robert Mitchum) rides into the town of Sheridan City in search of his estranged wife (Jan Sterling). It is a wild, lawless town, and Tollinger ends up taking the job of "town tamer," selling his services as a gunman for $500.

He shoots up a gang of outlaws, sets up a curfew, and outlaws firearms in town. The good citizens appreciate his cleaning up the town, but they begin to resent him—he is too violent. Once the threat is gone, they no longer want to have a gunman around. It is a cycle well understood by Henry Fonda in *Warlock* (20th Century-Fox, 1959), directed by Edward Dmytryk.

The film begins with a group of ruffians shooting up the town of Warlock—it is the fourth time in a month that they've done it. They run the sheriff out of town and murder the local Italian barber. The leading citizens decide that they've had enough and send for a town tamer—they've read about his exploits in a book. The town tamer (Fonda) and his sidekick (Anthony Quinn) arrive and set about cleaning up the town. The two gunmen are very much aware that they are losing their way of life. As Quinn says, "Civilization is stalking Warlock." As the West's towns become civilized, there is less call for gunmen.

Hawks and Wayne intended *Rio Bravo* to be a response to *High Noon*, but the film served to continue a theme begun in that film—society is weak. The townspeople were receding into the background of westerns, becoming unimportant features of the scenery. They were weak and needed to be protected by professionals—men like Fonda and Quinn in *Warlock*. The little groups of professionals in Hawks's westerns are the progenitors of *The Magnificent Seven*, *The Professionals*, and *The Wild Bunch*. The gunfighter rode into the fifties alone, looking for a chance to hang up his guns, marry the right girl, and settle down; he rode out of the decade as part of a group of professionals, a mercenary, proud of his skills, a man with no intention of settling down. *Rio Bravo* was very popular in Italy. Its Italian title—*Un Dollaro d'Onore* (*A Dollar of Honor*)—was soon to be echoed in a series of westerns by Sergio Leone, beginning with *Per un Pugno di Dollari* (*A Fistful of Dollars*).

Jean Simmons and Gregory Peck in The Big Country
(United Artists, 1956).

The
Professionals

1960-1969

Preceding pages (*left to right*): *Steve McQueen, James Coburn,*
Horst Buchholz, Yul Brynner, Brad Dexter, Robert Vaughn, and
Charles Bronson in The Magnificent Seven *(United Artists, 1960).*
Above: *Kirk Douglas (left) and John Wayne in a production*
shot from The War Wagon *(Universal, 1967).*

"Little by little, the look of the country changes because of the men we admire."

Hud

Someplace along the Mexican border, perhaps on one of the trails that lead to the Rio Grande, perhaps on the banks of the river itself, there is a certain spot where a great change took place. On some hot afternoon around the turn of the century, a rider heading north paused, thought awhile, and then turned around and rode back into Mexico. The lone rider may have looked up and seen a lawman, sitting in a Model T, waiting for him on the opposite shore. But it wasn't the thought of going to jail that made him turn around—it was the thought of going back to that strange country where, almost overnight, horses had become "manure spreaders" and individual freedom had become no more than a national fable.

Moments in time are hard to locate geographically, but American filmmakers have been searching for that spot for more than two decades, running their film crews along the border and in and out of Mexico in the hope of finding that moment when going home to Texas suddenly meant leaving freedom behind—that place where the ideals of a nation slammed into what the nation had become.

Long before anyone ever meant for it to happen, long before anyone even understood what it meant, the frontier ended. There was nowhere else to go. It happened so quickly that the men and the ideas of the past were caught, alive, by the men and ideas of the future: the last fierce Indian chiefs had their photographs taken seated behind the steering wheels of Fords. In many ways the future bought the past and took it on the road. At the same time that the Indian tribes were facing the bleak prospect of life within the confines of reservations, white actors in film studios were trying on wigs and practicing howling before galloping across the vast expanses of the celluloid West. In other ways, and in countless separate incidents, the future ran over the past, canceling it out so fast that it had no chance to adapt, and many men became anachronisms in their own lifetime. The first few years of the 1960s—years before the scope of the western was changed by foreign-made films—saw a series of beautiful movies about men caught by the end of one idea of America and the beginning of another. Most of these films take place at the turn of the century or later—even in contemporary America—for the filmmakers were seeking to explain how and why America changed and what happened to the men who were caught by that change.

The period of the Mexican Revolution—with its loud mixture of dynamite, automobiles, horses, machine guns, sixshooters, and easily overlooked politics—has always been a favorite with the makers of action films (it is especially appealing because it can be filmed so easily in Spain). During the sixties and seventies, Mexico became even more important as the scene of the "last act" of the West, the chosen refuge of men fleeing the civilization north of the border. Even before the chaos of the revolution, Mexico presented a new frontier for western Americans. Across the border, a man could still live by the old ways.

The 1950s began with *The Gunfighter*, the story of a lone man trying to hang up his guns; the 1960s began with *The Magnificent Seven* (United Artists, 1960), the story of seven men trying to find a way to continue living by their guns. The seven gunmen are hired to protect a Mexican village from a predatory gang of bandits. It is not the kind of work they would normally accept—they don't particularly like farmers, and the pay is paltry. Each man gives his own reason, a reason reflecting his character, for taking the work. One (Brad Dexter) believes the farmers must have a hidden treasure; the leader of the group (Yul Brynner) is amazed by the village's offer of everything it has ("I've been offered a lot for my work, but never everything"); the younger members are eager for an opportunity to prove themselves; and one of the seven (Charles Bronson) is a half-breed and understands the farmers' plight. But the reason they take part in the expedition is really the same for each of them: they have outlived their time, and the work defending the poor farmers is the only offer they have.

But seven American gunmen risking their lives to protect worthless peasants? When the leader of the bandits, Calvera (Eli Wallach), asks one of the seven, Vin (Steve McQueen), why he took the job, Vin answers him by telling a tale about a fellow he knew in El Paso who took off all his clothes and jumped into a cactus bed. When he was asked why he did it, he said only, "It seemed to be a good idea at the time." The explanation could be rephrased, "Why not?" Eventually, the proffered payment becomes unimportant, and the seven fight as much out of affection for the farmers as to live up to their own principles.

The strength of *The Magnificent Seven* lies in the characterizations of the seven gunmen. Yul Brynner, as Chris, the leader of the group, and the other six men—Steve McQueen, Horst Buchholz, Charles Bronson, Robert Vaughn, Brad Dexter, and James Coburn—are each given a recognizable personality based more on character than on a particular skill. In fact, their violent skills seem to mirror their personalities, and they become "magnificent"—heroic—figures in the ways in which they prove themselves individuals by fighting and dying according to their character.

The efforts of the seven to train the farmers in warfare and the battles against the bandits, with each of the seven fighting in his particular fashion, are dramatic and exciting, but it is the musical score—written by Elmer Bernstein—that provides the spirit of the film. The song, which evokes the bold courage and defiant individualism that are so important to our idea of the West, was enormously popular. It is no surprise that the song was used as the Marlboro cigarette theme song—even separated from the film, it seems almost inspirational.

The film is full of philosophizing about the nature of power and the life of violence. The seven mercenary heroes and the villagers defeat the gang of bandits, but there is something tragic in the victory. The final judgment on what has happened is delivered by a wise old farmer, who explains to the surviving gunmen, "Only the farmers have won. They will remain forever. They are like the land. You are like the wind . . . a strong wind . . . blowing over the land and passing on."

With the aid of the Bernstein score, the seven would seem to "pass on" back into the western legend whence they rode, but in fact the film is based on a very nonwestern story—Akira Kurosawa's *The Seven Samurai* (1954). It was John Sturges, who both produced and directed *The Magnificent Seven*, who hit upon the idea of adapting the Japanese film to a western setting. Sturges was not the only filmmaker paying attention to the Japanese samurai films, and *The Magnificent Seven*—with its moving portrayal of western gunmen at the end of the West—stands as the first indication of a trend that eventually changed the western film forever. Like cowboys going south for some "old-time action," the western was soon to cross borders (and oceans) in search of a new home.

The Magnificent Seven also outlines a new role for the "good guys" in the westerns of the sixties. As anachronistic gunmen, the seven become—like half-breeds and other people separated from society—morally superior individuals. The moral integrity of the leaders of the seven, Chris and Vin, is established at the beginning of the film, when they force a group of bigoted townspeople to bury a dead Indian in the town's "white" cemetery. During the sixties, the denizens of the old West reflect the dark mood of American society. Townspeople—the people for whom the courageous pioneers won the West—are bigots; lawmen and politicians are corrupt; uniformed soldiers are cold-blooded butchers. The hero in a sixties western lives by a personal code that separates him from ordinary men—men who eagerly believe in "progress"—and that almost invariably leads to his death. Nobody "wins" anymore. Evil cannot be defeated; the hero must die.

The Magnificent Seven made stars of its actors; McQueen, Bronson, and Coburn were reunited in Sturges's *The Great Escape* (1963). Brynner reprised his role as Chris in the first of *The Magnificent Seven*'s three sequels, *The Return of the Seven* (United Artists, 1966), directed by Burt Kennedy. "I never thought I'd come back," muses Brynner as he rides into the village. He gathers a group of professional gunmen to free the male population of the village: they have been kidnapped by a bandit gang. The role of Chris was given to George Kennedy in *Guns of the Magnificent Seven* (United Artists, 1968), directed by Paul Wendkos. Kennedy and six pros set off to free an imprisoned Mexican revolutionary leader. By the time of *The Magnificent Seven Ride* (United Artists, 1972), directed by George McGowan, the only traces of the original film were Bernstein's soaring score (which was used in all three sequels) and the magic number seven. Lee Van Cleef plays an Arizona marshal who, along with an unscrupulous journalist (Michael Callan), paroles five convicts so that they can help defend the women and children of a border town from a band of desperadoes that has massacred all their menfolk.

The Magnificent Seven's three sequels provide insight into how the western changed during the dozen years from 1960 to 1972. The original film was shot in Mexico—the sequels in Spain; the original film has philosophical depth—the sequels are merely excuses for violent action; the characters of the gunmen are of central importance to the first film—by the last film, the gunmen have become seven violent dwarfs, and their killing skills are all they have for character. The last sequel stars a man whose career was made in "spaghetti" westerns—an indication of one of the most dramatic changes in westerns. But perhaps the most important aspect of the last film is the fact that—in the tradition of Robert Aldrich's *The Dirty Dozen* (1967)—the professionals have to be recruited from prison. The only men tough enough for the job—the kind of wild, rough individuals who settled the West—now must be locked up. There is no room for them in the modern, civilized world.

There is no room for the tough gunman, and there is no room for his code. The freedom to roam at will would have meant very little had it not been supported by strong beliefs in personal ties and the value of the individual. The western hero has always been a man of strong loyalties, a man of determined honesty who takes pride in his name and knows right and wrong. He is composed of ideals that most Americans left behind long ago.

In 1956, American playwright Arthur Miller wanted to get a divorce from his wife, so he went to Nevada to set up legal residence. He found himself a place to stay near a dried-up lake bed about fifty miles from Reno—at that time the divorce capital of the country. While he was there, Miller met a group of cowboys who roped wild horses and sold them to dog-food manufacturers. Miller said that the men "represented to me the last really free Americans. They were misfits in our modern jet age."

Miller got his divorce and married Marilyn Mon-

roe. He wrote a story about the Nevada mustangers, sold it to *Esquire*, and then decided to make it into a screenplay; he wanted to create a vehicle for his new wife, an "ode to Marilyn." Director John Huston was delighted with the screenplay, as was Clark Gable, who was given the leading role of cowboy Gay Langland, "the last of the free men." Monroe was enthusiastic about the opportunity to work with Gable: "When I was growing up, Clark Gable represented everything I idealized—and to find that that ideal was all I ever dreamed of, plus so much more—more human, warmer!" She nicknamed Gable "Clarkie."

Gable, Monroe, and the rest of the cast—including Montgomery Clift, Eli Wallach, and Thelma Ritter—were assembled in the Nevada desert, where the average temperature reached 106 degrees. Even with the terrible heat, there was cause for joy—Gable announced that his wife was pregnant. At 59, he was finally going to be a father. He always referred to the expected baby as "he"—Gable wanted a son, but he had no intention of saddling the boy with the name Clark, Jr. He thought John Clark or Charles Clark might be nice.

Just as the members of *The Magnificent Seven*

demonstrated their character in the ways in which they fought and died, the protagonists in *The Misfits* (United Artists, 1961) display their characters in the ways they each seek some sort of human contact. They are anachronistic holdovers, the last romantics in a harshly antiromantic world. Roslyn Taber (Monroe) is in Reno to get a divorce, and she meets three out-of-work cowboys: Langland (Gable), Perce Howland (Clift), and Guido (Wallach). The three men take her with them to a house outside Reno, and she becomes, for each of them, a source of love, whether as wife, mistress, or mother. She rebels when she finds that they're using airplanes and trucks to capture the last wild horses—only to sell the animals for dog food. Langland's only explanation is, "They changed it all around."

The dialogue of the film is sometimes ponderously significant, as when Roslyn says, "You shouldn't believe what other people say. Maybe it's not even fair to them," or when Guido, the pilot, laments, "I can't make a landing, and I can't get up to God." At the end of the film, Gay and Roslyn are driving off together to start a new life and have her child—she's pregnant. "How do you find the way in the dark?" asks Roslyn.

Yul Brynner (left) repeats his role as Chris in the first sequel to
The Magnificent Seven, The Return of the Seven *(United Artists, 1966).*

"Head for the big star up ahead. The highway is right under it," assures Gay. But even this advice has a note of tragedy, for earlier in the film Guido explained that by the time the light from a star reaches earth, the star may no longer be there. Everything has been changed around, and the light from the stars cannot help them find their way.

There is a sweet poignance to the film, which is only increased by its aftermath. *The Misfits* was the last film for both Gable and Monroe. Gable died three days after the final scene of the film was made. He did not live to see the birth of his child. Had it been a girl, it would have been named Gretchen—but it was the boy Gable wanted, and he was named John Clark Gable. The marriage of Monroe and Miller did not survive the making of the film—they were divorced a week before it was released. Miller married the still photographer for the film; Monroe began work on another film, *Something's Got to Give*, but her inability to show up on time forced the producers to fire her. On the morning of August 5, 1962, Monroe's housekeeper found her lying naked and dead. The cause of her death has been the source of heated controversy for more than twenty years.

Montgomery Clift died in 1966; his last words were "Absolutely not"—his response to being asked if he wanted to watch *The Misfits* on late-night television.

And the wild horses? They were protected by the endeavors of another misfit resident of Reno, Velma Johnston, better known as Wild Horse Annie. In 1971, the "Wild Horse Annie Act" was passed, prohibiting the use of airborne and mechanized vehicles in rounding up horses.

"They changed it all around," laments Gay Langland in *The Misfits*. "They" changed it so much that cowboys who should be riding the wild horses in freedom are catching them so that the horses can be eaten by domestic dogs living in fenced-in backyards. Wild Horse Annie did what she could for the horses; there was nothing anyone could do to protect the cowboys, and the steel walls of the modern world have forced them into the dog's life. The lone, proud man on a horse has nowhere to go on concrete roads.

Dalton Trumbo based the screenplay for *Lonely Are the Brave* (Universal, 1962), directed by David Miller, on Edward Abbey's novel *Brave Cowboy*. The film relates a sweet fable about one last, lonely cowboy who gets run over by the future. Jack Burns (Kirk Douglas) has his horse, his friends, and his disposition. He is an anachronism, an independent man determined to go where he wants and to do what he pleases. But he is locked in by civilization. Douglas himself said of the film, "*Spartacus* had the same theme. This is about enslavement in the modern age." In many ways, Douglas's role in *Lonely Are the Brave* echoes his role in *Man Without a Star* (1955), in which he plays a roaming cowpoke with a hatred of barbed wire and a fascination for indoor plumbing.

The story begins in Albuquerque, New Mexico. Burns's best friend (Michael Kane) is caught giving food and shelter to wetbacks and is put in jail. In traditional cowboy fashion, Burns gets himself jailed so that he can spring his pal. But his friend, who has a wife and kids, doesn't want to escape—he would rather serve out his time and not risk a longer sentence. So Burns escapes alone and takes off on his affectionate horse, Whiskey, for the Mexican border.

He is chased by a posse equipped with all the ac-

coutrements of modern civilization—rifles with telescopic sights, jeeps, walkie-talkies, even a helicopter. The posse is led by a humorous and sympathetic sheriff (Walter Matthau) who has respect and a little admiration for his quarry—he also has an inept deputy (William Schallert).

Even though he is vastly outnumbered and his horse and Winchester should be no match for the vehicles and weapons of the posse, Jack Burns outwits and eludes his pursuers. He almost makes it to freedom, but crossing a wet highway in the dark, he is run down by a huge truck. The truck, owned by the Acme Bathroom Fixtures Company, is carrying fifty-six toilets to Duke City, New Mexico. Burns's horse is shot, and Burns is carried away, fatally wounded, on a stretcher. His bid for freedom has been ended by indoor plumbing.

The Man Who Shot Liberty Valance (Paramount, 1962), directed by John Ford, presents a somber, nostalgic view of how the West was transformed from a wilderness into a garden. The film seems at times like a lesson in civics, as it carefully traces how eastern law—freedom of the press; the freedom to congregate; freedom of education; racial equality—replaced the law of the West—the law of the gun and the tough-minded individual.

The film begins with a train pulling into the small western town of Shinbone. Senator Ranse Stoddard (James Stewart) and his wife, Hallie (Vera Miles), have come to pay their last respects at the funeral of Tom Doniphon (John Wayne). When an eager newspaper reporter asks the senator why he has come all the way from Washington for the funeral of an unknown man, the senator responds with a long flashback in which he tells, for the first time, the true story of Tom Doniphon. The senator, famous as "the man who shot Liberty Valance"—and therefore tamed the frontier—explains how he came west to set up a law practice, met Doniphon and Hallie—who were at that time sweethearts—and got involved in the local dispute over statehood for the territory. As the champion of the law, Stoddard befriended the local newspaperman, Dutton Peabody (Edmond O'Brien) and set about educating the townspeople, teaching them how to read and introducing them to the Constitution and the Declaration of Independence. It was not always an easy task—Pompey (Woody Strode), who worked for Doniphon, had particular trouble remembering a certain part of the Declaration: "All men are created equal."

Liberty Valance (Lee Marvin), a cruel outlaw in the pay of the cattlemen, does his best to thwart the efforts of Stoddard, and when Valance tears up the newspaper office, almost killing Peabody, Stoddard has to confront him with a gun. (In traditional Ford fashion, Valance is dealt the card hand of aces and eights—"the deadman's hand"—before he goes out to face

Stoddard.) The mild and meek easterner—Doniphon calls him Pilgrim—seems to have no chance against Valance, but he miraculously manages to shoot and kill him. On the basis of his fame for killing Valance, Stoddard's career soars—the territory becomes a state, and he becomes its first senator.

But it was not Stoddard who shot Valance: it was Doniphon, who stood in the shadows behind Stoddard and plugged Valance with his Winchester. Doniphon's sacrifice—he loses Hallie to Stoddard and fades into obscurity—is poignantly clear to both Stoddard and Hallie, but when Stoddard has finished recounting the story, the newspapermen show no interest in printing it. As one declares, "This is the West, sir. When the legend becomes fact, print the legend."

Lonely Are the Brave and *The Man Who Shot Liberty Valance* appeared during the summer of 1962. That same summer, audiences were treated to a memorable double feature. The film with top billing was *The Tartars*, an Italian-Yugoslavian production starring Orson Welles as a lustful Tartar chieftain. Welles was growing very wide—while describing him, one reviewer said he looked like a walking house. In the second slot on the double bill, buried beneath the lurid slash-and-smash spectacle, was one of the most beautiful westerns ever made and one of the best evocations of the end of the West: *Ride the High Country*, directed by Sam Peckinpah.

Ride the High Country was Peckinpah's second movie. His first, ***The Deadly Companions*** (Paramount, 1961), resembles the television westerns that Peckinpah wrote. The plot concerns an army officer-turned-gunfighter named Yellowleg (Brian Keith) who accidentally kills the son of a wealthy woman (Maureen O'Hara) in the course of stopping a bank robbery. The woman decides she wants to bury her son next to her husband in distant Siringo, and Yellowleg, as atonement, agrees to lead the funeral procession which must cross the territory of hostile Indians. There is a parallel plot involving Yellowleg's search for the Confederate soldier who tried to scalp him during the war. He has been searching for five years, and in the first scene of the film he finds the man—Turkey (Chill Wills).

The Deadly Companions did not earn Peckinpah great fame. Nor did ***Ride the High Country*** (***Guns in the Afternoon*** in Great Britain) (MGM, 1962)—at least not in the United States. However, in both Great Britain and France, the film was immediately recognized as a classic, and when American audiences went back to have a second look, they realized what they—and the studio that had entombed the film beneath *The Tartars*—had missed.

Ride the High Country takes place around the turn of the century, during the remarkable period when horses and automobiles shared the roads, but the film's theme is not just the end of the West—its real concern

Left to right: Clark Gable, Marilyn Monroe, Eli Wallach, and Montgomery Clift in The Misfits *(United Artists, 1961).*

is honesty and personal dignity. The two main characters are two aging westerners, men who have had the misfortune of living beyond their time. A large part of the film's beauty is due to the actors chosen (by producer Richard Lyons) for the roles: Randolph Scott and Joel McCrea, two old men whose faces are well-known from hundreds of western films. It was the first time the two had acted together, although they had been friends for years. No better men could have been chosen for a film about the end of the West, and in many ways the film is also a farewell to a period in the history of western films. Scott, the older of the two men, was born the year of *The Great Train Robbery*, and *Ride the High Country* was released just four years before the arrival of the first "spaghetti" western.

The film begins with a scene that immediately establishes the changes that have taken place in the West. Former lawman—a man who helped make the West "safe for decent folks"—Steve Judd (McCrea) rides into a town full of cheering townspeople. He believes they are cheering for him and shyly acknowledges the attention only to be yelled at to get out of the way—they are actually cheering a race, and before he gets much farther, Judd is nearly run over by a car. He has come into the town to see about a job. The local bankers want him to pick up a shipment of gold from a new

strike in the High Sierras at a place called Coarsegold. When he remarks about how small the shipment is— only $20,000—one of the bankers explains to him that "The days of the forty-niners are past, and the days of the steady businessman have arrived."

The amount doesn't really matter to Judd, for guarding a gold shipment is work he likes and is better than what he has been doing—working as a bouncer and stickman. But he fears he is too old to do the job alone and looks up an old pal, Gil Westrum (Scott), another former lawman who is also down on his luck. Westrum is working in a carnival, dressed up as the Oregon Kid, "the last of the western town tamers"— a cruel parody of the two men's real past. Westrum accepts Judd's offer of some "old-time activity," and they take along Westrum's young friend, Heck Longtree (Ronald Starr).

Westrum and Longtree plot to steal the gold, and along the way the three men pick up a girl, Elsa Knudsen (Mariette Hartley in her film debut), eager to escape the oppressive life with her religious father (R. G. Armstrong). They take her to marry Billy Hammond (James Drury), who lives in Coarsegold. But the Hammond family, including the groom-to-be, turns out to be a pack of sleazy, wicked-willed characters, and Judd and Westrum steal Elsa away and take off, with the

Above: *Brandon De Wilde (left) and Paul Newman in* Hud *(Paramount, 1963). Opposite: Randolph Scott (left) and Joel McCrea in* Ride the High Country *(MGM, 1962).*

Hammonds in hot pursuit.

There is an honest sincerity about *Ride the High Country* that makes it seem intensely personal. The film is like the men it is about—soft-spoken and disarmingly straightforward—and its conversations poetically state Peckinpah's personal views of the importance of loyalty and self-esteem and of the subjectivity of right and wrong. Elsa says to Judd, "My father says there's only right and wrong—good and evil—nothing in between. It isn't that simple, is it?" Judd answers, "No, it isn't. It should be, but it isn't."

Westrum and Longtree make their play for the gold, and Judd catches them and swears to see they get tried. Westrum can't understand Judd's determination to deliver the gold. "This is bank money, not yours," he says. "And what they don't know won't hurt them," replies Judd. "Not them, only *me!*" It isn't so much the act of stealing that outrages Judd, it is his friend's betrayal. Dressed in an old coat with frayed sleeves, Judd is an old man in a world that has forgotten him and his kind, but he doesn't want to get rich and doesn't covet what belongs to others. As he says, "All I want is to enter my house justified" (a rewording of Luke 18:14 and a direct quotation from Peckinpah's father).

Westrum makes his getaway, but when the Hammonds attack, he rides back to rescue his friend in a moving scene that wonderfully repeats all the valiant rescue scenes of a generation of western films. The two friends defeat the Hammonds in an old-time shootout, but Judd is fatally wounded. Speaking about the gold, Westrum says to Judd, "Don't worry about anything. I'll take care of it, just like you would have."

"Hell," says Judd, "I know that. I always did. You just forgot it for a while, that's all." Then he says, "So long, partner," and Westrum replies, "I'll see you later," and leaves Judd to die after one last glance up at the far, high mountains.

Only Judd's attachment to an old code prevents Westrum and Longtree from stealing the gold. By the time of **Hud** (Paramount, 1963), directed by Martin Ritt, the old ways are gone, recalled, if at all, only in songs. The time of the film is the present day—it is every man for himself, and Hud Bannon (Paul Newman) believes that the entire country is corrupt, "from television game shows to expense accounts." The only surviving exponent of the old ways is Hud's father, Homer "Wild Horse" Bannon (Melvyn Douglas), a man who hates Hud for what he has become. "You're smart," he says to Hud. "You can talk a man into trusting you." But Homer knows the truth: Hud doesn't give a damn about anyone or anything except himself. He passes his time satisfying his lust with other men's wives. He abuses everyone, eventually running off all the people who care for him.

One of those people is Alma (Patricia Neal), the Bannon's housekeeper. Hud's mistreatment of Alma is one of his most vicious acts—he purposely gets rid of the one woman who tries to understand him. But the person who cares most for Hud is his nephew, Lon, played by Brandon De Wilde, who a decade earlier had acted the role of little Joey Starrett in *Shane*. *Hud* and *Shane* have more in common than De Wilde: both are about a young boy coming of age and learning about the world from an admired role model. But there is nothing of the noble character of Shane in Hud, and as Homer says, "Little by little, the look of the country changes because of the men we admire."

Hud begins with a scene that is the logical next step from the first scene of *Ride the High Country*: across the long, flat Texas horizon rides a truck—carrying a horse. No one rides horses anymore; Hud, the modern cowboy, drives a pink Cadillac. When it is discovered that the Bannon cattle have hoof-and-mouth disease, Hud wants to try to sell the diseased animals to another rancher before the government can condemn the herd. Homer, an old-time cattle rancher who can remember the days of the longhorn cattle when the Texans made everything they needed—hats, ropes, clothing, furniture—from the bones and hides of the animals, is shocked at the idea. What good is a man's life if he doesn't live by principles? Homer accepts his fate with grim resoluteness. The cattle have to be shot. A bulldozer is used to dig an enormous pit, the cattle are herded into it, and lines of riflemen shoot the animals. With the cattle gone, Hud wants to dig for oil on the property, but Homer loves the land and doesn't

want anyone punching holes in it. And he doesn't want to make money without working. "I want mine to come from something that keeps a man doin' for himself," he says. With the death of the cattle, Homer's spirit is broken. He is an old man in a world that has changed. He is tired, and the one time he really wakes up is in a movie theater where he "follows the bouncing ball" to sing a loud chorus of "Clementine."

But it is all over. The cattle are dead—Homer even has to shoot the few remaining longhorns he had kept because "they remind me of how things were." Homer dies, and Lon, seeing his uncle for what he is, leaves him. Finally alone in the ranch house, Hud looks out a window with a slight smile, as though he were happy to be finally alone. The old ways are all gone, and no new values have been established to take their place. As Homer says at one point, "It doesn't take long to kill things like it does to grow."

The alienation of the hero that began in the westerns of the 1950s leads to Hud, the ultimate "antihero" who destroys everything around him. Paramount's working title for *Hud* was *Hud Bannon against the World;* the screenplay for the film, written by Irving Ravetch and Harriet Frank, Jr., is based on a novel by Larry McMurty called *Horseman, Pass By.* McMurty's title is taken from a poem by William B. Yeats, "Under Ben Bulben." The full quotation, which Yeats requested as his epitaph, reads: "Cast a cold eye on life, on death. Horseman, pass by!"

> "When you talk about the Duke, you're not just talking about an actor—you're talking about the spirit that made America great."
> —Archie Bunker, "All in the Family"

Many young filmgoers sympathized with cynical, amoral Hud. They understood his alienation. The more conservative viewers of the film saw him as one more indication of the collapse of American values. The "Establishment" was under violent assault during the 1960s, and many filmmakers sought to break all the rules, smash all the moral codes, and deny all the old traditions. Other filmmakers tried to reaffirm those very things, and the old West became a popular battleground between the warring ideologies. Have our current maladies always been part of American society, or are they recent developments? What is the truth about the famous heroes of the past?

John Wayne never had any doubt about who the good guys were. By 1959, Wayne was a wealthy man—he had invested wisely—looking forward to easing himself into retirement. He was 52 and slowing down, but there was still one story that he wanted to tell. He had always wanted to make a film about the Alamo, and the nation's problems made him think it was more important than ever. As he said, "It had to be made

into a motion picture. It has the raw and tender stuff of immortality, peopled by hard-living, hard-loving men whose women matched them in creating a pattern of freedom and liberty." When no one else showed any interest in the idea, Wayne decided to do more than just star in the film: he would also produce and direct it.

The screenplay for *The Alamo* (United Artists, 1960) was written by James Edward Grant, who had created the screenplay for *Angel and the Badman,* the first film Wayne had produced. Grant did nothing to disturb the legends of the epic battle and gave Wayne exactly what Wayne wanted—an intensely patriotic story full of dramatic reflections on the heroic virtues of Americans. The story of the film covers the events from the declaration of the Texas republic to the battle of San Jacinto, but most of the film takes place within the walls of the Spanish mission. (Wayne didn't use the original building—he had a new one built near Brackettville, Texas, about 100 miles from the original.) In fact, most of the film is taken up with the final battle, with the 7,000 Mexican troops methodically overrunning the garrison and killing the 180 volunteers.

Wayne plays Davy Crockett; Richard Widmark is Jim Bowie; Richard Boone is Sam Houston. Wayne also found room for his son Patrick and his daughter Aissa—and for Frankie Avalon, too.

Wayne didn't do such a bad job of directing, and his pal John Ford may have helped with some of the scenes. (Ford may even have shot a few scenes, but they were not used in the final print.) Dimitri Tiomkin wrote a suitably rousing score. But the film ran way over budget, finally costing more than $12 million. Wayne, who fervently believed in the message of the film, cashed in his personal fortune to bankroll the project, and when it made a very poor showing at the box office (it did eventually make a profit), Wayne found himself at the edge of bankruptcy. Instead of being one of his last films, *The Alamo* ushered in a decade full of a particular kind of western—the "John Wayne film," most of which were nothing more than vehicles to support Wayne's large persona and present his conservative politics. Wayne became an American institution.

Wayne's next western, *North to Alaska* (20th Century-Fox, 1960), resembles a cross between *The Spoilers* and a humorous Italian opera. Wayne and Stewart Granger are two prospectors who have struck it rich; Fabian is Granger's brother; Ernie Kovacs is a wily villain out to steal the partners' claim; and Capucine is the woman they all fight over. Directed by Henry Hathaway, the film has a lot of roughhousing and a lot of "lusty" humor.

In *The Comancheros* (20th Century-Fox, 1961), Wayne, as Captain Jake Cutter of the Texas Rangers, arrests Paul Regret (Stuart Whitman), a Louisiana gambler wanted for killing a man in an illegal duel.

John Wayne in The Alamo *(United Artists, 1960).*

A-S-27

Regret clobbers Cutter with a shovel and gets away, but Cutter catches up with him, and when Regret proves himself in a fight against the Comanches, he is made a Ranger. The two pose as rumrunners and infiltrate the Comancheros, a gang of outlaws selling weapons and whiskey to the Comanches. *The Comancheros* was directed by Michael Curtiz—it was his last film—and includes roles for both Patrick and Aissa Wayne. The plot appealed to someone, for it was reused in *Rio Conchos* (20 Century-Fox, 1964), directed by Gordon Douglas.

Wayne does not appear in *Rio Conchos*, but Whitman does. The film stars Richard Boone as a drunken, vengeful ex-Confederate soldier who kills Indians for the fun of it. He, Whitman, Tony Franciosa, and Jim Brown—in his screen debut—take off after 2,000 carbines that have been stolen from a cavalry shipment. It is 1867, and although the Civil War is over, a former Confederate general (Edmond O'Brien) has set up a new Confederacy along the Rio Conchos and is allying his army of outlaws with the Apache so they can all fight their common enemy—the United States.

John Wayne appears as General Sherman in *How the West Was Won* (MGM, 1962), a monstrous epic that required the services of three directors—John Ford, Henry Hathaway, and George Marshall—a host of stars—including Debbie Reynolds, James Stewart, Wayne, Henry Fonda, Richard Widmark, Gregory Peck, Robert Preston, Raymond Massey, Lee J. Cobb, George Peppard, and Karl Malden—and 12,617 extras. The whole thing, narrated by Spencer Tracy and based on a series of articles in *Life* magazine, cost more than $14 million and was the first dramatic use of Cinerama, which had until then been used for travelogues. The film covers a sixty-year period (1830–1890) in the history of the West and is divided into five segments: the Erie Canal and the settlement of the Ohio River territory; the wagon trains and the California gold rush; the Civil War; the building of the transcontinental railroad; and the bringing of law and order to the West. The various episodes are seen through the eyes of four generations of a pioneer family. *How the West Was Won* is not really about the "winning" of the West—it is a celebration of the western movie, with bit parts for everyone and lots of action that could have been lifted from any number of films.

Andrew V. McLaglen, son of the actor Victor McLaglen (who appeared as a whiskey-loving Irishman in John Ford's cavalry films) served as an assistant to Ford on *The Quiet Man* (1952), the popular film about love and fisticuffs in Ireland that starred John Wayne; Maureen O'Hara; and Victor McLaglen as the bullying Red Will Danaher. *McLintock!* (United Artists, 1963), directed by Andrew V. McLaglen, is *The Quiet Man*—and Shakespeare's *The Taming of the Shrew*—in a western setting. The film was produced by Wayne's eldest son, Michael; the screenplay was written by James Edward Grant.

George Washington McLintock (Wayne), cattle baron ("I work for everybody in these United States that steps into a butcher shop to buy a T-bone steak") and leading citizen of the town of McLintock, has everything except his wife, Kate (O'Hara), who left him when she suspected him of infidelities. When she returns, after a two-year absence, to get a divorce and take custody of their daughter, Becky (Stefanie Powers), she finds that McLintock has taken on an attractive new cook (Yvonne De Carlo). The cook has a 7-year-old daughter (Aissa Wayne) and a son (Patrick Wayne) who has eyes for Becky. The familial spats and problems with the local Indians are all presented as farcical slapstick comedy. The film includes an epic battle in a large muddy hole. (In reality, the hole was not filled with old-fashioned water-and-dirt mud—when real mud is photographed, it is "flat," even with color film. The hole was full of two tons of Bentonite, a chalk product used in oil drilling and chocolate syrup. Bentonite is far superior to real mud—its color is clearer and sharper, it clings to things, and actors can slide around in it with ease.)

After his comedy western with Wayne, Andrew V. McLaglen directed three westerns that were more serious: *Shenandoah*, *The Rare Breed*, and *The Way West*.

Shenandoah (Universal, 1965), which was the basis for the Broadway musical, stars James Stewart as the stubborn, isolationist head of a family of Virginia farmers (the film was shot in Oregon). The Civil War doesn't interest Stewart in the least until his youngest son (called "the boy") is kidnapped by Union scouts. Eventually, his entire large family is drawn into the war and, in a tear-jerking ending, is reunited after it.

The screenplay for *The Rare Breed* (Universal, 1966), written by Ric Hardman, deals with the introduction of the Hereford cattle to the Texas range. The "meatless, milkless, and murderous" longhorns were stringy but hardy—they could survive the rough climate of the American Southwest. The English Herefords—meatier and tastier—were not as tough as the longhorns, and it was feared they wouldn't survive. The idea was to create a new breed, and *The Rare Breed* is about a newly widowed Englishwoman (Maureen O'Hara) who comes to America with a prize Hereford bull named Vindicator. She hires James Stewart to help her get the bull to its buyer, a Scotsman (Brian Keith). The villain of the film is Jack Elam—he even sets off a stampede.

Elam appears in a more likeable role—as a traveling preacher named Weatherby—in *The Way West* (United Artists, 1967). The film follows the route of a wagon train from Independence, Missouri, to Oregon

Top: *Kirk Douglas in* The Way West *(United Artists, 1967).*
Above: *Kirk Douglas tossing Robert Walker, Jr., into the water in* The War Wagon *(Universal, 1967).*

in 1843. The wagon train is led by a stern visionary named Senator Tadlock (Kirk Douglas), whose rousing speeches inspire people to leave their homes and follow him. To guide the train Tadlock even manages to get famous scout Dick Summers (Robert Mitchum), who is grieving over the death of his squaw wife. (Summers has another problem—he is steadily going blind.) Lije Evans (Richard Widmark) doesn't need any inspirational speeches from the senator to make him join the caravan—he is an embodiment of the pioneer spirit, a true Yancey Cravat (*Cimarron*) who has to keep moving—and drinking. With all the religious righteousness from the senator keeping the wagons moving, the pioneers get nervous and things go wrong. Aside from the scene of fording a river and the Indians attacking ("We're all part Indian," says Summers for some reason), there are plenty of family problems, most of them brought on by an over-sexed Sally Field.

In 1964, Wayne lost the better part of one lung to cancer. "I licked the big C," he declared and went right on making films. *The Sons of Katie Elder* (Paramount, 1965), directed by Henry Hathaway, begins in Clearwater, Texas, with the funeral of Katie Elder, pioneer Texan. Her four sons—John (John Wayne), Tom (Dean Martin), Matt (Earl Holliman), and Bud (Michael Anderson, Jr.)—pay their last respects. When John discovers that the family spread is no longer theirs and that their father died under suspicious circumstances, he and his brothers set about investigating and get themselves involved in a lot of gunplay.

The loss of the lung slowed Wayne down. His breathing became audible, and he no longer moved with the smooth assurance he had displayed as the Ringo Kid in *Stagecoach*. When that film was remade in 1966, directed by Gordon Douglas, the role of the Ringo Kid went to Alex Cord. Of course, all the roles went to different actors—Doc Boone was played by Bing Crosby and Dallas was played by Ann-Margret. Buck, the stage driver, was played by Slim Pickens, who three years earlier had added a touch of the West to *Dr. Strangelove* by whooping and hollering and taking one last ride—on a hydrogen bomb.

Wayne was no longer the Ringo Kid, but he was still John Wayne, and he kept making westerns. Full of action and rough humor, *The War Wagon* (Universal, 1967), directed by Burt Kennedy, is a favorite with John Wayne fans. Made at the same time as *El Dorado*, Wayne appears wearing—in addition to his ever-present *Red River* belt buckle—a Montagnard bracelet. He plays a landowner who has been cheated out of his land, framed, and sent to prison by an evil conniver (Bruce Cabot). Released from prison, Wayne decides to take revenge by knocking over Cabot's gold-laden "war wagon," an armor-plated coach armed with a Gatling gun and manned by thirty-three guards—twenty-eight outriders and five in the coach.

143

Wayne calculates that it will take five men (not a magnificent seven) to take the coach, and he goes around collecting his pros. His first choice is Kirk Douglas, whose outfit includes a tight leather shirt and black leather gloves—he wears a large silver ring with a nice big stone over one of his gloved fingers. Douglas has been hired by Cabot to gun down Wayne, but when Wayne makes him a better offer—a large share of the gold carried in the war wagon—he changes his mind. There is also the slight matter of camaraderie—the two men don't trust each other, but they enjoy each other's company. They have a good time together. They both agree on the quality of the local whores—whores who are made more desirable because they don't speak English—and they compete in a sort of shooting contest. When they are approached by two of Cabot's henchmen, Wayne and Douglas quickly dispatch their opponents and then argue about their prowess. "Mine hit the ground first," says Douglas. "Mine was taller," says Wayne.

Wayne rounds out his little group with an Indian (Howard Keel), a safecracker (Keenan Wynn), and—a necessity in any group of professionals during the sixties—a dynamite expert (Robert Walker, Jr.). The wagon is no match for Wayne and his crew.

Throughout *The War Wagon*, Wayne seems to genuinely enjoy every opportunity to use his little—in his paws—pistols. Violence was part of the John Wayne hero at any age, and Wayne—as he had demonstrated in *The Alamo*—believed that courageous bands of fighting men were essential to the history of America. As he proved by wearing his Montagnard bracelet, Wayne felt strongly about the Vietnam War, and in 1968 he again decided to produce and co-direct a film. *The Green Berets* was the only film of the decade about Vietnam, and it is certainly no accident that the name of the besieged Green Beret encampment in the film is Dodge City.

In 1969, Wayne made two westerns: *The Undefeated* and *True Grit*. The first, full of brawling action, is a continuation of Wayne's other films of the decade; the second is a brilliant film in which Wayne has the opportunity to act his age.

Directed by Andrew V. McLaglen, *The Undefeated* (20th Century-Fox) begins with a Civil War battle being fought three days after the end of the war. Wayne, as a Union cavalry colonel, decides to keep his homeless and penurious bunch of men together, and they head out West to capture wild horses and sell them to the U.S. Army. When Wayne finds that the army contractors are unscrupulous, he decides to head for Mexico and sell the horses to the Mexican Army—this is the period of Maximilian's battles with Juarez. Rock Hudson, a Confederate cavalry colonel, finds the end of the war hard to take, and rather than see his Louisiana plantation fall into the hands of swindling

John Wayne in True Grit *(Paramount, 1969).*

carpetbaggers, he burns it down and sets off with his men and their families to fight as mercenaries in Mexico. So it is that the two groups meet in Mexico. The former Yanks help the former Rebs fight off a gang of Mexican bandits, which—along with a massive brawl as part of a Fourth of July celebration—helps relieve the tension between the two groups of former enemies. They have a few scraps with Maximilian's French horsemen, and the film ends with a stampede of the horses through Maximilian's lines—a scene reminiscent of *Alvarez Kelly* (1966).

John Wayne was 62 when he acted the part of Rooster Cogburn in *True Grit* (Paramount). He had been a star for forty years—*True Grit* was made thirty years after *Stagecoach*—and he had played old men before—as in *Red River* and *She Wore a Yellow Ribbon*—but now he really was old. Nor was Henry Hathaway, the director of the film, a young man—he was born in 1898. Wayne and Hathaway knew how to create the character of an old man, and paunchy, ornery, one-eyed old Rooster Cogburn was one of Wayne's greatest roles—he even won an Oscar for it.

The screenplay for *True Grit* is based on a novel by Charles Portis; indeed, Portis wrote the book with Wayne in mind and sent Wayne galleys to read. Screenwriter Marguerite Roberts used entire blocks of dialogue from the novel, and the words, phrases, and ironic politeness give the film a 19th-century charm.

When her father is killed by a hired hand named Tom Chaney (Jeff Corey), 14-year-old Mattie Ross (Kim Darby) sets off after the murderer ("I won't rest until Tom Chaney's barking in hell"). She goes to Fort Smith, Arkansas, where Judge Isaac Parker (the fa-

mous hanging judge encountered under a different name in *Hang 'Em High*) holds his court. She arrives in time to witness one of the judge's public hangings and asks the local sheriff for help. He turns her down but recommends to her Rooster Cogburn—"Fear don't enter into his thinking." When she meets the fat old man—he's not exactly what she had in mind—she asks him, "They tell me you're a man with true grit?" Crusty Cogburn agrees to help her find her father's killer and even lowers his fees: "I'm givin' you my kid's rate for doin' the job!" (Cogburn has a personal reason for taking the job; he believes Chaney has joined Ned Pepper's notorious gang, and Pepper is the only villain who has ever escaped him.) The unlikely pair are joined by a Texas Ranger named La Boeuf (Glen Campbell, in his screen debut), who is after the killer for another crime.

Cogburn and La Boeuf don't get along, and they don't want Mattie around, either. But when they try to ditch her, leaving her behind when they board a ferry, she just dives her horse into the water, prompting the old boozer to exclaim, "By God, she reminds me of me."

In the film's most famous scene, Cogburn comes upon Pepper (Robert Duvall) and his gang in a glade. Sitting straight on his horse, a pistol in one hand and his Winchester in the other, Cogburn calls out, "I mean to kill you in one minute, Ned, or see you hanged in Fort Smith at Judge Parker's convenience. Which will you have?"

"I call that bold talk for a one-eyed fat man," Pepper yells back.

"Fill your hands, you son-of-a-bitch!" responds Cogburn, and taking the reins of his horse in his teeth, he charges the four outlaws in true jousting fashion.

He kills only three of them. Pinned under his horse, he laments, "Dammit, Bo, first time ya ever gave me reason to curse ya."

The outlaws are done away with—the violence in *True Grit* is brutal—and Cogburn takes Mattie home, where she offers the old man a grave site next to her own. But Cogburn isn't ready to die yet, and as he rides away he calls back to her, "Come and see a fat old man sometime." (Audiences did just that in *Rooster Cogburn*, in 1975.)

"What was wrong with us? Nothing. Nothing. Just our color."

Tell Them Willie Boy Is Here

The sixties loved half-breeds—cut off from society, they are in a unique position to deliver scathing criticism—and the sixties finally admitted that there had been blacks—or at least Woody Strode—out West. But the sixties did little to change the ethnicity of westerns. The only real change was that more Mexicans bit the dust between 1960 and 1969 than Indians.

Elvis Presley plays a half-breed in *Flaming Star* (20th Century-Fox, 1960), directed by Don Siegel (who the year before had directed Fabian in *Hound Dog Man*). Presley doesn't sing in the movie—well, he sings the title song (unseen), and he takes on a few bars at a surprise birthday party—but he acts well. As the son of an Indian mother (Dolores Del Rio) and a white father (John McIntire), he finds himself in the middle of a war between the Kiowas and white settlers.

The Kiowas and another "half-breed" are the subject of *The Unforgiven* (United Artists, 1960), directed by John Huston and based on a novel, *The Siege at Dancing Bird*, by Alan Le May (who also wrote *The Searchers*). The film takes place in the Texas Panhandle shortly after the Civil War and concerns a pioneer family living in a sod house. The family is composed of three brothers (Burt Lancaster, Audie Murphy, and Doug McClure), their mother (Lillian Gish), and their adopted sister (Audrey Hepburn). A mysterious one-eyed stranger—more an apparition than a man—appears and proclaims himself the "sword of God." Dressed in a Confederate uniform and waving a sword, he claims that Hepburn is really a "red-hide whelp," a Kiowa Indian by birth. The mother won't divulge the secret of how she and her long-dead husband came by the child (he rescued the girl from a massacre of Kiowas), and the neighboring whites begin to resent having one of the "enemy" in their midst. Then the Kiowas decide that they want to have the girl back. The family refuses to give in to either the bigoted whites or the Indians, and when the Indians attack the cabin, Hepburn has to shoot at her own people.

Like the films of Ford's cavalry trilogy, *Sergeant Rutledge* (Warner Brothers, 1960), directed by John Ford, is based on a novel by James Warner Bellah. And like the three cavalry films, it concerns the cavalry and its ongoing conflict with the Indians. What sets *Sergeant Rutledge* apart is the fact that the title character is black. Sergeant Rutledge (Woody Strode), the "top soldier" in the Ninth Cavalry, is accused of raping and murdering a white girl and is court-martialed. Most of the film takes place in a courtroom, but as each of the various witnesses takes the stand, his or her testimony is related in a flashback, many of which take place, of course, in Monument Valley. The theme of the film is racism, particularly its basis in sexual fears, and Ford even manages to manipulate the viewer's racism—Strode's glistening muscles make him seem guilty.

Ford used Strode in his next two westerns, but not as the leading character. In *Two Rode Together*, Strode plays an Indian; in *The Man Who Shot Liberty Valance*, he plays Pompey, Tom Doniphon's (John Wayne) hired hand and sidekick.

Like *The Searchers*, *Two Rode Together* (Columbia, 1961) is about efforts to retrieve people who have been taken captive by Indians. The two who ride to-

gether are James Stewart (this was his first film with Ford) and Richard Widmark. Stewart plays a mercenary marshal of a border town. Widmark, a cavalry lieutenant, wants Stewart to help bring back people who have been taken—years ago—by the Comanches. Stewart, an expert in dealing with the Indians, is cynical and coldly realistic. He tells the relatives of the captives, who have gathered at the fort, that they shouldn't hope for anything, and he vividly describes what the Indians do to captives (including a description of the Sun Vow ceremony of *A Man Called Horse*). When the people insist that they want their lost relatives back, Stewart wants to charge them for his services—$500 for each captive returned.

It takes a remarkably short time for Stewart and Widmark to get to the Indian camp and locate the captives (who include silent film star Mae Marsh). As Stewart predicted, the captives don't want to go back. Stewart and Widmark finally take one boy and a Spanish woman (Linda Cristal)—who turns out to be the woman of Stone Calf (Woody Strode), and Stewart is forced to kill the Indian.

The larger part of the film concerns the prejudice the woman encounters back in white civilization. The white women can't understand why she didn't kill herself rather than suffer such indignities. Her explanation is that her religion—she's Catholic—forbids suicide.

There is the usual amount of Fordian humor in *Two Rode Together*—a comic three-way conversation, Widmark bumping his head on a tent lantern, Stewart trying to carry three glasses of punch—and there is the obligatory dance at the cavalry post. Even with the slapstick humor and the traditional music, the racism and bigotry make it clear that Ford was rethinking his views of the West.

He was also rethinking his views of the Indian, and in *Cheyenne Autumn* (Warner Brothers, 1964), his last western, he delivered his repentance for how he had treated the Indians in all his previous films.

Cheyenne Autumn is based on a historical novel by Mari Sandoz that tells a true story—in 1878, a group of nearly 300 Cheyenne Indians, confined to a reservation in the Indian Territory (Oklahoma) and suffering from disease and malnutrition, decided to go home and began walking toward their own country in Wyoming. It was a 1,500-mile trek, and very few of them made it, but it wasn't just the physical hardship that wore them down—they were pursued by the cavalry and harassed by the settlers whose land they crossed.

It is a moving story, poetically heroic and sorrowful, and it was a good choice for Ford's apology to the Indians. As he said, "This will be the first picture ever made in which Indians are people." The Indians—led by Ricardo Montalban and Sal Mineo—are indeed presented in a very sympathetic light, but *Cheyenne Autumn* is a Ford western and suffers from his addiction

to slapstick comedy. The scenes in Dodge City—a honky-tonk world that revolves around an ongoing poker game, with James Stewart comical as Wyatt Earp and Arthur Kennedy as Doc Holliday—are more easily remembered than the scenes of the long-suffering Indians. The *Harvard Lampoon* voted it one of the worst films that year, along with *The Greatest Story Ever Told, The Carpetbaggers*, and *Kiss Me, Stupid.*

Duel at Diablo (United Artists, 1966) was produced by Ralph Nelson and Fred Engel (Nelson also directed) and stars Sidney Poitier—the same three men who made *Lilies of the Field*. The film begins and ends with a knife cutting through the screen, and between the two slashes it tells a taut story of racism and bigotry. James Garner is a scout seeking revenge for the murder of his Indian wife; Sidney Poitier is a cynical, dandyish former cavalry trooper who makes his living breaking in horses for the army; Bibi Andersson plays a white woman who has been taken captive by the Apaches and has a half-breed child; her husband (Dennis Weaver) can't understand her—according to him any decent woman would prefer to die than be an Apache squaw—and she runs away to return to her child. The entire group sets off with a cavalry troop (led by Bill Travers) to carry a load of ammunition from Fort Creel to distant Fort Concho—en route they are attacked by Indians. The violence, combined with the unnerving musical score by Neal Hefti, gives the film a tense atmosphere. (The credits for *Duel at Diablo* list an Alf Elson, who is none other than the director, Ralph Nelson—he has a small scene as a cavalry colonel.)

One of the characters in Harold Robbins's novel *The Carpetbaggers* is Nevada Smith, an aging cowboy star of the silent screen. When the novel was made into a film, in 1964, the role of Nevada Smith was played by Alan Ladd. *Nevada Smith* (Paramount, 1966), directed by Henry Hathaway, is a "prequel" to *The Carpetbaggers*. The screenplay, by John Michael Hayes (who also wrote the screenplay for *The Carpetbaggers*) relates the early life of Max Sand, the half-breed who became Nevada Smith.

When young Max Sand's (Steve McQueen) father and Indian mother are brutally murdered by three men (Karl Malden, Arthur Kennedy, and Martin Landau), he sets off after them, determined to get revenge. He has the good fortune of encountering a traveling gunsmith (Brian Keith) who teaches him how to shoot and also teaches him that a gun is only a tool—in order to find and kill the three men, the young half-breed will have to learn a new way of thinking and acting. He learns his lessons well and goes to great lengths to track down the three killers (including getting himself put in prison to get near one of them).

One of the nice things about half-breeds—from the viewpoint of Hollywood filmmakers—is that they

Preceding pages: The Sons of Katie Elder (*Paramount, 1965*).

Ernest Borgnine (left) and William Holden in The Wild Bunch
(Warner Brothers, 1969).

Above: *Barry Sullivan (left) and
Robert Redford in* Tell Them
Willie Boy Is Here *(Universal,
1969). Right: Sidney Poitier
and Bibi Andersson in* Duel at
Diablo *(United Artists, 1966).*

Hang 'Em High *(United Artists, 1968)*.

Cleavon Little (left) and Gene Wilder in Blazing Saddles
(Warner Brothers, 1974).

don't have to look like Indians. Elvis Presley and Audrey Hepburn don't look much like Indians, nor does Steve McQueen. As Nevada Smith, McQueen doesn't have to suffer much prejudice. Paul Newman doesn't look much like an Indian, either, and as John Russell in **Hombre** (20th Century-Fox, 1967), he plays not a half-breed but a white man who has been brought up by the Indians. But even with his blue eyes, his status in society is that of a half-breed, and he has to suffer a lot of vicious bigotry.

Directed and produced by Martin Ritt, *Hombre* resembles a second remake (the first was in 1966) of *Stagecoach.* John Russell (Newman) has two names, a "white" one and an Indian one—Hombre. Carried off as a child by the Apaches, he was found and brought back to white civilization, only to run away to rejoin them. As an Indian—by choice—he cynically understands the Indian's abused role. His division between the Apaches and the whites has made of him a detached loner. He is identified as a man apart by his acerbic sophistication; Russell's superiority comes not from his self-image as an Indian but from his powerful inner-directedness. Suffering abuse has made him learn to endure, has made him stronger. He has had to realize and accept more things about himself and others than most people, and his understanding of the world is not blocked by fears or prejudices.

Russell is a breaker of wild horses. In the opening sequences of the film, it is firmly established that he considers himself an Indian and wants nothing to do with whites. When he inherits a boardinghouse (from the man whose name he bears), he has to take a trip in a "mud wagon" (stagecoach). (Careful viewers will note that the towns on the trip—Contention City and Bisbee—are the towns named in *3:10 to Yuma.*) With him on the stage are an Indian agent (Fredric March), who has been cheating the Indians and is absconding with his stolen wealth; the agent's wife (Barbara Rush), who has no fondness for Indians and makes Russell ride on the roof rather than inside the coach; the worldly and wise housekeeper of the boardinghouse (Diane Cilento); a young couple; and a nasty character who turns out to be an outlaw (Richard Boone). The only white person sympathetic to Russell at the beginning of the film is the stage driver (Martin Balsam). "You've been up in the mountains too long," he tells Russell, meaning that Russell should relinquish his Indian ways and rejoin white society. That is precisely what Russell does not want to do. When the stagecoach passengers are stranded and besieged in an abandoned mining camp by an outlaw gang, Russell (Hombre) saves them, but he does not do so because he has changed his mind about the corrupt and bigoted whites. Quite the contrary—he protects them, and dies for them, because his personal morality makes him responsible for them. He protects the weak.

Top: *Suzanne Pleshette and Steve McQueen in* Nevada Smith *(Paramount, 1966). Above: Martin Balsam (left) and Paul Newman in* Hombre *(20th Century-Fox, 1967).*

When last we met George Armstrong Custer, he was Errol Flynn in *They Died with Their Boots On* (1942), and he was energetically heroic. In *Custer of the West* (ABC, 1967), directed by Robert Siodmak, Custer is played by Robert Shaw, and although the accent is similar (Flynn was Australian; Shaw was English), Flynn's breathless enthusiasm is replaced by verbose nihilism. As Custer, Shaw plays a soldier with no political interests, a man who suffers for the stupidity of his government. He sees all evil as inevitable. "You're paying the price for being backward," explains Custer to an Indian. He also delivers a short polemic against modern war: "Trains, steel, guns that kill by thousands. No horses. Our kind of fighting is all over." "For the last time, then," responds an Indian. As is traditional, Custer is the last one to die at the Little Big Horn, and viewers are left with the sense that had he been the first, the catastrophe might have been averted.

The Black Hills of Dakota, scene of the Little Big Horn, got their name because they are so thickly forested that from a distance they look black. The treeless plain behind the action in *Custer of the West* is Spain. Making westerns in Spain necessarily changed the topography of the old West; because of its similar landscape, the Southwest became a popular location for westerns (its proximity to Mexico helped explain the abundance of foreigners), and the Apaches (so cunning that they are rarely seen) became the preferred tribe of Indians.

The Spanish scenery is of little importance in *Chuka* (Paramount, 1967), directed by Gordon Douglas—most of the film takes place inside a fort. The colonel in command of the outpost (John Mills) is a mean man, detested by those who know him. His men are plotting mutiny, but his loyal sergeant (Ernest Borgnine) stands by him. Rod Taylor (who coproduced the film) stars in the title role of Chuka, the lone gunfighter. When someone asks Chuka where his home is, he replies, "Anywhere I happen to be." This vagabond hero is savvy in the ways of the Indians and tries to save the fort from massacre—it is surrounded by Indians. Somewhat like Hombre, Chuka's superior skills make him feel responsible for the inhabitants of the fort. One of these is a wealthy Mexican widow (Luciana Paluzzi), who delivers a possible theme for the film: "In a lifetime of experience, I have learned that one man is the image of all men."

In *Shalako* (CIN, 1968), another made-in-Spain western, Sean Connery follows the heroic example set by Chuka. The screenplay for the film, written by J. J. Griffith, Hal Hopper, Scot Finch, and Clarke Reynolds, is based on a novel by Louis L'Amour; the film was directed by Edward Dmytryk. It must therefore be the cast that gives the film its peculiar feel: aside from Connery (who was already notorious as an international spy), there is Brigitte Bardot (who speaks recognizable English). Bardot's presence in Apache territory is handily explained—she is part of a natty assortment of European aristocrats who are on a hunting safari (presumably during Africa's off-season). Suitably bombastic pigs (they are served their evening meal by a butler and sip sparkling wine after each "kill"), the Europeans are treacherously double-crossed by the guide they have hired (Stephen Boyd), and Shalako—a lone gunfighter who knows the ways of the Indians—comes to their rescue. The Indians who mercilessly harass this group are led by a chief with magnificent long black hair—Woody Strode.

Ossie Davis doesn't play an Indian in *The Scalphunters* (United Artists, 1968), directed by Sidney Pollack. He claims he is a Comanche, but he is really a runaway slave. The Indians in the film, led by Armando Silvestre, aren't the villains—they aren't even the scalphunters of the title. The scalphunters are white bounty hunters who make their living killing Indians and selling the scalps for $25 each. The leader of this mean crew is Telly Savalas; his mistress, Shelley Winters, passes her time smoking cigars and reading astrology books. The Indians capture Davis, and when they steal a trapper's furs, they give Davis to him in recompense. The trapper (Burt Lancaster) wants his furs back; Davis wants his freedom. The Indians are slaughtered by the scalphunters, who then take possession of the furs. All of this supposedly takes place during the 1850s, but the film's humor—sometimes grim and sometimes too obvious in its significance—is very contemporary.

Blue (Paramount, 1968), directed by Silvio Narizzano, stars Terence Stamp as another "half-breed," a man divided between two conflicting ways of life. Azul ("Blue"—so-called because of his eyes) is the son of American parents who were slaughtered by Mexicans during the Texas Revolution. Adopted by a Mexican revolutionary-turned-bandit named Ortega (Ricardo Montalban), Azul learns to be a cold-blooded killer, just like his three stepbrothers. But when he takes part in a raid into Texas, Azul the wanton killer finds himself drawn to another, more peaceful way of life. He eventually is forced to choose between his own people (the Texas ranchers) and the Mexican bandits who attack them. The film, which is very violent and gory, makes use of some odd devices to tell its story, including silent chase scenes and close-ups of eyes and nostrils. Stamp does not speak for the first fifty minutes.

The basic structure of *Blue*—that of a man divided between two ways of life—and the actual making of the film, which involved taking a citified film crew out on location among rural folk, led to the making of *Fade In* (Paramount, 1968), directed by "Allen Smithee" (a pseudonym for Jud Taylor) and produced by Narizzano (who directed *Blue*). Filmed simultaneously with *Blue*, on the same locations, *Fade In* uses the making

Gregory Peck buying train tickets for Noland Clay and Eva Marie Saint in The Stalking Moon *(NGP, 1968).*

of *Blue* as its background (the stars of *Blue* appear in scenes in *Fade In*). *Fade In* is the story of a love affair between an assistant film editor (Barbara Loden) and a local rancher (Burt Reynolds) whose land is being used for the western. They are two different people: he believes in the old mores, she shocks him with the new ones. It is a very bittersweet little love story, not at all like *Blue*.

A stalking-horse is a horse—or even a figure shaped like a horse—behind which a hunter stalks game. In **The Stalking Moon** (NGP, 1968), directed by Robert Mulligan, the hunter is an Indian named Salvaje ("savage" in Spanish) who is hunting for his child, and he might as well be hiding behind the moon—he is everywhere, unseen but always threatening.

The film begins with a frontier scout named Sam Varner (Gregory Peck)—he has been a scout for twenty years and is ready to retire—taking part in one last roundup of Apaches. Among the Apaches are found a white woman named Sarah Carver (Eva Marie Saint) and her 9-year-old half-breed son (Noland Clay). She has been held captive by the Apaches for ten years and barely remembers how to speak English. Varner takes

responsibility for the woman and child and delivers them to a railway station. He means to leave them there, but it is clear that they cannot fend for themselves, so he takes them with him to his "passel of land" in New Mexico, which he has bought mail order.

They are closely followed by the child's father, Salvaje (Nathaniel Narcisco), who is never himself seen but who makes his presence known by killing everything—men, women, children, horses, dogs—he comes across. Varner and Carver—and the viewer—become the quarry. Each time the camera pans, it doesn't stop where the viewer thinks it will, but keeps going a little, as though it were looking for something. Nervousness pervades the film as the little group awaits the inevitable attack of the Indian. "You won't hear him," says Sarah. "I'll hear him," says Varner. "It doesn't happen that way," she continues. "He just comes."

When he does come, the final battle is very frightening, but no one ever reflects that perhaps the Apache father might have a right to his child. The question is avoided by making him into a kind of monster, an inhuman and indestructible killing machine.

Tell Them Willie Boy Is Here (Universal, 1969) is

an unusual film about Indians in that it takes place after the turn of the century, long after Wounded Knee, the last major "battle" of the Indian wars. The location of the film is Southern California's Riverside County, and the story involves the nation's last Indian manhunt. A young Paiute Indian named Willie Boy (Robert Blake) kills his girlfriend's father and runs off with her (Katharine Ross). According to Paiute law, what he has done is "marriage by capture"; according to the white man's law, it is murder, and a posse takes off after him. The members of the posse, led by Sheriff Cooper (Robert Redford) enjoy the opportunity to take part in this old-time activity. The most bigoted among them, Calvert (Barry Sullivan), misses the old days "with all the fighting and everything." He remembers that "in the morning you could look out and see the tepees, white in the sun," and he also remembers Sheriff Cooper's father, a lawman who was killed in a barroom brawl. "Your daddy was lucky," says Calvert. "He died while it was still good to live."

The hunt for Willie Boy is given impetus when it is announced that President Taft is about to pay a visit to the area. Nervous officials and eager newspapermen turn the lone Willie into an Indian uprising. The still-fresh memory of President McKinley's assassination leads to fears for the president's life, and while an enormous, thronelike chair is prepared for Taft (he was a very hefty man), the word goes out that Willie Boy must be caught.

Willie has nowhere to run. The world that he belongs to no longer exists. His tribe, confined to a reservation, is fading away, losing its identity. The legends are being forgotten. "What was wrong with us?" he asks, knowing the answer. "Nothing. Nothing. Just our color." He knows that he cannot escape, and so does his girlfriend. "You can't beat them," she says. "Never." "Maybe," he replies, "but they'll know I was here." Willie Boy has control over nothing about his future except the time and place of his death. Like the heroes of many westerns during the sixties, he has to die. He cannot live and remain true to himself and his beliefs. Either he changes or he dies.

Tell Them Willie Boy Is Here was the second film directed by Abraham Polonsky; he had directed his first, *Force of Evil*, in 1948. He had been blacklisted in 1951 after appearing before the House Un-American Activities Committee. At that time, Congressman Harold H. Velde had called him "the most dangerous man in America."

"If you go gettin' killed, don't come runnin' back here."

The Good Guys and the Bad Guys

Bringing civilization to the western frontier included bringing culture. Lola Montez, with her overtly suggestive Spider Dance (in which she danced around the stage, fighting off invisible spiders that attacked her in very private places), was not the only representative of European culture touring the western towns. Sarah Bernhardt made appearances out West in such plays as *Froufrou*, and Oscar Wilde, who dubbed Bernhardt "the divine Sarah," gave lectures on interior decorating. One of the most popular acts was the Mazeppa, performed by Adah Isaacs Menken. Apparently naked (she wore tights), Menken would be lashed to the back of a horse and would ride around the theater and then disappear offstage. It was thrilling—particularly because there was a dispute about whether or not she was really wearing anything.

Heller in Pink Tights (Paramount, 1960), directed by George Cukor and based on a novel by Louis L'Amour, recounts the travails of a troupe of actors traveling out West. The leader of the group is Anthony Quinn; the star attraction is Sophia Loren (in a blonde wig). They make their way from town to town, pursued by bill collectors, gunmen, and hostile Indians. In Cheyenne, they have to put up with a critical theater owner who doesn't like their rehearsal of *Helen of Troy*. "What's so classy about her running around with you instead of her husband?" he asks Quinn. He assures the actors that his audience won't go for that kind of thing, so they perform the ever-popular Mazeppa instead.

Just as any plucky European actor with a trunk could cross the ocean and risk raw eggs and catcalls on western stages, so any Hollywood actor—and any foreign tale—could be propelled into a western setting. The old West, hospitable to a fault, was defenseless.

Although its title echoes Rudyard Kipling's short story "Soldiers Three," the screenplay for *Sergeants 3* (United Artists, 1962), written by W. R. Burnett, is based on Kipling's poem "Gunga Din." The three sergeants are played by Frank Sinatra, Dean Martin, and Peter Lawford; their sergeant major is Joey Bishop. They're all in the cavalry out West, and the Gunga Din character—who rides a mule instead of an elephant—is played by Sammy Davis, Jr., in the role of a freed slave who attaches himself to the three madcap men in uniform. This comedy western of the Rat Pack out West was directed by John Sturges, who is better remembered as the director of *The Magnificent Seven*.

Robert Aldrich, another well-known director of westerns, directed *Four for Texas* (Warner Brothers, 1963), in which the Rat Pack is joined by the Three Stooges. Even Arthur Godfrey makes an appearance—as Arthur Godfrey. The plot of the film—Frank Sinatra and Dean Martin battle each other for control of a town's gambling casinos—frequently disappears, or is forgotten, as the two stars exchange quips. However, what seems like idle banter is occasionally fraught with a certain significance, as when Sinatra, watching Martin walk, remarks, "Some say boots are made for walking"—a plug for Nancy Sinatra's hit song. Ursula Andress, who had recently appeared in *Dr. No*, and Anita Ekberg, a former Miss Sweden, have speaking roles in the film, but both women spend most of their time silently leaning over. Cleavage was not new to the old West, but the producers of *Four for Texas* took great care to make sure it was just right: they held Hollywood's first nude screen tests for the film. (The nude scenes were excised by the censor before the film was released.)

The appearance of the Three Stooges in *Four for Texas* is saddening—the cruelest Apache torture could never match what they "humorously" do to each other—but not unreasonable. Slapstick comedy is a staple of westerns. *Advance to the Rear* (*Company of Cowards* in Great Britain) (MGM, 1964), directed by George Marshall, is a good example of pratfall humor out West. The film tells the comic tale of a company of Union Army misfits who are sent "so far West they'll never be heard from again." Led by a veteran officer (Melvyn Douglas) whose theory of warfare is not to disturb the enemy so the enemy won't disturb him, the group is composed of boobs, each of whom has an identifying shtick: one is a kleptomaniac, one is a flagpole

sitter, one is an incendiary, one has chronic hiccups, one is a punchy exfighter, and the deadly "Smiling Boy" hugs his pals to death. The only sane man in the group is Glenn Ford, and although their far-western exile is supposed to keep the rest of the world safe from their antics, they manage to get involved with a Rebel spy (Stella Stevens) and a gold shipment.

The humor in *Cat Ballou* (Columbia, 1965), directed by Elliot Silverstein, is of a different sort—it comes from within the western genre itself and threatens to make more sense of the West than any serious film. The wide-eyed and innocent Catherine Ballou (Jane Fonda) has to contend with a murderous pack of unscrupulous land-grabbing businessmen and their hired thug, Tim Strawn (Lee Marvin), who wears a tin cover to hide his missing nose. When Strawn murders her father, Miss Ballou stubbornly determines to fight back and sends for the famed Kid Shelleen (also played by Marvin). She has read about his heroic exploits in dime novels, but the Kid, like the rest of the West, has changed, and he arrives in no shape to face his look-alike, Strawn. The fact is that Shelleen and his steed share a drinking problem. Undaunted, Catherine becomes "Cat," and she and her gang hold up a train and then head for that famed outlaw roost, the

Sergeants 3 *(United Artists, 1962). The three heroes are Peter Lawford (top), Frank Sinatra, and Dean Martin.*

157

Hole in the Wall. The Wild Bunch they encounter has seen better days and wants to be let alone, but Cat's enthusiasm eventually wins everyone over (as do Nat "King" Cole and Stubby Kaye as they wander through the film, happily rendering the theme song). The film manages to make affectionately raucous references to a large chunk of western lore without offending anyone, and the scene of the drunken Kid on his drunken horse holding up a wall has become a classic (Marvin won an Oscar for his dual role in the film).

A Big Hand for the Little Lady (*Big Deal at Dodge City* in Great Britain) (Warner Brothers, 1966), directed by Fielder Cook, is about poker. Once a year, the wealthiest men in the territory around Laredo get together for an unlimited-stakes game. No matter what they may be doing—even attending a daughter's wedding—they leave and rush to the game. Among the men seated at the table are an undertaker (Charles Bickford), a lawyer (Kevin McCarthy), and a very well-to-do rancher (Jason Robards, Jr.). This particular year, they are joined in the game—against his poor wife's protestations—by a stranger (Henry Fonda). At the crucial moment in the game, with the pot worth over $20,000, the newcomer has a heart attack, and his wife—the little lady (Joanne Woodward)—has to

replace him. "How do you play this game?" she demurely inquires, picking up her husband's hand.

A Big Hand for the Little Lady is a very funny movie about poker with a very surprising ending. *5 Card Stud* is a very serious movie about poker and, although it is a murder mystery—a western whodunit—there is no surprise in its ending.

In *5 Card Stud* (Paramount, 1969), directed by Henry Hathaway, seven men sit down one night to play a game of poker. One of the men—a stranger in town—is caught cheating and is hanged. Not long after this event, another stranger (Robert Mitchum) arrives in town and sets himself up as a preacher. Immediately after his arrival, the various members of the card game turn up dead, each one killed by a lack of air (reflecting the belief that hanged men strangle to death—hell, the fall and the broken neck will kill you). One of the men, the owner of the general store, is "drowned" in a barrel of flour; another is strangled with barbed wire; the third is hanged from the bell rope in the church; the fourth is strangled by hand. Someone is out for revenge, and someone is tipping off the murderer to the identities of the participants in the game. Dean Martin solves the crime.

Burt Kennedy, who wrote the screenplays for

many of the Budd Boetticher-Randolph Scott films, likes to make westerns and has made a lot of them. His westerns share a relaxed atmosphere suitable for either comedy or violent action. There is more of the former in **Mail Order Bride** (**West of Montana** in Great Britain) (MGM, 1963), in which Buddy Ebsen sets about educating a recalcitrant Keir Dullea. A friend of the lad's dead father, Ebsen has in his possession the deed to a ranch, but (as directed by the father before his death) he won't give it to Dullea until the youth has proved his mettle as a responsible man. The sagacious former lawman decides—after an early morning visit to the privy with a copy of a Montgomery Ward catalog—that what the boy needs is a good wife. Selecting a suitable mate from the ads in the catalog, Ebsen sets off for Kansas City to pick up the bride (Lois Nettleton), who turns out to be a young widow with a child. Having tamed the wild boy (who falls for his mail-order bride) and dispatched a rustler (Warren Oates), the old-timer departs.

Not all cowboys like cowboying. Some don't even like horses. **The Rounders** (MGM, 1965), directed by Burt Kennedy, is a comedy about two unhappy cowboys (Glenn Ford and Henry Fonda) in the modern West who long for a place "where there ain't no grass, ain't no horses." The man they work for (Chill Wills) is a cheap scoundrel, and the horses they try to tame are too smart for them. What they really want to do is make enough money to go to Tahiti and open a bar. This was the first time Ford and Fonda had ever worked together. Peter Fonda has a part, too.

There isn't much humor in **Welcome to Hard Times** (**Killer on a Horse** in Great Britain) (MGM, 1967). Burt Kennedy both directed the film and wrote the screenplay, which is based on a novel by E. L. Doctorow. The Hard Times of the title is the name of a town, but "hard times" could just as easily describe the events that take place in the ramshackle little mud-puddle settlement. "The end of the line," Hard Times is populated by the dregs of the West, a bunch of losers who are led by a pacifist mayor (Henry Fonda). The town falls prey to a vicious gunman (Aldo Ray), known as "the man from Bodie." He rides into the town, gets drunk, and—as the townspeople and their mayor cowardly do nothing—rapes and murders a prostitute, kills three men, and then rapes the mayor's girlfriend (Janice Rule)—all without speaking a word. Before he departs, he sets fire to the town. Most of the town's residents desert the smoking ruins; those who stay are joined by a few newcomers, including a traveling saloon keeper (Keenan Wynn). (John Anderson plays both a storekeeper, Ezra Maple, who leaves the town and Isaac Maple, Ezra's twin brother, who arrives with the "new blood.") The efforts to rebuild both the town and the spirit of its people make up most of the film. The townspeople manage to keep Hard Times from dying,

and it is rebuilt to be better than it was originally. Then the man from Bodie returns.

The last line of Kennedy's **Young Billy Young** (United Artists, 1969) is "Somebody came to town." That somebody is a marshal named Kane (Robert Mitchum), who comes in search of the man who killed his son during a jailbreak. Marshal Kane is the name of the lawman in **High Noon**, and the character of Billy Young is based on Billy Clanton (of the notorious family that faced the Earps at the O.K. Corral), but this is not another film about the Earps; indeed, it begins with the assassination of a Mexican general on a train. **Young Billy Young** has a very ordinary plot: Marshal Kane jails the son (David Carradine) of the man who killed his son (John Anderson), and the man makes plans to break the youth out of jail.

It is a common and quite versatile plot; Kennedy used it in a comedy western called **Support Your Local Sheriff** (United Artists, 1969), which begins with a gold strike in the small town of Calendar (population: 150). During the burial of a penniless vagabond, Prudy (Joan Hackett), the mayor's daughter, spies something shiny in the grave—it turns out to be gold, and Calendar is rapidly transformed into a lawless boom town, desperately in need of law and order. Jason McCullough (James Garner)—on his way to Australia—is made the

sheriff and has to confront a family of villains. When he jails the son (Bruce Dern) of the local patriarch (Walter Brennan), the old man comes in and points a loaded gun at the seated sheriff. The sheriff calmly reaches over and plugs up the barrel of the gun with one extended digit. As played by Garner, the sheriff is completely unperturbable, a man who seems sincerely annoyed at all the bothersome turmoil brought on by the conniving of other people. He is assisted, albeit reluctantly, by Jack Elam as his deputy. The film manages to parody just about every western ever made, paying particular homage to a choice few, such as *High Noon*. It is a very funny western—so funny that Kennedy decided to do it again.

Support Your Local Gunfighter (United Artists, 1971) stars Garner again, this time as a smooth-talking gambler named Latigo Smith. To avoid forced matrimony, he abandons a train and finds himself in the mining town of Purgatory. The town is divided between two warring families—the Ameses and the Bartons—who are racing to reach the mother lode. Colonel Ames has sent for a gunman, Swifty Morgan (Chuck Connors), and when Latigo arrives, he is mistaken for the infamous quick-draw expert. Latigo meets a cowboy named Jug May (Jack Elam), and Jug assumes the role of the gunfighter. The beautiful daughter in this film is Patience ("the sidewinder") Barton (Suzanne Pleshette) who, when not taking potshots at Latigo,

whiles away her time wishing she were at Miss Hunter's College for Young Ladies of Good Family on the Hudson River, a finishing school in New York. The film ends happily, with Latigo and Patience and Jug all leaving on a train—Jug, describing the future, explains that Latigo and Patience go to Denver to get married, and although she never goes to the finishing school, she sends seven daughters there. He finishes by giving his future: "Me? I go on to become a big star in Italian westerns." True enough.

Burt Kennedy's *The Good Guys and the Bad Guys* (Warner Brothers, 1969) is a comedy version of a common theme in westerns during the sixties: the end of the West. Marshal James Flagg (Robert Mitchum) still rides a horse, but the streets of Progress, the town he tamed, are choked with automobiles. When he suspects that Big John McKay (George Kennedy), an old-time train robber and hero of pulp westerns, has resurfaced and is planning a train heist, the marshal wants to form a posse. But the civilized townspeople don't believe the marshal's story of an outlaw who has suddenly reappeared after a twenty-year absence. The only person who believes the marshal's tale is his friend Old Grundy (Douglas Fowley), who warns him, "If you go gettin' killed, don't come runnin' back here." It is an election year, and the mayor of Progress fears that a posse, with its implication of lawlessness, would mar his reputation. With suitable pomp and the gift

Walter Brennan and James Garner in Support Your Local Sheriff *(United Artists, 1969).*

of a watch, he forces the marshal to retire.

The retired lawman captures the aging outlaw. The two men were once friends. During the good old days—when the good guys weren't really all that different from the bad guys—they had a fine time fighting each other. They agree that "it ain't no fun anymore," and the outlaw, taken to the marshal's home in town, expresses the obligatory astonishment at indoor plumbing. The two team up to stop the train robbery.

Glad to be rid of the cumbersome old outlaw, the gang of villains (led by David Carradine, whose father, John, plays one of the guards on the train) goes ahead with the robbery. The old good guy and the old bad guy foil the heist, and the film ends with a chase scene reminiscent of Mack Sennett's Keystone Kops, with a wild menagerie of tin lizzies, wagons, horses, handcars, motorcycles—everything that rolls—involved in the chase.

"Maybe there's only one revolution: the good guys against the bad guys. The only question is, who are the good guys?"

The Professionals

Had *The Great Train Robbery* been remade during the sixties, the train robbers would have been presented as the heroes, and the pursuing posse—the men for whom the 1903 audiences wildly cheered—would have been presented as a bunch of mercenary lawmen, former friends of the bandits who have taken to working for big-business interests. The chase scene, with all four hooves of every horse at some point off the ground, has been essential to the western from its birth, but the roles of the participants have changed. It is still the men with badges chasing the men without, but the men representing the law have come to represent a corrupt society in which people do and think what they are paid to do and think. The participants in the chase are really the future—that peaceful place with churches and schoolhouses and paved roads for motorcars— chasing the past—with its cherished sense of loyalty and its subjective notions of right and wrong. When an exasperated Butch Cassidy (in *Butch Cassidy and the Sundance Kid*) complains, "Dammitall, why is everything we're good at illegal?" no one in the audience would suggest that he give up his free lifestyle and, like the rest of society, succumb to an unfulfilling, but lawful, job.

The lawman Pat Garrett chased down the outlaw Billy the Kid and shot him through the heart. A year later, in 1882, Garrett wrote a book about the event, *The Authentic Life of Billy the Kid.* In 1957, Charles Neider researched the history of Garrett and Billy, relocated the story to Northern California, and called the resulting novel *The Authentic Death of Hendry*

Jones. Sam Peckinpah wrote a screenplay based on Neider's book, adding his own research. Peckinpah eventually used his research in his *Pat Garrett and Billy the Kid* (1973): the screenplay he wrote based on Neider's book was rewritten and became the basis of **One-Eyed Jacks** (Paramount, 1960).

George Cukor was originally going to direct *One-Eyed Jacks*, but he had trouble with the film's star and left the project. The star, Marlon Brando, had his own very clear ideas about how the film should be made, and he took over the direction. "We're going to improvise," he said, and that is what the actors did. Starring with Brando was an old friend, Karl Malden, who had first met Brando in 1946 when they had worked together in Max Anderson's "Truckline Cafe." The two stars worked easily together. As Malden said, "We work like two jazz musicians who've been improvising in the same small band for years and can send each other." Brando encouraged improvising and offered rewards to the actors of up to $300 for the best reactions in important scenes. In fact, the picture does not end the way Brando had originally planned—the actors held a ballot and voted for the ending they liked best.

The title of the film, an allusion to the jack in a deck of cards, whose face is seen in profile, refers to people who show only one side of their faces, only one aspect of their character. Those who appear to be the "good guys" may actually be the villains. Rio (Brando) and his partner, Dad Longworth (Malden), rob a bank and make off with the gold, pursued by a posse. When they are surrounded on a hill, with the posse closing in, Dad goes for horses, promising to come right back. He buys the horses but then decides to take the gold for himself and rides away. Rio is captured and spends five years in a rat-infested prison in Sonora. He escapes, chained to another man, and takes off to seek revenge. In the meantime, Dad Longworth has become the sheriff of Monterey, California, with a wife (Katy Jurado) and a beautiful stepdaughter (Pina Pellicer). Dad is an important man in Monterey, a fine, upstanding citizen. But Rio knows him for what he is. "You're a one-eyed jack in this town," he says to Dad, "but I see the other side of your face." Rio sets about exacting his revenge.

Calling Longworth (the Pat Garrett character) "Dad" is only one of the many curious twists in the film, which abounds in symbolism. It is visually beautiful, however, including scenes of the ocean—a true rarity in westerns.

Brando's next western, *The Appaloosa* (*Southwest to Sonora* in Great Britain) (Universal, 1966), directed by Sidney J. Furie, is another moody film about a man in search of revenge. Brando plays a cowboy with a cherished horse, an appaloosa, with which he plans to begin a new life. When the horse is stolen by a Mexican bandit (John Saxon), Brando takes off across the border to retrieve what is his. Like *One-Eyed Jacks*, the film has a peculiar intensity—probably due to Brando's style of acting. It also has peculiar camera angles, including enormous close-ups of various parts of faces.

Revenge is a common theme in westerns, but in **One Foot in Hell** (20th Century-Fox, 1960), directed by James B. Clark, the revenge taken is quite elaborate—a man plans to destroy an entire town. An ex-Confederate soldier (Alan Ladd) blames the townspeople of a small Arizona town for the death of his pregnant wife—they refused to give her the $1.87 needed to pay for a necessary medicine. Becoming deputy sheriff of the town, the man gathers a group of helpers and plots to do more than kill the men he holds responsible—he wants to bring the town to its knees. His plans include robbing the bank in an effort to bring about financial ruin.

Dalton Trumbo wrote the screenplay for **The Last Sunset** (Universal, 1961), directed by Robert Aldrich, a film in which notions of right and wrong get confused in a muddle of personal problems and awkward interrelationships. Kirk Douglas, a sporty-looking gunman, kills the brother-in-law of Rock Hudson. Hudson sets off after Douglas, who makes it to the home of an old lover (Dorothy Malone) who is now married to an alcoholic rancher (Joseph Cotten). There is also a daughter (Carol Lynley). The entire group begins a cattle drive, and along the trail Lynley falls for Douglas, and he responds enthusiastically. What he doesn't know is that the enticing young woman is actually his daughter; when he finds out, he faces Hudson in a gunfight. What Hudson doesn't know is that Douglas's gun is empty.

In *The Magnificent Seven*, a poor Mexican village hires seven gunmen, led by Yul Brynner, as protection against an outlaw gang. In **Invitation to a Gunfighter** (United Artists, 1964), directed by Richard Wilson, a town "invites" a gunfighter to get rid of one bothersome man. It is 1865, and a former Confederate soldier (George Segal) returns to his hometown, Pecos, New Mexico, to find that his farm has been sold as "enemy property" and his girl (Janice Rule) has married a maimed Union veteran. The Rebel goes on a rampage. Since all the men in the town were either killed or wounded during the war, the town's leading citizen (Pat Hingle) decides to send for Jules Gaspard d'Estaing (Brynner), "the fastest gun in the West." The gunfighter turns out to be a suave, cultured (he plays the spinet and quotes poetry) Creole. Offered $500 to kill Segal, Brynner takes his time, and the town ultimately turns against him.

The Outrage (MGM, 1964), directed by Martin Ritt, is based on Akira Kurosawa's film *Rashomon*. A husband and wife (Laurence Harvey and Claire Bloom) encounter a Mexican bandit (Paul Newman). The bandit rapes the wife and kills the husband. A court is convened at which four versions of the story are presented, that of each of the three participants (the husband lived long enough to tell his story to a passing Indian) and a fourth observer. Each version of the story uses the same events to tell a very different account of what happened. Which version is the truth? The truth gets lost, or diffused, in the layers of personal motives and prejudices. Perhaps they are all telling the truth.

The Outrage was not the only adaptation of a Kurosawa film to appear in 1964; Italian audiences were responding enthusiastically to a film called *Per un Pugno di Dollari*, a reworking of Kurosawa's samurai film *Yojimbo* (1961). When it was released in the United States two years later (its title in English is *A Fistful of Dollars*), its version of the old West challenged the version presented by American filmmakers, which was already wobbling, troubled by an inability to believe in heroes.

Sam Peckinpah has been quoted as saying that *Rashomon* is his favorite film. Perhaps he likes it because of the way it weaves together myth, symbolism, and character to create a vision with so many facets that the "truth" becomes a very personal matter. Peckinpah's third film, **Major Dundee** (Columbia, 1965), has a familiar plot—soldiers out to rescue white children captured by the Apaches—but it tells a story that goes beyond the action of the plot. Even though a great deal of the film was cut by the studio that released it—an unfortunate but common fate for Peckinpah's films—and even though someone saw fit to add a marching song by Mitch Miller's Sing Along Gang, the film retains a sense of unity.

Charlton Heston, wearing his kepi at a rakish angle, is Major Dundee, a Union officer who has been put in command of a prison camp as punishment for fighting "his own war" at Gettysburg. Richard Harris is Benjamin Tyreen, the ranking officer among the Confederate prisoners, a former friend of Dundee's. When the Apache renegade Sierra Charriba and forty-seven of his warriors go on a killing spree and carry off three young boys, Dundee is sent to get the children back and takes along a mixed group composed of civilians, who serve to get out of jail; "six coloreds," who serve to prove themselves as soldiers; and Harris and some of the Confederate prisoners, who agree to serve "until the Apache is taken or destroyed." As this "command divided against itself" rides out in search of the Indians, there is a kind of singing contest: the Union troopers sing "The Battle Hymn of the Republic," the Confederates sing "Dixie," and the civilian scouts sing "Clementine." Not only are North and South divided—the West provides a third division. When a John Ford cavalry troop left a fort, all the men joined in a stirring chorus of the same song: in *Major Dundee* there is no unifying loyalty.

Top: *Paul Newman and Claire Bloom in* The Outrage *(MGM, 1964)*.
Above: *Battle scene from* Major Dundee *(Columbia, 1965)*.

They get the children back but have to face more than the Apaches. They ride into Mexico, where Dundee becomes a hero and "Viva Dundee" is painted on adobe walls. It is a personal war—personal for the "six coloreds," personal for both Dundee and Tyreen, the former friends who found themselves on opposite sides of the Civil War. The small command eventually has to battle French lancers (Maximilian's men), and patriotism of a different kind unites them in one, final dramatic battle.

In *Alvarez Kelly* (*The Richmond Story*) (Columbia, 1966), directed by Edward Dmytryk, a neutral representative of the West gets involved in the Civil War. Alvarez Kelly (William Holden), a cattle rancher, is hired to drive a herd of cattle from Texas to the Union Army besieging Richmond. The Mexican-Irish (hence his name) Kelly has no particular attachment to either side in the war. His "three deities" are "money, whiskey, and women"—he wants only to deliver the cattle and collect his money. His plans are changed by a one-eyed Virginia colonel (Richard Widmark), who takes Kelly's money and forces him to steal the herd for the Confederacy. Kelly does so by stampeding the cattle through the Union lines. (The film is based on a true

incident; Lincoln is supposed to have said of it that it was "the slickest piece of cattle stealing I ever heard of.") Kelly's loyalties don't change during the film, and both sides in the conflict are presented as being equally vicious. There are no heroes.

In *Vera Cruz*, the film that indicated the direction westerns were soon to take, Gary Cooper plays a role that would fit into any film of the sixties—a soldier of fortune out for personal aggrandizement who fights for whichever side offers him the most money. But Cooper eventually does the selfless, right thing, of course, and ends up having to kill his double-crossing partner, Burt Lancaster.

Burt Lancaster survived into the grim West of the sixties. In *The Professionals* (Columbia, 1966), directed by Richard Brooks, he plays one of four experts hired by a wealthy American businessman named Grant (Ralph Bellamy) to go into Mexico and rescue the businessman's young bride (Claudia Cardinale), who has been kidnapped by Captain Jesus Raza (Jack Palance), "the bloodiest cutthroat in Mexico." Each of the four men has a specialty: the leader, Lee Marvin, is a former Rough Rider who is a strategist and a weapons expert; Lancaster is the dynamite expert; Woody

William Holden (center) in Alvarez Kelly *(Columbia, 1966).*

Left to right: Burt Lancaster, Lee Marvin, Robert Ryan, and Woody Strode in The Professionals *(Columbia, 1966).*

Strode, a bounty hunter, is an expert tracker and a marksman with all weapons, including the bow and arrow; Robert Ryan, a ranch foreman, is a professional wrangler. The year is 1916 (Marvin first appears driving a car), and Mexico is in turmoil, with "Viva Villa" chalked on the walls of ruined haciendas. The four Americans are not unfamiliar with Mexican politics, but they have become cynical observers. They still have some of the "old" code, however. When he learns that there is a treasure in gold buried nearby, Lancaster is tempted to leave off the expedition for the girl and look for the gold, but Marvin reminds him that he gave his word. "My word to Grant ain't worth a plug nickel," says Lancaster. "You gave your word to *me*," says Marvin. When he is asked why Americans would take part in a Mexican revolution, Lancaster explains, "Maybe there's only one revolution: the good guys against the bad guys. The question is, who are the good guys?"

The professionals prove that they are "good" guys by following their sense of right and wrong, even though it leads them to turn against their employer.

The Mexican landscape that they travel across is full of danger. As one of the four says, "Nothing's harmless in this desert unless it's dead." It is an apt description of another country in another series of films, the never-never land of Sergio Leone's West, which both physically and spiritually resembles Sicily more than any corner of the United States. Particularly in his three "Dollars" films—*A Fistful of Dollars, For a Few Dollars More,* and *The Good, the Bad and the Ugly*—the West is presented exactly as it never was: static and feudal. There are no trees, there are no Indians. The sun shines bright every day all day. And,

perhaps its most salient feature, it is a moral wasteland. Machiavelli's guidelines have been followed to their inevitable conclusion: no one trusts no one.

Leone made *A Fistful of Dollars* (United Artists, 1966) at a time when Italian westerns were in a slump—there had been too many of them. Indeed, in order to disguise the fact that the film was another Italian-made product, Leone and the other Italians involved in making the film hid behind American-sounding pseudonyms: Leone became "Bob Robertson"; Massimo Dallamano, the photographer for the film, became "Jack Dalmas"; Ennio Morricone, who wrote the score, was "Dan Savio." Although Leone's film resembles its predecessors, which were composed of a series of violent shootouts joined by a vague plot, he added a wonderful artistry, and his film changed both the Italian—"spaghetti"—westerns and, in some ways, the westerns made in the United States. Leone's innovative style of directing and the "musical" score written by Ennio Morricone—which was more than music, supplying sounds to previously silent things, such as thoughts and attitudes—created a totally new vision of the West.

The star (who is neither a hero nor a good guy) of Leone's "Dollars" trilogy, Clint Eastwood, needed no pseudonym, although he was not exactly famous. His role as Rowdy Yates on television's "Rawhide" had not made a star of him. Leone tried to get numerous American actors for the lead role of the Man With No Name. He wanted Henry Fonda (he finally got him for his last western), but ended up with Eastwood. Eastwood turned out to be what Leone wanted; in fact, Leone altered the character of the Man With No Name to

accommodate Eastwood. But Eastwood did have to adapt himself to the role—he had to learn to smoke, a difficult chore, but one he accomplished so well that the smoking cheroot became an integral part of him.

Calling the lead character the Man With No Name makes sense within the framework of the traditional western, in which the unknown hero appears out of nowhere to solve someone else's problems. Shane had only half a name and could easily have operated with no name at all. But the Man With No Name does not arrive to offer assistance. Very little character can be ascribed to him beyond the facts that he doesn't talk much and he smokes cheroots. He is completely detached, absolutely disinterested. He is out for personal gain and nothing else. He doesn't even seem to belong to the culture within which he operates. In the Italian version of the film he is sometimes referred to as "Il Monco" ("the monk"), which might explain his detachment but not his affinity for "dollars." Indeed, it is never clear what Leone's characters want with the gold they are seeking. No one believes that they want to buy a little spread and settle down. Instead, they battle for this gold as though it were a prize, a proof of their superior skills.

Leone lifted the plot for *A Fistful of Dollars* from Akira Kurosawa's *Yojimbo*, sometimes following the Japanese film scene for scene. *Yojimbo* (the title means

"bodyguard") is about a samurai who hires himself out to two opposing clans and then, for his own amusement, sets the two groups against each other. In *A Fistful of Dollars*, the Man With No Name (Eastwood) arrives in a small town and puts himself in the middle of a conflict between two families. The notion of warring families is not alien to the West—the Graham-Tewksbury feud is a fine example—but the kind of clan loyalty in Leone's films belongs more in southern Italy than the American Southwest. But it is the violence, the sadistic brutality of the films, that alternately repels and attracts American viewers. Most of the so-called bounty hunters in the old West collected rewards for dispatching dangerous or destructive animals—in Leone's films they become bounty "killers," and they ruthlessly stalk men.

The fabulous success of *A Fistful of Dollars* allowed Leone to spend more money on his next western, *For a Few Dollars More* (United Artists, 1967). Leone had enough extra dollars to add another Amercan star, Lee Van Cleef. Based loosely on Kurosawa's *Sanjuro*, the second film is much better than the first, and if it doesn't make it as a western in the Hollywood tradition, it succeeds wonderfully as a comic-book version of the same material.

For a Few Dollars More begins with a scene recognizable as the first scene in countless American westerns: a lone rider, probably the hero of the film, is seen from above, riding across rough terrain. But, coming from somewhere out of view, there is the sound of contented whistling. This invisible whistler then loads a gun and strikes a match. He waits. A shot rings out, and the rider falls. Even before the titles appear, the "hero" has been killed. As if this weren't enough, titles appear informing the viewer that "Where life had no value, death sometimes had its price. That is why the bounty hunters appeared." Eastwood, repeating his role as the Man With No Name, and Lee Van Cleef, as Colonel Mortimer ("the best shot in the Carolinas") are both bounty killers. Their murderous skills are established early in the film. Mortimer coolly locates the man he is out after in a hotel room. The man escapes out into the street and starts running. Mortimer unrolls his saddle blanket to reveal a gun-lover's dream—a veritable arsenal of western weapons, including three rifles and a Buntline Special with a detachable stock. He calmly assembles the latter and shoots the fleeing victim (he has to finish the man off with a weapon better suited to such close-range work). This weapons fetishism runs through all of Leone's films, and regardless of how incongruous the weapon is in the period depicted, it is usually well displayed. Colonel Mortimer is a wise old bounty killer. He even smokes a meerschaum pipe, proof of his professional ease. The Man With No Name is younger than Mortimer and has not yet attained his elder's patience (he smokes cheroots). The two meet—they're both after the same man—and, of course, don't trust each other. Each goes off to do research on the other. Mortimer looks up the Man With No Name's record in some old newspapers. In a great comic scene, the Man With No Name visits the Old Prophet (played by German actor Josef Egger), a crusty old fellow who stubbornly refused to sell his land to the railroad, so now the tracks run right by his house, and each time a train goes by his little home is nearly shaken to pieces. Resigned to working together (after a shooting match in which they shoot each other's hats around), the Man With No Name inquires of Colonel Mortimer, "Were you ever young?"

"Yes," reveals Mortimer, "and just as reckless as you. Then one day something happened."

In fact, Mortimer has a personal reason for stalking the evil Indio (Gian-Maria Volonté)—Indio raped and killed the colonel's sister. It is refreshing to find that Mortimer is in this for revenge, not money. The thoroughly evil Indio (who smokes marijuana throughout the film and seems to share flashbacks with Mortimer about what he did to Mortimer's sister), has a wicked laugh. He is always laughing his wicked laugh. He laughs so much that his wanted poster shows him laughing. When Mortimer and the Man With No Name look at the poster, however, they see only the nice zeros in $10,000 (Mortimer momentarily forgetting that he is in this for revenge). As they stare at the zeros, dreams of gunshots bounce through their brains. These are very simple men.

The teamed bounty killers manage to slaughter the "villains," and, his revenge satisfied, Mortimer starts to ride away as the Man With No Name heaps the bodies on a wagon and adds up his bounty. He comes out short of the expected sum and finds one more man to kill. Hearing the shot, Mortimer calls back, "Any trouble, boy?"

"No," responds the Man With No Name. "Thought I was having trouble with my adding. It's alright now."

For his third film, *The Good, the Bad and the Ugly* (United Artists, 1967), Leone had even more money to spend, and Eastwood (the "good") and Van Cleef (the "bad") were joined by Eli Wallach (the "ugly"). The dense iconography and fetishism of Leone's previous two films reach their peak in this film, in which Leone piles on so many details that some viewers have been led to believe the film is historically accurate. It isn't, but it really doesn't matter. Leone's Civil War, with its rows of gleaming Gatling guns, owes more to Verdun than Shiloh; his prisoner-of-war camp, with its inmate musicians, resembles Auschwitz more than Andersonville—and well they should, for Leone manages to tell a remarkable tale about war, anarchy, and morality in a film filled with a wistful sadness.

The three lead characters end up looking for a cache of gold buried in a cemetery, but they arrive there along separate routes. In the beginning of the film, Blondy, or No-Name (Eastwood), and Tuco (Wallach) are involved in a money-making venture: there is a reward on Tuco's head, and he allows himself to be turned in by Blondy, who collects the reward money and then, at the last minute, saves Tuco's life by shooting the hanging rope. Blondy eventually tires of the game and, taking the money, strands Tuco in the middle of the desert. Tuco complains about the behavior, and Blondy remarks, "Such ingratitude. After all the times I've saved your life." Tuco survives, of course, and the three men run into each other, meet and separate, as they wander in and out of the Civil War, changing uniforms as the situation warrants, being taken captive, even taking part in battles. The anarchy of the war means freedom, but it also means that moral judgments—even such simple ones as "good," "bad," and "ugly"—become meaningless. The individual killings carried out by the amoral three men are compared to the organized mass slaughters sponsored by governments ("I've never seen so many men wasted so badly," says Blondy). The useless carnage of the war makes the avarice of the three gold-seekers appear sensible—almost. The film ends with a justly famous three-way gunfight.

The Good, the Bad and the Ugly was Clint Eastwood's last film with Sergio Leone. Eastwood returned to the United States and began making his own films, first with other directors and eventually directing the films himself. He did not stop smoking cheroots, and he did not stop playing loners with superhuman prowess. But his popularity grew, and even before John Wayne died, Eastwood had become the leading star of American westerns. (Eastwood became quite a sex symbol: Rosemary Rogers dedicated her first novel, *Sweet Savage Love*, to him.)

Eastwood is only the most obvious "change" wrought by Leone on American-made westerns. Before the arrival of Leone, romanticism was on its way out of westerns and graphic violence was on its way in, but Leone managed to rearrange the essential ingredients of the western film in a way that, perhaps unfortunately, made sense. Westerns were already headed in the direction of that place "where life had no value"; Leone and the music and sound effects of Morricone helped make that wasteland seem like a reasonable substitute for the real West.

Clint Eastwood's first American western, *Hang 'Em High* (United Artists, 1968), directed by Ted Post, takes place in another kind of West—the violent Oklahoma Territory of 1873. The film begins with Eastwood—who looks a lot like the old Rowdy Yates but still puffs on cheroots—driving a herd of cattle across a river. He is met by a posse composed of nine men led by a Captain Wilson (Ed Begley). They claim he stole the cattle. He explains that he is Jedediah Cooper, a former lawman from St. Louis. He even has a bill of sale for the cattle. But this impromptu jury is impatient, and egged on by Wilson they string him up. He is saved from death by the fortuitous arrival of Ben Johnson (who appears in the film only to disappear—his death is spoken of in passing). Cooper is taken, along with a cartload of prisoners, to Fort Grant, where he is tried before Judge Fenton (Pat Hingle). (Fort Grant stands for Fort Smith, Arkansas, and Fenton stands for Judge Isaac Parker, the hanging judge met with in *True Grit*. Parker was quite a judge. He sentenced 168 men to death; 88 were hanged.) The judge believes Cooper's story and hires him as a marshal (a dangerous job—65 of Judge Parker's lawmen were killed performing their duty). With his neck scarred by the lynchers' rope, Marshal Cooper sets off to methodically track down the nine men, and the film carefully compares his personal vengeance with the public justice meted out by the judge. Cooper rebels against the judge's methods, but he eventually learns to adjust his personal views to the needs of the law. While he deals with the men who made the mistake of not finishing the job of lynching him, the judge holds group hangings, with as many as six men lined up along the huge scaffolding. The rapists, murderers, and rustlers, their heads hooded, are dropped to their doom.

A very similar public hanging ends in a very different way in *Bandolero!* (20th Century-Fox, 1968), directed by Andrew V. McLaglen. The film begins with a foiled bank robbery in the town of Val Verde, Texas, in 1867. The would-be robbers, led by Dean Martin, are outsmarted by the local sheriff (George Kennedy) and thrown in prison to await their hanging. Far away in San Antonio, Martin's brother—James Stewart—learns of the imminent hanging from the hangman himself, a spry Oklahoman on his way to Val Verde. The hangman is proud of his work and delights in describing the more difficult aspects of his profession. Stewart does away with the talkative executioner, takes the man's gear, and assumes his role. Thus, at the last minute, the members of the gang, nooses around their necks, are freed by Stewart and take off out of town. Just outside the town they encounter Raquel Welch (widowed in the robbery), and they take her along on their flight toward Mexico. This group is followed by the sheriff and his posse. Pulling up the rear is Stewart, who takes the time to rob the bank on his way out of town—"Seemed like the thing to do," he later explains.

Reunited, the two brothers (Dee and Mace Bishop) argue about their pasts and their future. The Civil War has left them homeless and directionless. Stewart served with Sherman; Martin rode with Quantrill—one wrought destruction as a soldier, one as an outlaw. Stewart wants to buy a little spread up in Montana (which he describes as though he had seen it in an Anthony Mann movie); Martin is chary of the Indians and isn't ready to settle down. In a motley way, Martin's little gang prefigures Peckinpah's Wild Bunch. As one of them (Will Geer) says, "There ain't but one way for us. This way," he says, holding up his gun, "The way we know. The way we growed."

As the outlaws and the pursuing posse travel further south in Mexico, they enter "the territory of the bandolero," where the local outlaws kill every gringo. Martin and his gang take refuge in an abandoned town, the inhabitants of which have been driven off by the bandoleros. The sheriff—who happens to be enamored of Welch and is an honest, straightforward lawman, very good at his job—is not far behind. He again proves his skill by getting the drop on the group of outlaws. But no sooner has he captured them than the Mexican bandits ride into town. Just about everyone is killed in the ensuing bloodbath. (Americans holding off Mexicans in a scene of grim carnage was not new to the set of the film; McLaglen used the same buildings near Brackettville, Texas, that John Wayne had used in *The Alamo*.) Before he dies, Stewart has time to deliver an epitaph on his dead brother: "It was always hard for Dee to see the light at the end of the trail."

The Magnificent Seven made their first encore appearance in 1966 in *The Return of the Seven*. That same year, "the gunfighter" came back in *Return of the*

Gunfighter (MGM, 1966), directed by James Neilson. Robert Taylor stars as Ben Wyatt, an aging gunslinger who, in the tradition of Gregory Peck in *The Gunfighter*, is constantly being forced to defend his reputation. "Why won't they leave me alone?" he asks. When Mexican friends ask him to come help them in their struggle against a gang of outlaws, he sets off and arrives too late—the friends have been killed, and only the daughter (Ana Martin) is still alive. So the two of them (joined by Chad Everett) set off to seek revenge.

John Sturges, who directed *Gunfight at the O.K. Corral*, continued the story in *Hour of the Gun* (United Artists, 1967). James Garner plays Earp; Jason Robards, Jr., is Doc Holliday; Robert Ryan plays Ike Clanton. The film begins with the famous gunfight and follows Earp in his quest for personal revenge.

In *Day of the Evil Gun* (MGM, 1968), directed by Jerry Thorpe, a professional gunman, Glenn Ford, returns home after a long absence to find that his wife and two daughters have been kidnapped by Chiricahua Apaches. He takes off after them, joined by Arthur Kennedy, a neighbor who has been courting Ford's wife in his absence. The two searchers encounter Indians, Mexican bandits, army deserters, and, in one of the film's most striking scenes, pass through a town ravaged by a cholera epidemic. The sage gunman uses his weapon reluctantly; the peaceable farmer, however, begins to enjoy killing. As Ford says to him at one point, "It gets easier all the time, doesn't it?" They get the women home okay, but the jealous and gunhappy Kennedy insists on a shootout with Ford.

Gunfighters were not the only heroes of westerns during the late sixties. *Will Penny* (Paramount, 1968), directed by Tom Gries, tells a very different story of the West and provides a rare glimpse of the workaday world of the cowboy during the late 1880s. Charlton Heston stars in the title role of an aging cowpuncher who is anything but heroic. Drifting from job to job, he is beginning to realize that life has passed him by. Coarse and illiterate, a loner all his life, he has little to show for his years in the saddle except for some remembered bruises and his loyalty to his few friends (who include Anthony Zerbe and Lee Majors). The film begins with the end of a cattle drive. Collecting his pay, Penny rides off toward the north, in search of work for the winter. He finds a job as a line rider, which will mean spending the winter alone in an isolated shack (the man who hires him says, "I don't want to hear from you till spring"). He finds the shack already inhabited by a "cultured" woman (Joan Hackett) and her son. During the long, cold winter, the uncouth cowboy and the young woman—who claims to be on her way to join her husband—grow fond of each other. The villains of the film are a murderous gang of "rawhiders," led by a self-ordained Preacher Quint (Donald Pleasance). Penny has already had one encounter with

the gang, and they show up at the shack, seeking revenge. Zerbe and Majors show up, too, to help in the battle, and in the end the woman asks Penny to stay with her. But he is too old to change his life. "I'm damn near fifty years old," he says. "What do I know about love? It's too late for me."

There is a quiet, lyrical beauty to *Will Penny*. The mountains that Penny rides through appear cold, and the ground he sleeps on is visibly hard. It is not a very exciting life, and Penny has very little to look forward to (when he is on the trail, he can look forward to warm biscuits in the morning). Indeed, the gun battle with the rawhiders seems to be added just to make Penny's story more palatable. Without the distraction of the gunfire, the story would be a little too sad.

Villa Rides! (Paramount, 1968), directed by Buzz Kulik, appeared at a time—just after the assassination of Robert F. Kennedy—when film critics felt audiences might respond poorly to violent films. The critics were wrong. The screenplay for *Villa Rides!* was written by Robert Towne and Sam Peckinpah based on a book by William Douglas Lansford. The film stars Yul Brynner as Pancho Villa. He is aided in his fight by Charles Bronson as Fierro—"the butcher of the Revolution"— a murderous lieutenant who kills as many as 300 prisoners at a time. Robert Mitchum appears as a freelance aviator who uses his sputtering biplane to sell guns to counterrevolutionary forces. Captured by Villa, he agrees to become Villa's one-man air force. Herbert Lom plays the double-crossing General Huerta. The good guys are every bit as murderous as the bad guys; the difference between the two may lie only in the greater calm displayed by the good guys—the bad guys are liable to get excited and sweat. What is more, they may be unattractive.

Villa Rides! was filmed in Spain. So was *100 Rifles* (20th Century-Fox, 1969), directed by Tom Gries, which takes place during the same period and expresses the same disdain for the lives of prisoners. In *100 Rifles*, the prisoners are rebellious Yaqui Indians, and they are lined up and shot three at a time in an effort to save ammunition. As Fernando Lamas, the evil Mexican general, explains, "The bullets, they are worth something; the Yaquis, *nada*." Like the Mexican general in *The Wild Bunch*, Lamas has a German adviser (Hans Gudegast) and a Mercedes automobile. His entourage also includes an American (Dan O'Herlihy), a representative of the Central Pacific Railroad. Opposing this evil crew is a tribe of Yaqui Indians led by Raquel Welch and a half-breed called Yaqui Joe (Burt Reynolds). Reynolds robs a bank in Phoenix and uses the $6,000 to buy rifles for his people. An Arizona lawman (Jim Brown) pursues Reynolds and follows him all the way into Mexico. Both Reynolds and Brown get involved in the Yaqui battles against the machine-gun-equipped army; Brown gets involved with Welch, and their love scenes, in which their two remarkable bodies roll around—a black man and a white woman—were considered scandalous. The exciting battles include an attack on a train (Welch distracts the guards by taking a shower—scantily clad—under a water tower) and the final shootout, which begins when a train is run into a town and off its tracks.

One of the more interesting features of *Firecreek* (Warner Brothers, 1968), directed by Vincent Mc-Eveety, is that it stars Henry Fonda as the leader of an outlaw gang. He has been wounded in a gunfight, and he and his gang stop in the small town of Firecreek. The town is similar to the town in *Welcome to Hard Times*. "It's a town full of losers," says one of the residents, and most of the town's citizens are not courageous westerners—they are people who came West to escape failures in the East. The part-time sheriff of this town (James Stewart), who gets $2 a month for his services, doesn't carry a gun. He wears a badge made for him by his kids which reads, "SHERAF." The outlaws take over Firecreek, and the sheriff has to decide what to do. His wife is about to give birth; his friends tell him the town is not worth dying for. But when Fonda's gang lynches a local halfwit, Stewart's mind is made up, and the remainder of the film resembles *High Noon*.

Although he plays the leader of an outlaw gang, the character portrayed by Fonda is not completely unsympathetic. In fact, there is something heroic about him and something tragic about his death. Henry Fonda could never play a thoroughly evil character. Or could he?

Sergio Leone thought he could. For his fourth and most ambitious western, Leone finally got Henry Fonda. He got a lot more, too. For *Once Upon a Time in the West* (Paramount, 1969), Leone traveled to the United States and even shot some scenes in Monument Valley. In addition to Fonda, the film stars Charles Bronson, Jason Robards, Jr., Claudia Cardinale, Keenan Wynn, Frank Wolff, Jack Elam, and Woody Strode. (Elam, Strode, and Al Mulock are gunned down in the first scene of the film. Leone had wanted to kill off the heroes of his previous film, *The Good, the Bad and the Ugly*, but the stars wouldn't agree—it would have been Leone's way of bidding a fond farewell to the three "Dollars" films.) Bronson, who usually plays a heavy, plays a "hero," a character named Harmonica; Robards plays another recognizably good character, a man named Cheyenne; Fonda, however, plays a character named Frank, a hired gunman working for the railroad, an evil man. Fonda first appears during the cold-blooded slaughter of a family of set-

Yul Brynner in Villa Rides! *(Paramount, 1968).*

tlers, the McBains. When the shooting stops, there is one McBain left alive, little Timmy. "What shall we do with this one, Frank?" asks one of the murderers. "Since you call me by name," responds Frank, taking out his pistol and blasting the innocent little boy point-blank. The famous blue eyes shine like ice; Henry Fonda is a killer.

Once Upon a Time in the West is an epic fairy tale. It is not based on American history but on the myths of the West presented in penny dreadfuls, Wild West shows, and Hollywood films (many of the lines of dialogue in the film are lifted from other westerns). The story of the film—the inevitable end of the West brought on by the arrival of technology in the form of the railroad—is not new to westerns, but Leone presents it with his usual cynical pessimism, and the film seems, with all its American actors and American scenery, very foreign.

Part of the foreignness is the result of the film's obvious concern for what might be called the socio-political aspects of the West, almost as though the film were based on a dime novel by Marx. It is not a personal story, and its symbols are lifeless. Frank, the outlaw who works for the railroad boss, Morton (Gabriele Ferzetti), is helping the railroad end the West of which he is part. He plans to save himself by becoming a businessman. At one point, he seats himself at Morton's desk. "How does it feel, sitting behind that desk?" asks Morton. "It's like holding a gun," responds Frank.

"Only much more powerful." But Frank cannot save himself—he is part of the West that must die. So are Cheyenne (Robards)—a heroic outlaw who gives his life in an attempt to destroy the railroad—and Harmonica, who is surviving only for revenge against Frank, who killed his brother. As Cheyenne says of Harmonica, "People like that have something inside, something to do with death."

Frank eventually finds that he cannot turn himself into a businessman, cannot save himself. "So you found out you're not a businessman after all," the wise Harmonica says to him.

"Just a man," says Frank.

"An ancient race," concludes Harmonica.

Frank, Cheyenne, and Harmonica have to die to make room for the new America, the hungry masses who will be fed by the former whore (Cardinale).

There is something of the fairy tale in *MacKenna's Gold* (Columbia, 1969), directed by J. Lee Thompson. The film stars Gregory Peck as a U.S. marshal taken captive by a Mexican outlaw named Colorado (Omar Sharif). It happens that the marshal has seen—and destroyed—a map to a canyon supposedly full of Apache gold. This legendary horde—variously referred to as the "lost Adams" and Canyon del Oro—is of spiritual importance to the Apache. The marshal is nabbed by the bandit, who wants to get the gold so he can emigrate to Paris and become a fancy gentleman. These

Above: *Henry Fonda (left) and Charles Bronson in* Once Upon a Time in the West *(Paramount, 1969).*

two and the bandit's gang are joined by "the gentlemen from Hadleyburg," the upright men of a nearby town who come running to get their share of the gold. (The screenplay for the film was written by Carl Foreman, and he admitted that the town of Hadleyburg bears more than a passing resemblance to the Hadleyville of *High Noon*.) This group includes the town's newspaper editor (Lee J. Cobb), its preacher (Raymond Massey), and a certain Old Adams (Edward G. Robinson), an old-timer who has seen the canyon only to be subsequently blinded by the Apaches. The gold-seekers are chased by both the Apaches and the cavalry. Telly Savalas plays a cavalry sergeant who kills three of his own troopers in order to join the expedition. The film ends with a scene that belongs more to either a fairy tale or a science-fiction thriller than to a western, and *MacKenna's Gold* may be best remembered for an odd scene of Omar Sharif swimming nude and then sitting on a rock—his legs shyly crossed—grinning.

The last year of the sixties saw three films that deal with the theme that began the decade: the end of the West. The first of these films, *Death of a Gunfighter* (Universal, 1969), directed by Robert Totten and Don Siegel under the combined pseudonym "Allen Smithee," stars Richard Widmark as Marshal Frank Patch, an aging lawman who still rides a horse and wears a gun even though the town he tamed is on its way into a new century—its homes are lit with Mazda bulbs instead of gaslight. Looking forward to the future and wanting to appear as modern and progressive as possible, the townspeople ask the marshal to resign. They see no need for him—he is nothing more than an awkward reminder of the violent past that they would all prefer to forget. (He also knows all their past histories, including some things that they would like very much to see forgotten.) When the marshal refuses to resign, the townspeople (making use of the violence they deplore) turn against him. The only person to help the marshal is his mistress of twenty years (Lena Horne), whom he marries on his last day, before facing the well-armed townspeople.

It was quite a group. There was Ben Kilpatrick ("the Tall Texan"), Deaf Charley Hanks, Black Jack Ketchum, George "Flat Nose" Curry, Harvey Logan, Harry Severynns (alias Harry Tracy), Butch Cassidy, and the Sundance Kid. The group had a number of names, including the Hole-in-the-Wall Gang, the Powder Spring Gang, and the Robbers' Roost Gang, but they are best known as the Wild Bunch, and their daring train robberies provided the inspiration for Edwin S. Porter's *The Great Train Robbery*. Those same robberies also brought about the eventual end of the gang, and the Wild Bunch was broken up and hunted down. In August of 1902, the deadly marksman Harry Tracy

died in a wheat field in Washington State, the victim of a massive manhunt. Other members met similar ends. But the gang's most famous members avoided that fate—they left the country.

Butch Cassidy and the Sundance Kid is about the two who got away; the title of *The Wild Bunch* does not necessarily refer to the same gang, but the film is based on the same spirit and tells a similar story about the end of the West.

Butch Cassidy and the Sundance Kid (20th Century-Fox, 1969), directed by George Roy Hill, begins with a mild disclaimer: "Not that it matters, but most of what follows is true." Most of it is "true" to the legend of the two outlaws. Screenwriter William Goldman followed the accepted version of their story (which includes Butch's fondness for bicycles), with only one deviation: there is no proof that the two Americans died in South America. They may have spread the rumor of their deaths themselves, just to get the law off their trail.

One of the most popular westerns ever made, the fame of *Butch Cassidy and the Sundance Kid* is attributable to its two stars, Paul Newman as Butch and Robert Redford as Sundance. It is their friendship—expressed not in caring words but in an ongoing exchange of wry, sarcastic humor—that makes the film so endearing. The optimistic Butch does most of the talking. As he says, "Everybody else wears bifocals, but I got vision!" Sundance puts up with his partner. When called on to respond, Sundance expresses himself in either searing glances or caustic retorts. The language of this sophisticated repartee is very "contemporary," and the two heroes would fit into almost any story. The famous bicycle-riding scene, to the tune of "Raindrops Keep Fallin' on My Head," by Burt Bacharach, contributes in no small way to the contemporary feel of the film. Until the end, *Butch Cassidy and the Sundance Kid* is a comedy, an adult fairy tale about two very likeable men who are good at only one line of work—a line that just happens to be against the law.

When Butch and Sundance rob the Union Pacific Flyer for the second time, they use a little too much dynamite to open the safe: the blast destroys the train car and sends the money flying into the air. While they are gathering the banknotes, a second train appears, and in a scene that goes back to *When the Daltons Rode*, the doors of the train cars open and mounted riders emerge. The members of this special posse, led by a feared Pinkerton agent, are never introduced, never seen in close-up. They are tireless professionals employed by the railroad for only one purpose—to catch the two outlaws—and they chase them with a frightening seriousness. "I think we lost 'em," says Butch at one point. He looks hopefully at Sundance. "Do you think we lost 'em?" he asks. When there is no reply, Butch agrees, "Neither do I." Nothing the two

Gregory Peck in MacKenna's Gold *(Columbia, 1969).*

outlaws do fools the relentless posse. "Who are those guys?" they both wonder.

"Those guys" are not an ordinary posse, and as Butch and Sundance learn from Sundance's girlfriend, Etta Place (Katharine Ross), the men in the posse will not go home when they get tired of looking—they will not go home until they get the two train robbers. It is Butch, of course, who hits upon the idea of going to South America, where there are plenty of banks and no dangerous lawmen. Etta agrees to go with them with the understanding that she won't stay. "I'm twenty-six, and I'm single, and I teach school, and that's the bottom of the pit. And the only excitement I've ever known is sitting in the room with me now. So I'll go with you, and I won't whine, and I'll sew your socks and stitch you when you're wounded, anything you ask of me I'll do, except one thing: I won't watch you die."

They go to New York. Their sojourn in the city—related in a series of over 300 still photographs—is a lot of fun; Bolivia doesn't turn out to be exactly the way Butch described it. In particular, there is a language problem to contend with. Etta tutors the two stubborn students in the phrases necessary for their profession—"Esta es un robo" ("This is a robbery"); "Manos arriba!" ("Hands up!")—and even takes part in a few heists. When the reputation of the two gringos spreads, Etta sees it is time to leave. With her gone, the two try their hand at going "straight" and serve as payroll guards. Butch, who has never shot anyone, has to learn to kill. They return to outlawry.

Butch and Sundance are recognized when they sit down at an inn in a public square. They shoot it out with the local garrison and take refuge in a small building. Badly shot up and surrounded, they mend each other's wounds while Butch makes plans for the future. He has a new idea: Australia. Sundance says he doesn't want to hear about it, but Butch knows that he really does, and as hundreds of Bolivian soldiers take up positions outside, Butch explains the advantages of Australia. The place has a lot going for it and one thing in particular: Australians speak English. Butch still hopeful and Sundance still skeptical, they run out of the building.

As they emerge from the building, the camera stops them in a freeze frame. The volleys of rifle fire are heard, but Butch and Sundance remain standing. Spared their death, the viewer is allowed to dream of their immortality.

In Arthur Penn's *Bonnie and Clyde* (1967), viewers were not spared the scene of the two outlaw heroes—Warren Beatty and Faye Dunaway—being riddled with bullets. The final scene of their death was presented in slow motion, making the viewer painfully aware of the impact of each bullet. Such violence would not have been in keeping with the lighthearted

mood of *Butch Cassidy and the Sundance Kid*, but it suited the mood of **The Wild Bunch** (Warner Brothers, 1969), directed by Sam Peckinpah.

The basic plot of *The Wild Bunch* is familiar. Aging outlaws, men who have lived to see the end of the West and with it the end of the only way of life they know, are chased by professionals hired by the railroad. They take refuge in Mexico, become involved in the local revolutionary chaos, and, following their outworn code, die in a final battle. The story may be familiar, but Peckinpah relates it in a unique way. The violence of the film—its famous "ballets of death"—has been a source of controversy since its release, but the power of the film lies elsewhere. It has the depth of a true work of art. It is such a coherent view, its various parts are so intrinsically true, that it seems to deliver the right answers to questions that cannot even be formulated. With all its terrifying violence, it does not present a pessimistic view of the world. It presents a world that is both very dangerous—with cruel men and corrupt ideas—and very romantic and beautiful. And the beauty—the dreamed-of possibilities—seem heartbreakingly near. All the blood and bullets do nothing to extinguish the film's sense of optimism.

Like all of Peckinpah's films, *The Wild Bunch* was chopped apart before—and even after—it was released. Among the scenes cut were flashbacks important to understanding the motivations of the characters. But despite the cuts, the film retains a sense of wholeness.

The story of the film takes place in 1913. The Wild Bunch, dressed in army uniforms, rides into the Texas town of Starbuck to rob the bank of a railroad payroll. As they ride down the street, they pass a crowd of children intent on a game. The laughing children have placed scorpions on an anthill and are delighting in the spectacle of the ants attacking the scorpions. It isn't long before the action of the film mirrors the children's pastime. The gang has been set up for an ambush, and as they leave the bank, bounty hunters open fire from all around, cutting down both gang members and countless townspeople. This first shootout establishes the Wild Bunch as cool professionals and the bounty hunters as moronic murderers. The men who escape the ambush—Pike Bishop (William Holden), Dutch Engstrom (Ernest Borgnine), Lyle Gorch (Warren Oates), Tector Gorch (Ben Johnson), and Angel (Jaime Sanchez)—join up with another member of the gang, Old Sykes (Edmond O'Brien), and take off for Mexico, pursued by the bounty hunters.

The members of the Wild Bunch are not reincarnations of the members of *The Magnificent Seven* or *The Professionals*. The identities of the outlaws in the Wild Bunch do not hinge on special skills (there is no dynamite expert), nor are they particularly likeable—they're not nice, polite, or even very smart. Very little

Richard Widmark and Lena Horne in
Death of a Gunfighter (*Universal, 1969*).

175

separates them from the vicious bounty hunters, but that very little is very important and is composed of their sense of loyalty and their pride in who they are. The leader of the group, Pike, is not infallible: the foiled bank robbery, which netted the Bunch only bags of metal washers, was a mistake, and he has made many mistakes before. The bounty hunters are led by a former friend of Pike's, Deke Thornton (Robert Ryan), who, as the result of another of Pike's errors in judgment, was captured and put in prison. He has been released by a cruel railroad boss named Pat Harrigan (Albert Dekker) for the specific purpose of going after his old friend. He doesn't like the mangy gang of bounty hunters he has to work with and would much rather be riding with Pike. "We're after men," he says to the bounty hunters, "and I wish to God I was with them."

The robbery in Starbuck was to have been the last job for the Wild Bunch. Pike wants to pull off one big job and then retire. It isn't that he has seen the error of his outlaw ways, but he knows he is getting old and that the law is catching up with him. "We gotta start thinking beyond our guns," he says. "Those days are closin' fast." In a conversation with Dutch, he says, "I'd like to make one good score and back off." "Back off to what?" asks Dutch. Pike has no answer.

Although he spends his time talking about the future, it is the past that Pike is thinking about. (Unfortunately, the flashbacks that explain his relationship to Thornton and how he lost the woman he loved are missing from most of the release prints of the film.) The past weighs heavily on Pike. His memory of how it was, troubled by memories of his past mistakes, makes him even more determined to live by the old code. When Sykes, the oldest member of the Wild Bunch, trips up the horses, the younger members make fun of him and want to ditch him. Pike will listen to none of that: "We're gonna stick together just like it used to be. When you side with a man you stay with him, and if you can't do that, you're like some animal, you're finished—we're finished, all of us." When Dutch complains about Thornton's having sided with the railroad, Pike, defending his old friend with the old code, says, "What would you do? He gave his word." "Gave his word to a railroad," counters Dutch. "It's his word!" says Pike. "That's not what counts," says Dutch. "It's who you give it to!" Although Dutch has the last word, Pike remains unconvinced, and Peckinpah does nothing to resolve the question.

Chased by the bounty hunters, the Wild Bunch goes into Mexico, a country divided by revolution. Angel is a Mexican and feels strongly about "my people, my village—Mexico." He is committed to the revolution. He takes the Bunch to his village, where the outlaws relax in scenes of peaceful beauty. Even the beastly Gorch brothers act like gentlemen. Pike points out their astonishing behavior to an old Mexican named Don

José (Chano Urueta). "Hard to believe," says Pike. "Not so hard," responds Don José. "We all dream of being a child again, even the worst of us—perhaps the worst most of all."

The beauty of Angel's village is sharply contrasted with Aqua Verde, a town in the control of the maniacal antirevolutionary general Mapache (played by Emilio Fernandez, a Mexican director and actor, born in 1904, who himself took part in Mexican revolutionary activity). The general has two German advisers (westerns rarely explain the presence of Germans in Mexico; they were there to try to convince the Mexican government to side with the Axis during the coming world war). The general also has a gift from the Germans: an automobile ("Now what in Hell is that?" exclaims Dutch when he first sees it). The Wild Bunch enters into a business agreement with Mapache. The general needs weapons for his battle against Villa, and they agree to hold up a U.S. Army munitions train. The train robbery is successful—it even nets a machine gun. But Angel's revolutionary connections are discovered, and he is tortured by Mapache.

The remaining four members of the Wild Bunch see Angel dragged behind Mapache's car. They watch him "play his string out to the end." Someplace outside Aqua Verde is the gang of bounty hunters; inside the town are hundreds of *mapachistas* with their German advisers and their machine gun. Pike, Dutch, Lyle, and Tector spend a night carousing in the town. The next morning, Pike walks into the room where Lyle and Tector are arguing with a whore over her price. "Let's go," he says. There is a pause, and then Lyle says, "Why not?" Joined by Dutch, the four of them walk off together to rescue Angel or die trying.

Their gun battle with Mapache and his men saves them from the hopeless task of trying to find a new future and allows them to die according to the way they lived. It is a rude lesson about violence. One of the special effects experts for the film claimed that more ammunition (blanks, of course) was used in the final battle than had been used in the entire 1913 Revolution in Mexico: 90,000 rounds. To display the effects of all those projectiles, more than 3,000 "squibs" (wired charges) were used. The battle is awesome, frightening, and at times beautiful. When it is over, when the four American outlaws are dead, riddled with bullets, the bounty hunters gleefully descend on the scene and take off with the bodies. Thornton and Sykes arrive, too. The two men ride off together, agreeing, "It ain't like it used to be, but it'll do."

The Wild Bunch, one of the most important westerns ever made and one of the most important American films ever made, provides a connection with *The Great Train Robbery*, another film told from the point of view of the robbers. In that first western, the wounded villains dramatically clutch their bodies and fall to the ground dead; in *The Wild Bunch*, they remain standing long past all reasonable belief, and the screen is doused with blood. It took a long time to kill the last bad guys—it took even longer to chase them down. The chase that began in those New Jersey woods in 1903 ended across the Mexican border in 1969, where it wasn't the good guys who finally "got 'em." It was the future that finally caught up with the bad guys, a future well armed with modern weapons and a helpful disinterest in individual men. The westerns of the seventies inherited no bad guys to chase and no good guys to do the chasing. The violence of *The Wild Bunch* became, in the hands of other men, anger, the filmmaker's anger at the audience for believing in (or putting up with) the western myth. Many filmmakers during the seventies seemed to be saying, "Maybe there never were any heroes, neither good guys nor bad guys. Maybe we should look again at all those stories and see how evil everyone really was."

Robert Redford (left) and Paul Newman in Butch Cassidy and the Sundance Kid *(20th Century-Fox, 1969).*

The Way It Should Have Been

1970–1979

"Sometimes the magic works, sometimes it doesn't."

Little Big Man

Broncho Billy Anderson, who had tumbled from the saddle as a wounded outlaw in *The Great Train Robbery* and gone on to become the first star of westerns—the first movie star—died in 1971. By the time he died, at age 88, the old West on film had lasted longer than the actual period of the West. From the days of the pioneers to the end of the frontier, when there was nowhere else to go, the West lasted little more than the length of one man's life. That is part of the West's sad beauty: individual men lived to see enormous changes within their own lifetime. Standing by railroad tracks in empty fields, old men could spit on the ground and declare that they recalled when the teeming buffalo herds had been spread across the hills as far as the eye could see.

The story of the West presents a very personal kind of epic. The same names of famous men and famous towns appear over and over; the same events were witnessed and participated in by the same small group of people. The possibilities for outlandish coincidences were amazing. It almost seems that it would not have been impossible for one man to have seen it all.

Such a man is Jack Crabb, the 121-year-old narrator of *Little Big Man* (NGP, 1970), a man who claims to be the sole survivor of Custer's Last Stand. The story he tells is like his given age: it is unbelievable but not impossible. Directed by Arthur Penn, *Little Big Man* is based on a novel by Thomas Berger, and some of the changes made by Penn and screenwriter Calder Willingham are unfortunate. When reading the book, one never knows whether or not Crabb is telling the truth: his narrative flows smoothly from the plausible to the seemingly impossible. When he describes a gunfight he had with Wild Bill Hickok in which he saved himself by using a special ring to reflect sunlight into the famous gunman's eyes, he is repeating a scene that could have been taken from a dozen dime novels. It has to be a lie—but if the rest of what he is saying is true, perhaps even that incredible account is true. A man divided between life with the Indians and life among whites, Jack Crabb's search for his own identity becomes the search for the truth about the West. His story is like the West itself—a mixture of history and fictional inventiveness, pure fable and dramatic accounts of human tragedy and courage. The Indians he lived among were always ready for a miracle; his story tests the willingness of the reader to believe the personal miracle of Jack Crabb, who "knowed Custer for what he was" and knew the Indians for what they were.

Although the movie captures some of this, it loses itself by trying to politicize. From the moment Crabb—

an invalid in a nursing home being interviewed by a timorous collector of western memorabilia with a tape recorder—says, "Turn the damn thing on," he is angry, and the story he tells about the mistreatment of the Indians drowns out the story of the book.

Jack Crabb (Dustin Hoffman) and his sister (Carol Androsky) survive the Pawnee massacre of their family. They are found by Cheyenne. His boyish sister (miffed at the Indians' failure to rape her) escapes (no one tries to stop her); Jack stays and learns to be an Indian, becoming Little Big Man. The rest of the film follows him through his many adventures as he lives alternately with the Indians and in white society. When he is not living among the Cheyenne as Little Big Man, he is busy as Jack Crabb taking part in nearly every aspect of the West. He goes through what he calls "periods"—a religious period; a gunfighter period, during which he befriends Wild Bill Hickok (Jeff Corey); a stint as co-owner of a general store; a period as a con man with a medicine show; a period as a drunk; a period as a hermit; another as a scout for the cavalry. He experiences the major confrontations between Custer (Richard Mulligan) and the Indians from both sides. He sees how the Indians were lied to and cruelly massacred. He has a white wife whom he loses in an Indian attack; he has an Indian wife whom he loses in a massacre. The film relates Crabb's life with droll humor, its various phases serving to expose the West and westerners for what they were.

The Indians Crabb lives with are quite unlike the Indians in other westerns. They don't pass their time dancing around the campfire. Rather, they are individuals with identifiable characters. (Some of the characterizations are taken too far, particularly that of Little

Horse, the *heemaneh*. His portrayal of a homosexual—with an overriding interest in the interior decoration of tepees—owes more to the vaudeville stage than the Great Plains.) The leader of the tribe, Old Lodge Skins, is a wonderful character with a wise benevolence, who is never surprised by the tricks of fate. (The fact that the character is played by Chief Dan George—a leader of the Canadian Salish tribe—was such a trick. The part was first offered to Sir Laurence Olivier, then to Paul Scofield, and finally to Richard Boone before being offered to Dan George.) When, after the Battle of the Little Big Horn, Old Lodge Skins decides that it is time to die, he and Little Big Man go up on a mountain, where the chief prepares his bier and sings his death song. Then he lies down to die. It begins to rain. "Am I still in this world?" asks the old Indian, opening his eyes. "Yes, Father," replies Little Big Man. "Whee, I was afraid of that," says Old Lodge Skins, concluding, "Sometimes the magic works, sometimes it doesn't." In the novel, the chief lies down and dies right away, for in the book we are challenged to believe in the magic; in the movie, not even the Indians believe in it, and all we believe in is the terrible perfidy and cruelty of the cavalry and its insane leader, George Armstrong Custer. The scenes of the various massacres are truly horrifying and graphically violent. It is regrettable that the magic of filmmakers allows them to show us the blood and gore of history but not the miracles performed by Old Lodge Skins.

The central massacre in *Little Big Man* is based on the Battle of the Washita, November 27, 1868, in which Custer led a dawn attack on a village of Indians. The central massacre in *Soldier Blue* (EMB, 1970), directed by Ralph Nelson, is based on another dawn massacre of Indians, this one led by Colonel John M. Chivington, "the Fighting Parson," on November 29, 1864, on a tribe camped at Sand Creek, Colorado. The victims of both massacres were Cheyenne, both tribes had been guaranteed safety where they were by the government, and in both battles women and children were indiscriminately butchered. Like *Little Big Man*, *Soldier Blue* is based on a novel (*Arrow in the Sun*, by Theodore V. Olsen, who also wrote the novel on which *The Stalking Moon* is based); like *Little Big Man*, *Soldier Blue* uses the basic outline of the novel to deliver an angry polemic on the mistreatment of Indians. The "soldier blue" of the title is Private Honus Grant (Peter Strauss). He joins Cresat Lee (Candice Bergen), a white woman who has been held captive by the Cheyenne for two years, and the two of them make a long trek together to reach an army outpost. During her captivity, the woman has become the squaw of a warrior named Spotted Dog (Jorge Rivero). Somehow, the experience has turned her into a nonstop blasphemer. "Balls!" and "Bullshit!" she exclaims as the two make their way toward distant safety. There is something of

a romantic comedy about their relationship, but there is nothing romantic in the battle scenes, in which bloodthirsty cavalrymen commit atrocities, such as slicing off the breast of a squaw and tossing it back and forth on the ends of their sabers.

Little Big Man and *Soldier Blue* began the decade of the seventies with violent denouncements of the old West as racist and imperialistic. The parallels to the Vietnam War were clear. By reexamining the past, filmmakers sought an explanation of the present. If there were problems today, then the past must have been tainted. Bereft of its heroes, the only thing left of the West was violence, and the leading characters in films no longer tried to fight evil—they merely tried to survive.

The Indians fared well in this reexamination. Having fought the corrupt system from the beginning, they were recognized as heroic figures. They had been right all along in their battle against the encroaching whites, and their final defeat became a symbol of tragedy. The plight of contemporary Indians became an important concern. In *Journey Through Rosebud* (GSF, 1972), directed by Tom Gries, a young draft dodger (Kristoffer Tabori) passes through the Sioux Indian Rosebud reservation and learns the realities of the Indians' life. When Marlon Brando was awarded an Oscar in 1972 for his role in *The Godfather*, he refused to accept it and, protesting the treatment of American Indians by the film industry, sent an Indian woman named Satcheen Littlefeather (actually an actress named Maria Cruz) in his place to deliver a short speech.

Filmmakers showed their liberal views by making the Indians more civilized and morally superior to the whites who massacred them. In many films, the Indians seem more like members of a sophisticated counterculture than heathens. *A Man Called Horse* (NGP, 1970), directed by Elliot Silverstein, presents a different view of the Indians, a view in which they seem alien and frightening. The film was put together with such care for historical details that it was, inevitably, attacked for being inaccurate. More than 500 Sioux Indians appear in the film—they are not Hollywood extras; 80 percent of the spoken dialogue in the film is in the Sioux dialect (most of it is not translated); and the headdresses, artifacts, huts, clothing, and ceremonial songs were recreated as accurately as possible (the color blue was not used, for the simple reason that nineteenth-century Sioux, who used earth paints, had no way to produce it).

The story of the film takes place in 1825. Lord John Morgan (Richard Harris), an English aristocrat on a hunting expedition, is captured by a Sioux hunting party while taking a bath. The leader of the Indians (Manu Tupou) gives Morgan to his mother, Buffalo Cow Head (Judith Anderson), who treats the English-

man like a horse. The world that he has been thrust into is strange and bewildering—the film makes clear the naturalness of life and death to the Indians, and Horse (Morgan) suffers agony at taking part in the life of his captors. Thanks to the presence in the Indian camp of a French half-breed who "speaks" Sioux, Morgan is able to understand—and so therefore is the viewer—some of what is happening to him. When Morgan helps defend the camp against Shoshone raiders, he is recognized as a man by the Sioux. In the film's most famous sequence, he takes part in the Sun Vow ceremony—his chest is pierced, ropes are threaded through the holes, and he is suspended from the ceiling of a hut. He marries an Indian (Corrina Tsopei) and eventually becomes chief of the tribe. Thus, regardless of the authenticity of the artifacts, language, and ceremonies of the film, *A Man Called Horse* relies on a standard notion—that a white man's superior intelligence will make him the leader of any group of savages. Morgan ultimately leaves the tribe to go back to England.

The producer (Sanford Howard), screenwriter (Jack DeWitt), and star (Richard Harris) of *A Man Called Horse* collaborated on another film about survival in a hostile environment, **Man in the Wilderness** (Warner Brothers, 1971), directed by Richard C. Sarafian. The film is based on the true story of a fur trapper named Hugh Glass who was mauled by a bear and left for dead by his companions (the character, played by Harris, is renamed Zach Bass in the film).

The events take place in the Pacific Northwest in 1820 (the film was made in Spain). The Captain Henry Expedition, laden with beaver pelts, is heading back to the Missouri River. The group of trappers presents a strange sight, for they have with them their 50-foot keelboat (the boat in the film was built according to specifications left in the papers of Lewis and Clark). The boat is used to sail up rivers. When it is necessary to travel overland, it is mounted on wheels and dragged by mules. The boat, with its mast and sail, seems as out of place in the wilderness—a boat out of water—as the men who travel with it. One of them, Zach Bass, is attacked by a ferocious bear. He is gravely wounded and is not expected to live. The leader of the expedition, Captain Henry (John Huston), delivers a brief sermon—"Zach fought against life all his life; now he fights with you, God"—and appoints two men to stay behind to watch the body and bury him when he dies—and if he doesn't die by the next morning, to kill and then bury him. Indians frighten off the two men, Bass survives, and he takes off on a 600-mile trek in pursuit of the expedition, troubled by his wounds, flashbacks of his earlier life, and close encounters with Indians.

Sanford Howard, Jack DeWitt, and Richard Harris reprised *A Man Called Horse* in **Return of a Man Called Horse** (United Artists, 1976), directed by Irvin

Kershner. Actress Gale Sondergaard returned to films in *Return of a Man Called Horse*: she had been blacklisted in 1951 after refusing to appear before the House Un-American Activities Committee.

This sequel begins with a 17-minute foreword that recounts the events of the previous film, which ended with Lord John Morgan (Harris) returning to England. Dissatisfied with life in England, Morgan returns to the West to find his tribe in dire straits: their land is being taken from them by a conniving trader (Geoffrey Lewis), and their women and children are being sold into slavery. In order tó cleanse himself and rid the tribe of the evil spirit that is plaguing it, Morgan must again undergo the Sun Vow ceremony (a scene that lasts a grueling 20 minutes). Morgan teaches the Indians how to use firearms and leads them in a successful assault on the trading post. The Indians return to their sacred land, and Morgan stays with them.

Endeavors to regain possession of tribal lands is the theme of a comedy western called **Flap** (**The Last Warrior** in Great Britain) (Warner Brothers, 1970). The film was directed by Sir Carol Reed, the British director who also directed such films as *Odd Man Out*, *The Third Man*, and *Oliver!* Clair Huffaker wrote the screenplay based on his novel *Nobody Loves a Drunken Indian*, a story about modern-day Paiute Indians in Arizona. The title of the novel was originally going to be used for the film, too, but in an effort to avoid offending anyone, it was changed to *Nobody Loves Flapping Eagle*. A group of Indians who read the screenplay wanted the title changed back—they felt the film had an important message. Somehow, it ended up being *Flap*. The film stars Anthony Quinn as Flapping Eagle, the second most decorated Indian veteran of the Second World War. Flapping Eagle's frustrations with life on the reservation are brought to a head when he learns of plans to construct a superhighway through the tribal homeland. He organizes the tribe, tries to attract public attention to the plight of the Paiutes, and takes part in numerous comic antics. He becomes a martyr to the cause when he is gunned down by a half-breed police sergeant (Victor French). The film ends with the Indians taking over the city of Phoenix, basing their claims on treaties dating to 1892. The film's theme song, "If Nobody Loves," was written by Marvin Hamlisch with words by Estelle Levitt: it is sung by Kenny Rogers and The First Edition.

The Jicarilla Apaches in New Mexico have tribal land rich in oil, natural gas, and timber, and their reservation is a popular tourist attraction. In search of wise investments, the tribe decided to finance a film and raised the $2 million for *A Gunfight* (Paramount, 1971), directed by Lamont Johnson—a western that has nothing to do with Indians. The film stars Kirk Douglas and Johnny Cash as aging gunfighters in Texas around 1885 who hit upon a novel money-making scheme. The two legendary quick-draw artists are always being asked to prove who's fastest, so they decide to hold a gunfight in a bullring and sell tickets—the winner (the one left standing) to take all the proceeds. The two men, who are friends, come to this decision not merely to satisfy public curiosity—both men need money. The film exposes a tired melancholy in the two men that adds to its atmosphere of impending doom. Cash's performance as a weary gunfighter is excellent; Douglas's son Eric has a role; and Keith Carradine appears in a part that reverses his role in *McCabe & Mrs. Miller.*

"I got poetry in me."

McCabe & Mrs. Miller

The poetry in the westerns of the seventies was the poetry of names, the names of men and women, like identifications scrawled on the backs of old photographs: Chisum, Cahill, Hannie Caulder, Monte Walsh, Big Jake, Josey Wales, Joe Kidd, Jeremiah Johnson, Junior Bonner, J. W. Coop, Chato, Ulzana, Santee, Valdez, Buck, Zachariah. With no larger truths to believe in, the West was divided up into individual stories, the faces in old photographs brought to life to tell their personal tales, their small truths. Like folk songs, the films are about people on their way into legend—their names are what they have in place of history, and their stubborn, unforgettable characters are what they have in place of heroism.

The seventies began with two movies about memorable individuals, *The Ballad of Cable Hogue* and *McCabe & Mrs. Miller.* Both films are about entrepreneurs, small businessmen who, perhaps understandably, love whores. Both men die in encounters with the future, the future composed of corporate America. Cable dies in the desert; McCabe dies in the snow. *The*

Ballad of Cable Hogue is a warm, funny film; *McCabe & Mrs. Miller* is cold and saddening.

The Ballad of Cable Hogue (Warner Brothers, 1970), directed by Sam Peckinpah, is the story of a man who found water where there wasn't any. Abandoned in the desert by his two partners (Warren Oates and Strother Martin), Cable Hogue (Jason Robards, Jr.) wanders for four days without water, talking to God, not complaining but reminding Him of his growing thirst. In the middle of nowhere, Hogue finds water, discovers that the water happens to be on a stageline, and realizes there is money to be made. Things are not easy for the capitalistic Hogue—he has to kill his first customer (the man doesn't want to pay for the water), and he has trouble getting financing for his operation—but he establishes Cable Spring, the only stop for stagecoaches between Gila City and Deaddog. The ornery Hogue cheats people, charges too much, and has his own rough way of doing business, which includes nailing the dinner plates to the table because it makes them easier to wash—he just throws a bucket of water over the table. But Hogue is a wonderfully likeable man, endearingly individualistic, the ruler of his small kingdom ("I'd be nothing in town," he admits). His friends include the Reverend Joshua Duncan Sloane (David Warner), "preacher to all of eastern Nevada and selected parts of northern Arizona" (his sermonizing serves only to gain access to other men's wives), and a prostitute named Hildy (Stella Stevens) who comes to live with him in the desert.

The Ballad of Cable Hogue is a romantic comedy (complete with a song that Hogue and Hildy sing together) with a serious side—it delivers a poetic ballad about the end of individualism. Cable, the last of his kind, dies after being run over by an automobile—a vehicle that signals both the end of his business and the end of his world. Cable is not brought into his house to die; instead, his bed is brought out to him, and he is placed in it for one of the longest death scenes in a movie—long because more than a man is being buried. His friend the preacher arrives to deliver a sermon. He asks God to take Cable—"but not too lightly"—and reminds Him that "out of the barren wastes, he carved himself a one-man kingdom." He adds, "When Cable Hogue died, there wasn't an animal in the desert he didn't know, there wasn't a star in the firmament he hadn't named, there wasn't a man he was afraid of."

Just as horses pulling stagecoaches need water, miners mining zinc need whiskey and whores. The plot of *McCabe & Mrs. Miller* (Warner Brothers, 1971), directed by Robert Altman, concerns a wandering gambler named John McCabe (Warren Beatty) who establishes himself in a small mining town on the Canadian border and, with the help of a Cockney madam named Mrs. Miller (Julie Christie), builds a saloon and whorehouse. When his business prospers, a corporation sends representatives to buy him out; when he refuses, the corporation sends gunmen to kill him. That is the plot, but the film does not move in that direction except when it has to. There are more important issues, chief among them the search, on the part of both the actors in the film and the members of the audience, for a warm place in which to calm down and relax.

Advertised as the picture "that finally shows the West as it really was," *McCabe & Mrs. Miller* makes use of conventions and characters from countless other films, but it delivers them as in a dream. Like the Leonard Cohen songs that provide the music, the details of the film—the muddy streets, overcast skies, and visibly cold winds—create a compelling atmosphere. The town in which most of the story takes place was constructed for the film—it grows as the film progresses—and Altman, famous for his attention to detail, filled the town with items from the period depicted: the Pacific Northwest in 1902. (Dresser drawers that are never opened in the film were filled with period articles. Closets that are never opened were filled with period clothes.) From any angle, the film tells the same story.

McCabe rides through mist and cold rain into the settlement of Presbyterian Church, looking for a poker game. Seeing business opportunities in the town, he brings in three slatternly whores and sets them up in tents. Mrs. Miller arrives on a remarkable steam-driven car and gets right to business. "Listen, Mr. McCabe," she says, "I'm a whore and I know an awful lot about whorehouses." She takes over the running of the whorehouse, and the entrepreneurial skills of McCabe and Mrs. Miller bring the growing town a certain decency—the men have to wash up in the new bathhouse before visiting the whorehouse. As soon as the town is enjoying this prosperity, a corporation sends two men to buy out McCabe. He refuses—he wants to hold out for more money. The corporation then sends three gunmen: Dog Butler, a giant with a cannonlike rifle; Breed, a half-breed Indian; and Kid, a grim youth who enjoys killing and shows off his prowess in one of the film's most dramatic scenes in which he kills a young cowboy (Keith Carradine). McCabe goes to the city of Bearpaw to get legal help. A lawyer (William Devane) offers his services free of charge. "When a man goes into the wilderness and with his bare hands gives birth to a small empire . . . ," says the lawyer and goes on to talk about "busting up trusts and monopolies," assuring McCabe that the corporation is a ruthless exploiter of the "small businessman . . . the soul of this great nation." The lawyer ends with a slogan for the campaign: "McCabe strikes a blow for the little man." The lawyer does nothing, of course, and McCabe goes back to face the three gunmen alone.

The beauty of the film is in the relationship between McCabe and Mrs. Miller. Nervous, pushing ahead of himself his own invented image, a gambler who makes his living making bluffs, McCabe can't find the way to express himself to Mrs. Miller. "I got poetry in me," he says. "I do. I ain't gonna put it down on paper, but I got poetry in me." Mrs. Miller, hardened by her profession, her tenderness protected by her businesslike manner and her addiction to opium, doesn't want to risk closeness—she knows what is going to happen. "You're freezin' my soul," McCabe says to her.

It is ironic that in the company of whores there is an intense sensitivity about closeness. Just as the two main characters argue over the space between them, so the camera and the viewer argue. The viewer feels like an uninvited guest compelled to sit at the farthest table. There is too much to watch, too much to listen to, and in the midst of all the details, all the information, a sad story is unfolding just beyond reach. Altman's habit of having all the actors talk at once—used to great effect in his earlier film *M*A*S*H*—creates a cluttered soundtrack in which the story of McCabe and Mrs. Miller becomes just one story lost in a dozen concomitant stories.

John Huston called *McCabe & Mrs. Miller* "the greatest forgotten movie of our time." It is a western—the final gunfight proves that beyond a doubt—but it is also a very contemporary story about people who turn away for the wrong reasons, about the inability to make ourselves understood. The muted colors of *McCabe & Mrs. Miller*, so beautiful that the film sometimes resembles a series of paintings, were the work of Vilmos Zsigmond, a Hungarian cinematographer who left Hungary and came to the United States following the 1956 uprising. (Zsigmond came with a friend, Laszlo Kovacs, also a cinematographer—and, in fact, in 1980, the two cophotographed *Close Encounters of the Third Kind*.) *McCabe & Mrs. Miller* was not the only film with photography by Zsigmond to appear in 1971: there was also **The Hired Hand** (Universal, 1971), directed by Peter Fonda, who also stars in the film. Fonda plays an errant cowboy who, in the company of his saddle buddy (Warren Oates), returns to his wife (Verna Bloom) and child after seven years of wandering. The wife takes them on as hired hands. When the other man leaves, the husband and wife slowly grow back together. But when word comes that his friend is in trouble with an outlaw (Severn Darden), the husband rides off to help him. The film, essentially about two men looking for their place in America, is reminiscent of *Easy Rider*.

"Nobody gets to be a cowboy forever."
Monte Walsh

It wasn't old age that killed the cowboy—it was bad weather and hard times. A series of terrible win-

Top: *Warren Oates (left) and Peter Fonda in* The Hired Hand *(Universal, 1971)*. Above: *Lee Marvin in* Monte Walsh *(NGP, 1970)*.

ters matched with summer droughts during the late 1880s brought an end to the open range and the life of the cowboy. The independent ranchers were forced to sell out, and big businesses—run by accountants "back East"—took over. *Monte Walsh* (NGP, 1970), directed by William A. Fraker, is an affectionate portrait of a cowboy caught by the changes. The novel by Jack Schaeffer on which the movie is based follows the life of Monte Walsh from his birth to his death; the movie deals only with the period around 1889 when, one by one, all the big ranches were bought up and all the land fenced in, leaving the cowboys without work. Monte Walsh (Lee Marvin) and his pal, Chet (Jack Palance, gleaming with a handsome charm), two middle-aged cowpunchers, come into town after a winter riding fences only to find that the ranch they worked for has been sold. They are offered a job by the foreman (Jim Davis) of another ranch, who explains that a big company named Consolidated is buying up the land. The company's accountants—"They never mention money—talk about 'capital' "—have not yet decided what to do with the land and the cattle. Monte and the other cowboys try hard to understand what is happening to their world. A diehard cowboy, Monte doesn't want to change his life: "I ain't doin' nothin' I can't do from my horse." Monte and Chet are among the lucky few to get jobs: the other cowboys head south or, after starving for a while, take up a life of crime, rustling cattle and robbing banks. Chet sees more clearly than Monte that the days of cowboying are over. He decides to marry a widow who owns a hardware store. "Mary and I are gonna get married," he says to Monte.

"How's that gonna work out, you bein' a cowboy?"

"I'm gonna be a hardware man," replies Chet.

"You gonna live in town?"

"Monte," says Chet, "you have any idea how many cowhands there were ten or fifteen years ago?" He warns Monte, "Nobody gets to be a cowboy forever."

Monte, too, has a woman he could marry, a whore named Martine (Jeanne Moreau). But Monte can't change, or can't make up his mind that he has to. He is bewildered—things are changing too fast for him. The accountants make up their corporate mind to fence in the land. Monte loses his job—the horses are sold to Colonel Wilson's Wild West Round-Up. Monte is offered a job by the owner of the Wild West show. The man wants Monte to take on the role of Texas Jack Butler (the original Texas Jack got run down by a streetcar in Chicago). Monte tries on the fringed buckskin jacket, looks at himself in a mirror, and then takes it off, saying, "I ain't spittin' on my whole life." His pride and his ongoing stories about the past are all Monte has left by the end of the movie.

Monte Walsh presents a vivid portrayal of cowboys: the scenes of cowboys working cattle are reminiscent of paintings by Charles Russell and Frederic Remington; the dialogue of the cowboys is humorously ironic, and their sincerity, honesty, and generosity shine. The villains of the film are the hard times, and the story of out-of-work cowboys becoming outlaws and towns emptying out and becoming ghost towns is based on history.

Wild Rovers (MGM, 1971), written and directed by Blake Edwards, is another film about cowboys, in this case an old one (William Holden) and a young one (Ryan O'Neal, fresh from his role in *Love Story*). Tired of cowboying and longing for a better life, the two partners decide to rob a bank (it's safer than getting married). They pull off the robbery—it nets them $36—and light out for Mexico, pursued by the sons of a ranch boss and former friend of Holden's (Karl Malden), who has become a serious businessman and doesn't want his other employees getting the wrong ideas. The film mixes pratfall humor with slow-motion scenes of death.

Like *Red River*, *The Culpepper Cattle Company* (20th Century-Fox, 1972), directed by Dick Richards, is about a cattle drive. Although many of the dangers that the trail hands encounter (in black and white) in *Red River* show up along the trail (in color) in *The Culpepper Cattle Company*, the two films are very different: in the earlier film, the cattle drive is a great event shared by heroic cowboys; in the later film, the cattle drive is a dirty job performed by antiheroic men who complain that "cowboyin' is something you do when you can't do nothing else." But *Red River* is about the men, and *The Culpepper Cattle Company* is about the cattle drive itself. The dusty cowboys in *The Culpepper Cattle Company* look alike—spit alike and cough alike—and the plot follows the cattle, not the lives of the men. The story of the film is really the viewer's experience of the cattle drive brought to life by the beautiful photography (by Alex Phillips, Jr.), the score (by Jerry Goldsmith and Tom Scott), and a remarkably sensitive soundtrack that revels in the sounds of guns being loaded and horses being saddled.

Gary Grimes (who played a lovesick teenager in *Summer of '42*) plays a 16-year-old boy who hires on to Frank Culpepper's (Billy "Green" Bush) cattle company "cause I wanna be a cowboy." He is given the job of Little Mary—cook's helper—and he suffers the indignities of being a timid novice among men who make fun of any hesitancy or meekness. Like *Will Penny* and *Monte Walsh*, the film presents the workaday world of the cowboy as a brutal routine full of dust and rudeness. The cowboys treat each other with a coarse affection. They look out for one another but also fight over minor offenses to their pride. Their work is dirty and thankless—the cattle are stampeded by rustlers, the horses are stolen, there are shootouts in sa-

186

Top: *Ryan O'Neal (left) and William Holden in* Wild Rovers *(MGM, 1971).* Center: *The cook's Little Mary (Gary Grimes, seated in center) in the middle of rude cowhands in* The Culpepper Cattle Company *(20th Century-Fox, 1972).* Above: *Gary Grimes in* The Culpepper Cattle Company.

loons, and men get buried along the trail—all for the salary of $1 a day plus "found" (food).

The film ends with a giant shootout that is not in keeping with the rest of the story. Grimes, the cook's Little Mary, decides to protect a group of religious squatters from a cruel landowner, and although they know better, the rest of the cowboys help him. Standing behind a wagon waiting for the landowner's gunmen to arrive, Grimes says to the cowboy next to him, "Bet you'd sure like to be back in Texas."

"Texas?" asks the cowboy.

"Isn't that where you're from?"

"Rhode Island."

The cowboys die defending the squatters—who then decide they can't stay "in this field of death." Grimes makes them bury his dead companions and then takes off his gun and throws it on the ground—a much different ending from that in John Wayne's contemporaneous film, *The Cowboys*.

Even before motorized vehicles replaced horses, newspapers began sponsoring endurance horse races. Such races became popular around 1880; they were still being held in 1910, and many men who found that they couldn't be cowboys forever took part in them. *Bite the Bullet* (Columbia, 1975), written and directed by Richard Brooks, is about an endurance horse race sponsored by *The Denver Post* in 1906. The prize is $2,000, and there are eight contestants in the 600-mile race: Gene Hackman and James Coburn, as two former Rough Riders; Candice Bergen; Ian Bannen; Ben Johnson, playing a character named Mister; Mario Arteaga, as a Mexican suffering from a cruel toothache and making liberal use of the then-legal heroin to ease the pain; Jan-Michael Vincent, as a dangerous young man looking to make a reputation for himself; and Robert Hoy. It is a grueling race (a newspaperman follows the participants on a motorcycle), and, as Mister says, "Who remembers a loser, or even cares? If you win, you're somebody."

Cars eventually replaced horses, and all of cowboying's roping and riding would have become a thing of the past had it not been preserved in rodeo. Some of the winners on the rodeo circuit, men like Hoot Gibson, Casey Tibbs, and Larry Mahan, have become nationally famous, but most professional rodeo riders content themselves with making a living doing something they love. Both the winners (driving cars or flying airplanes) and the losers (any way they can) get on down the road from year to year, from Calgary to Cheyenne, from San Francisco's Cow Palace to New York's Madison Square Garden, hoping to win a belt buckle at the National Finals Rodeo and enjoying the company and the beer along the way.

In 1972, there was a small stampede of rodeo films. The heroes of the films are not rodeo's big-money winners. Rather, the films are meditations on both contemporary American life and the fate of the cowboy.

Cliff Robertson made his debut as a director in *J. W. Coop* (Columbia, 1972), a film he also produced, wrote, and starred in. Described as "the guy with the greatest heart ever seen in rodeo," J. W. Coop (Robertson) gets out of prison after serving ten years (for passing a bad check and roughing up a sheriff), determined to become a champion. A lot has changed in a decade, however, and J. W.—"too lazy to work, too nervous to steal"—finds himself in a society that has only one goal: financial success. While J. W. bounces down the road from rodeo to rodeo, his competition flies in airplanes and worries about their stock portfolios. The film ambles along with J. W., meeting other rodeo riders, truck drivers, and assorted folk, their conversations providing their portraits. He even meets up with a hippie named Bean (Christina Ferrare)—her name is short for "human being."

The Honkers (United Artists, 1972), the only film directed by actor Steve Ihnat (who died shortly after it was completed), covers three days in the life of a rodeo rider (James Coburn). From dawn on the first day to dusk on the third, Coburn manages to win and then lose all the things that are important to him. He wins back the affections of his estranged wife (Lois Nettleton), only to lose her again because of his philandering ways; he tries to get to know his young son, teaching him how to steal and lie, only to lose his respect; he loses his best friend (Slim Pickens), a rodeo clown who dies saving his life. He has one special day, scoring the highest ever for bronc riding, but he ends up alone. Larry Mahan ("so good he makes it tough on everybody else") appears in the film, and Slim Pickens sings a song he composed himself, "I'm a Rodeo Cowboy."

Junior Bonner (CIN, 1972), directed by Sam Peckinpah, is about rodeo, but it is also about the contemporary West and American values. The film is a gentle portrait of a rodeo rider and his family, and like most Peckinpah films, its main concern is personal dignity. Junior Bonner (Steve McQueen) arrives in his hometown, Prescott, Arizona, to take part in the July 4 Frontier Days Rodeo. The town, like the rest of the West, has changed a lot since the days of the frontier, and Junior's brother, Curly (Joe Don Baker), is leading the way. Whereas the penniless Junior is still trying to beat the eight-second rodeo clock, Curly is "working on his first million," buying up land to make mobile-home developments. Their father, Ace (Robert Preston), a veteran rodeo rider, doesn't like the changes—he wants to go to Australia. Their mother (Ida Lupino) knows that Ace, "all dreams and sweet talk," and Junior, "as genuine as a sunrise," can't change. Money is not important to them (as Junior says, "Money's nobody's favorite"); they're working on a different kind of success. The modern-day cowboys in Prescott still go to saloons, where they drink, play cards, and get into good-natured brawls. Junior proves himself in front of his hometown crowd by riding a bull named Sunshine, a bull that had never been ridden and that had defeated him before. He uses the prize money to buy Ace a first-class ticket to Australia.

Stuart Millar, who produced *Little Big Man*, made his debut as a director with **When the Legends Die** (20th Century-Fox, 1972), a beautiful movie that uses the world of the rodeo circuit to tell a story about an Indian. Thomas Black Bull (Frederic Forrest), a young Paiute Indian schooled by his parents in "the old ways"—the songs, rituals, and traditions of his tribe— is taken to the reservation school to learn "the new ways" (his first lesson is how to diagram a sentence: "The crowd, after a thrilling finish, applauded enthusiastically the act"). Thomas Black Bull does not do well in school, but his skill with horses brings him to the attention of a former rodeo performer (Richard Widmark) who "buys" him—agrees to take custody of him until he is 21. Widmark teaches him bronc riding and takes him on the rodeo circuit. An alcoholic con, Widmark also teaches him to lie, swear, distrust, and cheat (by intentionally falling off one horse to raise the bets against him on his next ride). Widmark finally drinks himself to death, and Thomas Black Bull returns to the reservation, saying, "I've learned the new ways."

Riding Tall (MGM, 1972), directed by Patrick J. Murphy, stars Andrew Prine as Austin (his father named him after the city) Ruth, a tired bronc rider who meets a world-weary Vassar dropout named Chase (her father named her after his favorite bank) Lawrence (Gilmer McCormick). Chase has a Cadillac convertible, a fixed hatred for all authority, and a mean mouth. The two would-be lovers travel around in her car, making frequent stops so that she can smoke a joint in the nearest restroom (he thinks she has a weak bladder). Not until he gets free of the harridan does Austin (his friends call him "Aus") make a success of himself— on a horse named Last Chance. The film has so much swearing in it that when shown on television, it is very quiet—except for the censor's bleeps.

Pocket Money (NGP, 1972), directed by Stuart Rosenberg, was the first movie made by First Artists, the company formed by Paul Newman, Sidney Poitier, Barbra Streisand, and Steve McQueen. The film stars Paul Newman (Rosenberg had directed him in *Cool Hand Luke*) and Lee Marvin; its plot deals obliquely with a shady business proposition concerning cattle for the rodeo circuit. Newman, a slow-witted and gullible soul, is hired by a conniving Strother Martin to go to Mexico and buy 200 head of cattle. Newman is "assisted" by an old pal (Marvin), an inveterate con man. The two shuffle around below the border in a humor-

ous sort of way. The title song is sung by Carole King.

"The stink of slavery"
Buck and the Preacher

One other film about rodeo appeared in 1972: *Black Rodeo* (CIN), a documentary of a rodeo held on Randall's Island, New York, in September of 1971, in which all the participants were blacks. Produced, directed, and edited by Jeff Kanew, the film is narrated by Woody Strode, who discusses the importance of his role in John Ford's *Sergeant Rutledge*—the first starring role given to a black actor in a Hollywood western. There was nothing strange about a black rodeo—more than a quarter of the cowboys out West were black, and it was a black cowboy, Bill Pickett, who invented the rodeo event called steer wrestling (bulldogging). It is strange, however, that Hollywood has never accurately presented the importance of blacks on the western frontier. The cavalry that fought the Indians was made up in large part of black soldiers (the Indians dubbed them buffalo soldiers because of their hair), and between 1870 and 1890, fourteen black soldiers were awarded the Medal of Honor. The troopers riding to the rescue—bugles blaring and flags waving—were as likely to be black as white. Blacks took part in all facets of frontier life, from fur trappers and forty-niners to army scouts, farmers, and cowboys. Until the 1960s, however, blacks rarely appeared in westerns, and then only in minor "humorous" roles (such as Stepin Fetchit in *Bend of the River*). Strode's role as Sergeant Rutledge in 1960 helped pave the way for other black actors in westerns, and during the early seventies Hollywood recognized the existence of a black audience.

Not all westerns are made in the United States, of course, and both Jim Brown and Woody Strode have appeared in foreign-made films. In *El Condor* (NGP, 1970), a made-in-Spain "spaghetti"-type western directed by John Guillermin, Brown joins Lee Van Cleef as two soldiers of fortune who enlist the aid of a tribe of Apaches, led by a chief named Santana (Iron Eyes Cody), to go after a fortune in gold in a Mexican fortress named El Condor. Strode, who had gained international fame in the Italian film *Black Jesus* (1968), appears in *The Deserter* (Paramount, 1971), directed by Burt Kennedy, an international production also filmed in Spain. The cast of *The Deserter* includes John Huston, Chuck Connors, Ricardo Montalban, Brandon De Wilde, Slim Pickens, Albert Salmi, and Patrick Wayne, but the star of the film is Israeli actor Bekim Fehmiu; the plot concerns revenge wrought on a tribe of Apaches by a daring group of professionals.

Sidney Poitier directed (this was his first film as director) and stars in *Buck and the Preacher* (Columbia, 1972), a film based on the Exodusters, groups of former slaves who traveled west after the Civil War "to settle . . . where the stink of slavery ain't in the air." Poitier plays Buck, a former Union cavalryman who acts as frontier scout, guiding groups of ex-slaves west; the Preacher (Harry Belafonte) is a Bible-toting con man who tags along and becomes Buck's partner. (Belafonte learned how to chew and spit tobacco for the part. To give his teeth the proper stained appearance, he coated them with mascara and clear nail polish—he frequently has difficulty delivering his lines over the mess.) The wagon train of black pioneers has to deal with more than the usual dangers along the trail—they are pursued by a gang of white southern "labor recruiters" (led by Cameron Mitchell) who want to force the blacks to return to Louisiana. The escapades of Buck and the Preacher sometimes give the film the sense of a comedy caper, but the tone of the film—helped by a good score—is underplayed seriousness.

Bill Cosby made his film debut in *Man and Boy* (IND, 1972), directed by E. W. Swackhamer. Cosby plays a former Union cavalryman named Caleb Revers who has a wife (Gloria Foster), a son (George Spell), a fourteen-acre farm, and a horse. The horse is stolen by an aging black outlaw named Lee Christmas (Douglas Turner Ward) who is on his way to Mexico because "It's warm across the border. I hear tell the arthritis just melts away." The father and son set off on foot after the outlaw to retrieve the horse.

Man and Boy is sometimes referred to as a "black-sploitation" film, a film made with black actors for

Opposite: *Lee Marvin (left) and Paul Newman on the road in* Pocket Money *(NGP, 1972).* Above: *Harry Belafonte (left) and Sidney Poitier in* Buck and the Preacher *(Columbia, 1972).*

black audiences. The early seventies saw a slew of such films, among them *Shaft* (1971), *Shaft's Big Score* (1972), and *Super Fly* (1972). The most famous "black-sploitation" westerns were two films starring Fred Williamson and D'Urville Martin. The fame of the films is due in large part to their titles: *The Legend of Nigger Charley* and *The Soul of Nigger Charley*. After more than forty years of trying to eradicate the word *nigger* from the American vocabulary, southerners, in particular, were not pleased to see it on billboards. When *The Legend of Nigger Charley* was first released in Atlanta, Georgia, many local newspapers altered the title to *The Legend of Black Charley*.

Like Jim Brown, who smashed numerous National Football League records during his nine seasons with the Cleveland Browns, Fred Williamson played professional football for a decade before making his film debut in *M*A*S*H*. In *The Legend of Nigger Charley* (Paramount, 1972), directed by Martin Goldman (who co-wrote the screenplay with Larry G. Spangler), Williamson plays a slave who escapes from a Virginia plantation with two other slaves (one of whom is D'Urville Martin). They make their way west, pursued by a nasty gang of professional slave catchers. Williamson makes the transition from slave to lethal gunfighter smoothly enough and even finds the time to protect a white settler and his half-breed wife and children from another gang of white hoodlums.

The Soul of Nigger Charley (Paramount, 1973), written and directed by Spangler, stars Williamson and Martin and concerns their battles out West with ex-Confederate soldiers.

Charley One-Eye (Paramount, 1973), directed by British director Don Chaffey and produced by David Frost, has nothing to do with the two previous films. It features Richard Roundtree, who became an instant star in *Shaft*, as an army deserter pursued by a white bounty hunter.

Fred Williamson produced, directed, wrote, and stars in *Adios, Amigo* (IND, 1976), but it is Richard Pryor who is forever delivering the phrase that gives the film its title. Williamson plays an honest rancher who loses his spread to corrupt whites. He is arrested and sent off to prison in a stagecoach. Pryor holds up the stage, freeing Williamson. Prison would have been safer for Williamson than traveling with Pryor, whose con-man schemes get them both into no end of trouble. Pryor always manages to escape at the last minute, leaving Williamson in the worst possible situation with the flip farewell, *"Adios, amigo."* The film is remarkable for its slow-paced horse chases.

Perhaps the most "realistic" depiction of blacks in the West appears in *McCabe & Mrs. Miller*. A sophisticated, well-dressed black couple arrives in Presbyterian Church. They are ignored. They play an important part in putting out the fire in the church, but no one

190

speaks to them. Relegated to the background, they are not permitted to become members of the town, but must exist as peripheral citizens.

"Maybe this isn't the way it was . . . it's the way it should have been."

The Life and Times of Judge Roy Bean

As in all previous decades, the old West on film during the seventies reflected the prevailing attitudes of Americans, and the claims of many westerns made during the seventies that they present the West "as it really was" are unfounded. Thanks to the salesmanship of dime-novel authors and Wild West show promoters, the facts of the old West are inextricably blended with the legends of the old West, leaving filmmakers free to interpret the West according to their own lights. It is not surprising that the old West as seen through the eyes of the 1970s was the scene of urban blight, racism, sexism, imperialism, homosexuality, drug addiction, wanton violence, and loneliness. The only western heroes during the seventies were the mountain men in children's movies who got away from it all and befriended bears; everyone else out West was tainted, a progenitor, through degeneracy, of modern despair.

Where there were horses, there must have been horseshit. The streets of Tombstone (actually Almeria, Spain) in *Doc* (United Artists, 1971), directed by Frank Perry, are therefore littered with manure. Where there were politics, there must have been corruption: *Doc* "demythologizes" the story of Doc Holliday (Stacy Keach), Wyatt Earp (Harris Yulin), and the gunfight at the O.K. Corral, revealing the entire affair to have been the result of Earp's sleazy opportunism. Earp is running for sheriff (he wants the post because it offers opportunities for graft) on a law-and-order ticket;

Above: *D'Urville Martin (left) and Fred Williamson in* The Soul of Nigger Charley *(Paramount, 1973). Opposite:* *Kris Kristofferson (on floor) and James Coburn in* Pat Garrett and Billy the Kid *(MGM, 1973).*

when Johnny Ringo holds up a stagecoach, Earp offers a reward to Ike Clanton (Mike Whitney) and his family if they'll bring in Ringo and allow Earp to claim credit for nabbing him; the deal falls through, and Earp frames the Clantons for the holdup, provoking them into the famous shootout. Meanwhile, the consumptive, opium-puffing Doc and Kate Elder (Faye Dunaway) arrive in Tombstone. She hires on at the local bordello; he sets himself up as a gambler, using his spare time to teach Ike Clanton's nephew, The Kid (played by Denver John Collins, singer Judy Collins's younger brother), how to shoot. Doc becomes a friend of Wyatt's (there are implications of homosexuality in their rapport) and joins him for the gunfight.

Perry, whose previous films included *Diary of a Mad Housewife* and *David and Lisa*, peopled his fictional Tombstone with interesting faces, many of which he found in New York City. A bartender in the film is played by an official from Mayor John Lindsay's administration; and Mr. Clum, the editor of *The*

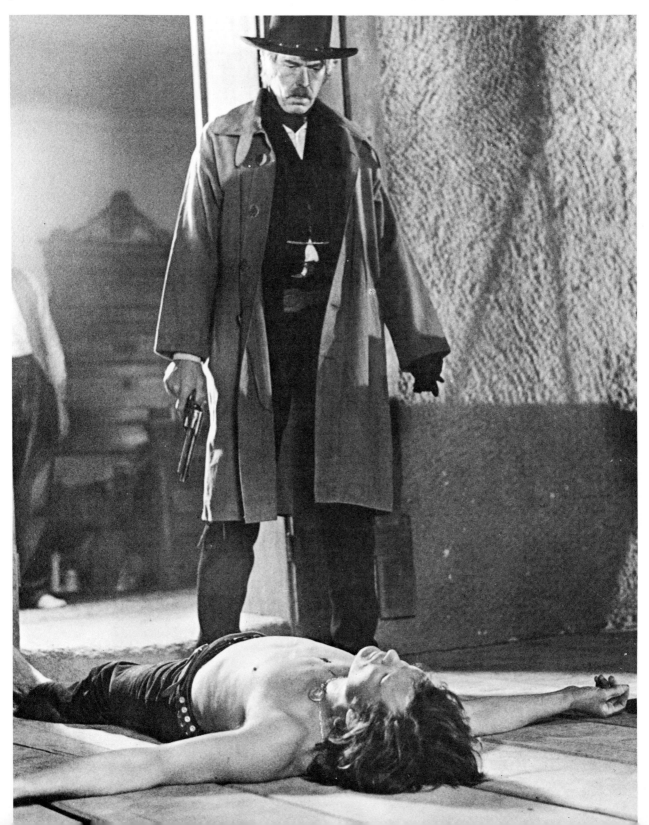

Tombstone Epitaph, is played by Dan Greenburg, author of *How to Be a Jewish Mother*. Greenburg was sitting next to Perry at a dinner party and was surprised to hear Perry exclaim, "That face—I've got to have that face in my film."

With its grubby anti-idealism and cynical politics, *Doc* pleased some reviewers. "Our mythic heroes were sick, dirty, violent, decadent, and otherwise far-from-perfect creatures. So that's why the nation's values are screwed up," stated one. Another wrote: "Implicitly, even Vietnam has its roots in the blood-drenched turf of the O.K. Corral."

That "blood-drenched turf" had been visited many times before, in such films as *Law and Order, My Darling Clementine, Gunfight at the O.K. Corral*, and *Hour of the Gun*. The story of Judge Roy Bean, "the law west of the Pecos," had been told before, too, in *The Westerner*. **The Life and Times of Judge Roy Bean** (NGP, 1972), directed by John Huston, begins with the statement, "Maybe this isn't the way it was . . . it's the way it should have been." The notorious hanging judge is played by Paul Newman ("I know the law, since I have spent my entire life in its flagrant disregard"), and his murderous antics are presented as comical. The film is episodic and full of cameo appearances. Stacy Keach appears as an albino outlaw named Bad Bob; Huston, the director, appears as a mountain man named (what else?) Grizzly Adams, who is accompanied by a pet bear named Zach (played by a bear named Bruno). Zach, who drinks beer, becomes a fixture in Bean's saloon. Bean's infatuation with Lily Langtry is not forgotten: he writes her fan letters and subscribes to the *New York Times* so that he can read about her career. Langtry herself is played by Ava Gardner, who hadn't appeared in an American film for more than seven years.

The screenplay for *The Life and Times of Judge Roy Bean* was written by John Milius, who also wrote the screenplay for **Jeremiah Johnson** (Warner Brothers, 1972), directed by Sydney Pollack. Like *The Life and Times of Judge Roy Bean, Jeremiah Johnson* is based on a historical character. Milius used two sources for the screenplay: *Mountain Man*, a historical novel by Vardis Fisher, and "Crow Killer," a short nonfiction biography by Raymond W. Thorp and Robert Bunker. Better known as "Liver-Eating" Johnson—a nickname based on the belief that he cut out and ate the livers of more than 100 Crow Indians—Jeremiah Johnson was a fearsome mountain man who managed to become a legend in his own time. The film does not dwell on Johnson's savage appetites, but concerns itself with the environment—ecology—and man's relationship with nature. Robert Redford stars in the title role of a man who, disgusted with civilization, becomes a mountain man in the Rockies. He meets an old trapper named Griz (Will Geer) and marries an Indian (Allyn

Mick Jagger in Ned Kelly *(United Artists, 1970).*

Ann McLerie). He is called upon by the cavalry to help locate a lost convoy, and to do so he must pass through a sacred Crow burial ground. He does this against his will and returns home to find his family slaughtered. He seeks revenge, killing all the Crows he can find. In the end, he makes peace with the Indians and becomes a legend: "Some say he's dead . . . some say he never will be."

Jeremiah Johnson was very popular. It inspired a class of seventh graders in Lancaster, California, to do research on Johnson, and they discovered that when he died, in 1900, he was buried in a veteran's cemetery in Los Angeles near the San Diego Freeway. Johnson had expressed the wish that he be buried in the mountains, and the students eventually saw his wish fulfilled. His body was dug up and flown to Wyoming, where it was buried, with Robert Redford present at the ceremony.

The screenwriters for *Bonnie and Clyde*, David Newman and Robert Benton, wrote the screenplay for **There Was a Crooked Man** (Warner Brothers, 1970), the first western directed by Joseph L. Mankiewicz. The film stars Kirk Douglas as Paris Pitman, Jr., a grinning outlaw who—along with a group of very peculiar characters—is thrown into a territorial prison run by a reform warden (Henry Fonda). Prisoner Pitman and the warden end up together, outside the walls of the prison, looking for a stash of loot. The film is not remarkable (although a few people claim to be offended by its surprise ending), but its seedy characters and grimy violence anticipate another film written by Newman and Benton—**Bad Company** (Paramount, 1972), which Benton directed.

Like *Bonnie and Clyde, Bad Company* is about outlaws, in this case the making of outlaws. Drew Dixon (Barry Brown) flees his family's home in Ohio to escape conscription into the Union Army (his brother has already been killed at Chickamauga.) In St. Joseph, Missouri, he meets Jake Rumsey (Jeff Bridges), leader of a gang of teenagers. The six draft dodgers set off for the West, where they are sure things will be better. Things aren't. The West they travel through is unlike the West usually depicted in westerns—it is barren and dusty, peopled by wicked homesteaders, vicious outlaws, and disillusioned pioneers returning to the East (one of whom offers the youths the sexual favors of his wife for $1 apiece). The violence is senseless and random—the youngest of the group is shot dead in the act of swiping a pie that has been left to cool on a windowsill. The original innocence of the boys—Drew, a pious and morally upright lad, reads them passages of *Jane Eyre* by the light of a campfire—is eventually destroyed, as they are forced to steal to stay alive. Only two of them, Drew and Jake, survive, and the film ends as they are about to pull off their first robbery.

Was Billy the Kid born mean or did bad company and squalid surroundings make him so bad? Michael J. Pollard, who first came to national attention in *Bonnie and Clyde*, stars in *Dirty Little Billy* (Columbia, 1972), directed by Stan Dragoti, a humorous version of the story of Billy the Kid, according to which Billy was a species of animate smudge. Ads for the film declared that "Billy the Kid was a Punk."

In 1972, being a "punk" had nothing to do with playing mean rock-and-roll music, but the idea of identifying a nineteenth-century rebellious youth who became an outlaw with a twentieth-century rebellious youth who became a rock star had already led to *Ned Kelly* (United Artists, 1970), a British film directed by Tony Richardson. Ned Kelly, a "wild colonial boy," was an Australian outlaw during the 1800s. (*The Story of the Kelly Gang*, made in 1906, was Australia's first feature film.) The son of an Irishman deported to Australia for stealing two pigs, Ned Kelly tried to lead a lawful life—he even opened a sawmill. But he and his two brothers just couldn't keep out of trouble; circumstances were against them. They became horse thieves, graduating to more serious robberies. They sometimes donned armor, including steel helmets that covered their faces, to pull off their heists. Surrounded in a saloon, Ned's brothers committed suicide; he surrendered and was hanged. The star of the film version of Ned Kelly's life is the Rolling Stones's Mick Jagger.

The star of *Bobbie Jo and the Outlaw* (AIP, 1976), directed by Mark L. Lester, is Marjoe Gortner, the famous child evangelist who had already played himself in *Marjoe* (1972), an Oscar-winning documentary about his life. In *Bobbie Jo and the Outlaw*, he plays "the outlaw" (Lynda Carter plays Bobbie Jo) a youthful criminal in contemporary New Mexico who decides he is Billy the Kid and goes on a killing spree accompanied by a bevy of female groupies.

The evangelical aspects of outlawry—or at least of Jesse James—are of importance in *The Great Northfield Minnesota Raid* (Universal, 1972), written and directed by Philip Kaufman. The film is another retelling of the story of the James gang and their ill-fated raid on the town of Northfield, Minnesota, during which the townspeople opened fire on the outlaws. True to the tradition of the seventies, the film attempts to debunk the myth of Jesse James. In this film, Jesse (Robert Duvall) is no Robin Hood hero—he is murderously neurotic. He believes his robberies are guerilla warfare against the wicked northerners; led by divine guidance, he gets his ideas in visions—or in outhouses. The film begins with Jesse and Frank (John Pearce) sitting together in a privy. The toilet paper is not a Sears catalog but a brochure from the Northfield bank.

As in many films of the seventies, the plot of *The Great Northfield Minnesota Raid* is frequently lost in the film's determination to accurately depict the period, a period of great national change. The symbols of modernism include a steam-driven tractor reminiscent of the steam-driven car in *McCabe & Mrs. Miller*; a bank vault with a time lock; and baseball. Baseball made a sudden appearance in westerns during the seventies, and there are games in *Ulzana's Raid* and *Posse*. In *The Great Northfield Minnesota Raid*, Cole Younger (Cliff Robertson) happens upon a game being played in Northfield. "It's the new national pastime," explains one of the townspeople. Younger blasts the baseball with his shotgun. "Our national pastime is shooting and always will be," he says.

Times changed, of course, and the men for whom shooting was "a national pastime" had to make way for the modern America of machines and corporations. That change—"the end of the West"—is the common theme of most of Sam Peckinpah's films, and *Pat Garrett and Billy the Kid* (MGM, 1973) may be its clearest statement. At one point in the film, Garrett (James Coburn) says to Billy (Kris Kristofferson), "Times are changing, Bill." Billy coolly replies, "Times maybe, but not me."

Rudolph Wurlitzer is credited with writing the screenplay for the film, but Peckinpah finally had a chance to make use of material about Billy the Kid he had assembled—material that had been used in Marlon Brando's *One-Eyed Jacks*—and *Pat Garrett and Billy the Kid* is not a simple retelling of the story of the lawman who chased down and killed his former friend, the outlaw Billy the Kid. In Peckinpah's hands, the chase becomes the future chasing down the past, the old ways being replaced by the new. The new ways are the impersonal corporation and political corrup-

Above and right: *Paul Newman as Judge Roy Bean in* The Life and Times of Judge Roy Bean *(NGP, 1972).*

tion; the old ways are lawlessness and defiant individualism. Even though he seems older and more sophisticated than the traditional Billy the Kid, Kristofferson makes a reasonable Billy because his career as both a singer and an actor identify him with rebellion. He has as a sidekick another symbol of youthful rebelliousness, Bob Dylan, playing a character named Alias. (When Garrett asks him who he is, Alias responds, "That's a good question.") The presence of Dylan (his screen debut) and the use of Dylan's songs for the musical score further clarify the oppositions in the film.

"This country's getting old," says Garrett. The truth is that he is getting old. He sees the changes that are coming, and rather than fight them, he sells out to the Establishment, to the Santa Fe business interests that are taking over and that have no room for men who have "too much play in them," the wild ones like Billy. Garrett is hired to go after his old friend; he hunts him down and finally kills him. Like all of Peckinpah's films, *Pat Garrett and Billy the Kid* was chopped up before its release—nearly sixteen minutes were cut—and the deleted portions include an important prologue and epilogue. Some of the cut scenes were restored to the film when it was shown on television, but the prologue and epilogue are gone. They are important because they show the murder of Garrett, nearly twenty years after he killed Billy—a murder paid for by the same business interests that hired him to kill Billy.

That Garrett, like Billy, was part of an old order is presented in a scene that dramatically relates the violence of the West. Garrett, camped for the night on the bank of a river, hears gunfire and looks up to see a raft coming down the river. On the raft is a man shooting at a bottle floating in the water. Garrett shoots at the bottle. The man looks at Garrett and aims his rifle at him. Garrett aims back, and the two stare at each other as the raft moves along with the current. The possibility of a violent death—for no apparent reason—is clear.

The cast for *Pat Garrett and Billy the Kid* includes Jason Robards, Jr., Barry Sullivan, Chill Wills, Slim Pickens, Jack Elam—a host of characters recognizable from other westerns—even Peckinpah himself, who appears near the end to push Garrett along toward the inevitable. "You finally figured it out," he says to Garrett. "Well, go on, get it over with." Even with all its missing scenes, *Pat Garrett and Billy the Kid* is an interesting movie—like all of Peckinpah's westerns, it is clear and hard and more than a little mean.

In 1974, in an article in *The New Yorker*, Pauline Kael declared that westerns were dead. In 1974 and 1975 it did seem that way, but 1976 saw an explosion of westerns. For America's Bicentennial celebration, there were no films glorifying the American Revolution (American filmmakers have made only ten films about

the Revolution—it is not a popular subject), but there were more than a dozen westerns, including John Wayne's last film (*The Shootist*) and Joel McCrea's last film (*Mustang Country*). The only financially profitable western was Clint Eastwood's *The Outlaw Josey Wales*; among the horde of forgotten westerns was *Buffalo Bill and the Indians, or: Sitting Bull's History Lesson* (United Artists, 1976), directed by Robert Altman.

"I'm going to Cody-fy the world," declares Nate Salsbury (Joel Grey), Buffalo Bill's business manager in *Buffalo Bill and the Indians*, and the film implies that a whole lot of truth got lost when the West was "Cody-fied." As one character states, "Truth is whatever gets the most applause," and crowds applaud spectacles, particularly spectacles that reinforce the crowd's distorted opinions. The action of the film takes place at Buffalo Bill's winter camp sometime in the 1880s (the film was shot in Alberta, Canada); the story of the film, based on Arthur Kopit's 1969 Broadway play *Indians*, involves encounters between Buffalo Bill (Paul Newman) and Sitting Bull (Frank Kaquitts). The Indian is a figure of true heroism; Cody, with his long, flowing hair and his colorful beard, is a hollow showman perpetrating a vicious myth. Present at these encounters and in other random scenes are a host of characters, including Ned Buntline (Burt Lancaster), the dime-novel author who brought Cody to fame; and Annie Oakley (Geraldine Chaplin), the crackshot artist who tirelessly blasts cigars out of the mouth of her husband (John Considine). The high point of the film is a special nighttime performance put on by the troupe for a visiting President Grover Cleveland (Pat McCormick), who happily declares of Cody, "It's a man like that that made this country what it is today." The president's traveling speechwriter is played by author E. L. Doctorow (at the time Altman and Doctorow had been discussing the film version of Doctorow's *Ragtime*, a project eventually filmed by Milos Forman in 1981).

Very much like a history lesson, *Buffalo Bill and the Indians* was an oddly suitable film for the Bicentennial, teaching as it does that America was made into what it is today by speechwriters, dime novelists, and eager press agents: the myth of our history that we applaud sometimes has little to do with the true history of the nation.

Along with Buffalo Bill and Sitting Bull, 1976 saw a film about Wild Bill Hickok and Crazy Horse. In *The White Buffalo* (United Artists, 1976), directed by J. Lee Thompson, Hickok (Charles Bronson) suffers from a venereal infection that gives rise to delirious nightmares in which he is attacked by a ferocious albino buffalo. Deciding that he must kill the animal, he leaves Buffalo Bill Cody's Wild West show in New York and heads west, assuming the alias of James Otis. Although he is told that such white buffalo are extinct, one at-

tacks and destroys an Indian village, killing the daughter of chief Crazy Horse. Crazy Horse is told that his daughter's spirit cannot enter the other world until her dead body is wrapped in the hide of the white buffalo. To succeed in his hunt for the buffalo, Crazy Horse must give up his title and travel under the name Worm. Eventually, the two aliased hunters join forces and confront the enormous white beast.

A lot of *The White Buffalo* takes place in the snow, with all the attendant avalanches and blinding blizzards. There is a lot of snow in another Charles Bronson western released in 1976: *Breakheart Pass* (United Artists, 1976), directed by Tom Gries. "There's a murderer amongst us," grimly announces one of the characters in the film. That there should be a murderer about is no surprise, for the full title of the film is *Alistair MacLean's Breakheart Pass*—the screenplay for the film was written by the famous British writer of thrillers. *Breakheart Pass* was MacLean's first western, and it resembles *Murder on the Orient Express* (by Agatha Christie) more than any western. Most of the picture takes place on a train passing through snowy mountains, and various characters disappear from the train or are found dead, leading to the remarkable conclusion that there is a murderer on board. The train is loaded with crates of medicine being taken to a small fort near a place called Breakheart Pass, where there has been an outbreak of diphtheria; government undercover agent Charles Bronson is on the train in search of a group of gunrunners. The second-unit direction by Yakima Canutt is exciting.

The female lead in *Breakheart Pass* is played by Jill Ireland. Bronson and Ireland, husband and wife in real life, starred together in another film in 1976—their eleventh film together—*From Noon Till Three* (United Artists, 1976), written and directed by Pulitzer Prize-winning playwright Frank D. Gilroy. Like *Buffalo Bill and the Indians*, *From Noon Till Three* is a humorous version of the creation of a western legend. Graham Dorsey (Bronson), an aimless drifter, joins an outlaw gang. He rides off with the gang to pull a bank job, but his horse breaks a leg, and he is left behind at a house on the outskirts of town. The house is run by an attractive widow (Ireland), and Dorsey spends a pleasant three hours seducing her. Meanwhile, his compatriots don't do well in their robbery attempt—one is killed and the other two are caught. Dorsey makes his getaway wearing clothes belonging to the widow's dead husband. He later changes clothes with a dentist, who is assumed to be the outlaw and is shot dead. The widow creates a very romantic story about her three-hour love affair with the "dead" outlaw. Her love story becomes the subject of plays and stories—there is even a song. When the very-much-alive outlaw reappears, no one—not even the widow, who has come to believe her fabulous tales of a tall, handsome stranger—believes he is who he claims to be.

Top: *Charles Bronson (that's Ben Johnson in the snow) in* Breakheart Pass *(United Artists, 1976).* Above: *Burt Lancaster suffering torture in* Valdez Is Coming *(United Artists, 1971).*

"Their probable intention is to burn, maim, torture, and kill."

Ulzana's Raid

In *Valdez Is Coming* (United Artists, 1971), directed by Edwin Sherin, Burt Lancaster plays a Mexican-American lawman, a former cavalry scout ("I used to chase Indians before I knew better") who makes his living riding shotgun for a stageline. When he kills an innocent black man as the result of a cruel cattleman's game (Jon Cypher), he tries to collect money for the man's Indian widow. The result of his efforts is that he is tortured by the cattleman's henchmen. The aging lawman dons his old uniform, loads his old buffalo gun, and sets off, pursued by the gunmen. He kills them off one at a time, exacting revenge for racial injustice.

In *Ulzana's Raid* (Universal, 1972), directed by Robert Aldrich, Lancaster plays an old cavalry scout named Mr. McIntosh, a "willful, opinionated man with contempt for all discipline." Unlike *Little Big Man* and *Soldier Blue*, in which the Indians are presented as morally superior to the white cavalrymen, *Ulzana's Raid* portrays both sides as equally sadistic (the Indians may be a little more "moral" because what they do—including cutting out a man's heart and playing catch with it—is in keeping with their religion, whereas the barbarities committed by the cavalrymen go against their avowed Christianity). The film begins with a baseball game played by cavalry troopers, the pitches being called by a young lieutenant named DeBuin (Bruce Davison). The game is interrupted by news that Ulzana (Joaquin Martinez) has left the reservation with nine other Apache warriors. When one of the officers asks what the Indians' probable intention is, Mr. McIntosh says, "Their probable intention is to burn, maim, torture, and kill." The sage old scout is correct: in the film the Apache do all those things—plus rape—savagely and repeatedly. Lieutenant DeBuin, McIntosh, an Apache scout named Ke-Ni-Tay (Jorge Luke), and a cavalry force are sent out after Ulzana. They are not expected to have much luck. As one sergeant remarks, "You ain't gonna see too much of him except dead things," and, indeed, the Apache kill almost everything they come across. The soldiers chasing the Apache are not very heroic—they, too, torture and disfigure their enemies. They also refuse to help the settlers they are supposed to protect. When word comes that Ulzana has escaped, the families inside the fort request cavalry escorts home. They are refused. In one of the film's most dramatic scenes, a woman and boy riding on a wagon are chased by Apaches. The soldier riding with them at first rides away, but when he hears the woman's pleas for help, he rides back to the wagon, takes out his pistol, and shoots her. He then commits suicide.

The moral argument between the two sides is battled out by two members of the cavalry force. The leader of the group, the inexperienced Lieutenant DeBuin, son of a minister who believed it was possible to be both a soldier and a Christian, cannot understand the cruelties wrought by the Apache. Ke-Ni-Tay explains to him that "Each man that dies, the man who kills him takes his power. Here in this land, man must have power. Ulzana is a long time in the agency. His power is very thin." Lieutenant DeBuin also cannot understand the cruelties wrought by the Christian soldiers. Mr. McIntosh responds to that. "What bothers you, Lieutenant, is you don't like to think of white men behaving like Indians. Kind of confuses the issue, don't it?" The cruel Ulzana actually operates very much like the cavalry—he even uses binoculars, and one of his warriors carries a bugle. McIntosh's opinion of the whole thing is that "Ain't no one of us right."

Ulzana's Raid was the last major western about Indians to date. Indians were no longer the enemy; the enemy was corrupt society, with its weak laws, racism, and bigotry. *Chato's Land* (United Artists, 1972), directed by Michael Winner, begins with Pardon Chato (Charles Bronson) provoked into a fight by a white sheriff. The lawman taunts Chato, calling him a "redskin nigger." Chato kills the sheriff and flees. The local saloon keeper (Jack Palance), a former Confederate cavalryman eager for action, organizes a thirteen-man posse, the members of which are pleased to have the excuse to kill an Indian. The posse captures Chato's wife and son. They kill the son, rape the wife, and then stake her out, naked, in the desert. Chato rescues her and, becoming the hunter rather than the hunted,

Joaquin Martinez (right) as Ulzana and Henry Camarge as his son in Ulzana's Raid *(Universal, 1972).*

pursues the posse into the desert, killing them off, carefully, one by one.

Director Michael Winner and star Charles Bronson repeated the basic scenario of *Chato's Land* in *Death Wish* (1974), in which Bronson, seeking revenge for the rape and murder of his wife and the rape of his daughter, takes it upon himself to personally exterminate New York City's hoodlums. Fittingly, Bronson learns his prowess with handguns while on a business trip out West.

Clint Eastwood had already made the transition from the West to the streets of New York in *Coogan's Bluff* (1968), and in 1971 he gave vigilantism a proud name in *Dirty Harry*. The ease with which Eastwood could exchange his city clothes and Magnum .44 for a poncho and Colt provides a clue to understanding some of the westerns of the seventies. Outlaws become "criminals," and crime becomes a personal matter.

The Revengers (NGP, 1972), directed by Daniel Mann, stars William Holden as a well-to-do rancher whose family is slaughtered by a gang of horse-stealing renegade Indians led by two white men. The law can do nothing—the renegades have crossed the border into Mexico—so Holden sets out for revenge alone. He realizes he needs help, however, and recruits six convicts—including Woody Strode and Ernest Borgnine—from a Mexican prison. The seven (thanks to *The Magnificent Seven*, always an important number in groups of gunmen) revengers kill one of the two white men. Holden is wounded (by one of his recruited prisoners), putting a temporary end to the chase for the other man. He is brought back to health by an Irish nurse (Susan Hayward, in her last film), who teaches Holden that "You live in your heart, and you've got to be careful what you put in your heart." Holden eventually decides that he doesn't want any "worms" (revenge) in his heart.

There is a different lesson to learn in *The Deadly Trackers* (Warner Brothers, 1973), directed by Barry Shear. Richard Harris stars as the peace-loving sheriff of Santa Rosa. He has never shot anyone and doesn't wear a gun—he has his own ways of dealing with violence. When a group of outlaws tries to rob the local bank, Harris nearly succeeds in capturing them all without firing a shot. But the leader of the gang (Rod Taylor) gets hold of the sheriff's young son, and the lawman—not wanting to risk any gunplay—allows the outlaws to leave town. When the wicked Taylor kills the sheriff's wife as she tries to save her son, and then the son himself, the sheriff becomes a vicious killer, intent on revenge. The outlaws are outrageously disgusting: their leader enjoys recounting the story of how he killed his own father; and one of them has, in place of an amputated hand, a large piece of a railroad tie (he uses it for smashing open watermelons and other men's skulls). The outlaws are so crude they even dis-

dain the use of flatwear when they eat, preferring to push food into their mouths with dripping fingers. These ill-mannered murderers cross the border into Mexico; the sheriff follows and becomes involved with a Mexican lawman (Al Lettieri) who is tracking the same bunch. The Mexican wants to bring the villains in alive—he has a witness to one of their crimes and wants to try the criminals in a court of law. Harris is no longer interested in such legalities; he wants to kill. Alternately together and apart, the two bickering lawmen pursue the hoodlums. Each time the two groups meet, the result is buckets of blood. The violence in the film is inexcusable, and the ending of the film—in which the moral is delivered with one last gun blast—is obnoxious.

The film was originally going to be called *Riata*; Samuel Fuller began directing it in Spain. Fuller was dropped, the film was relocated to Mexico, and Shear took over the direction. When Fuller and Lukas Heller—who wrote the screenplay—saw the film, they wanted their names removed from the credits, and Fuller's was; Fred Steiner—who wrote the musical score—wanted his name removed even before the first showing, and it was. The producer of the film, Fouad Said, and director Shear were not new to movies about crossing borders to relish in absurd violence—the year before they had created *Across 110th Street*.

The notion that only personal revenge inspires the dedicated pursuit of criminals is refuted, in a sense, in another film directed by Michael Winner. In *Lawman* (United Artists, 1970), Burt Lancaster plays a law officer named Jarred Maddox, a man thoroughly devoted to his duty. Hunting seven men who accidentally killed an old man during a drunken binge, Maddox rides into a strange town and finds that the men he is after all work for the local rancher, Vincent Bronson (Lee J. Cobb). Even when he has the entire town against him, the lawman persists in his efforts to bring in the culprits. Amazed at the man's determination, a storekeeper figures that it must be a matter of personal vengeance. "Kin?" he inquires. "No," responds Maddox, "just a lawman."

Most films are more personal. In *Shoot Out* (Universal, 1971), Gregory Peck plays an ex-convict named Clay Lomax seeking revenge on his former partner, who has betrayed him. The film was made by the same producer (Hal Wallis), director (Henry Hathaway), and screenwriter (Marguerite Roberts) who created *True Grit*, and, sure enough, before long Peck is teamed up with a young girl (Dawn Lyn, who had made her film debut as Elliott Gould's daughter in *I Love My Wife* (1970) and had appeared as a regular on television's "My Three Sons"). Peck thinks the girl may be his daughter; she prefers horses to people. Roberts based the screenplay on a novel, *The Lone Cowboy*, by Will James.

In *Santee* (IND, 1973), directed by Gary Nelson, Glenn Ford plays an aging bounty hunter seeking revenge for the murder of his son. He kills an outlaw and adopts the outlaw's son (Michael Burns). Jay Silverheels is on hand to take care of the horses. For some reason, the music for the film includes a song by Paul Revere and the Raiders.

Personal revenge provides the basic plot of *The Last Hard Men* (20th Century-Fox, 1976), directed by Andrew V. McLaglen, but in this film it is an outlaw who is seeking revenge on a retired lawman. Zach Provo (James Coburn) escapes from a Yuma prison chain gang and with an entourage of cronies sets out to get revenge on a lawman named Sam Burgade (Charlton Heston). It was Burgade who put Provo in prison, and Provo blames Burgade for the death of his young Navajo wife. But that was a long time ago. The film takes place in Arizona in 1909—Provo was imprisoned during the previous century, and the country has changed. There are cars and telephones (the first time Provo hears one ring, he is startled and opens fire on it), and in place of cattle drives there are refrigerated train cars packed with frozen meat. The retired lawman ("I quit the law because I thought it was over"), wearing the suit and bowler of a modern man, comes out of retirement to deal with his former enemy. His reason for returning to the violent ways of the past is simple: "Because I never knew how to do anything else." Provo captures Burgade's daughter (Barbara Hershey), lets his men molest her, and provokes a final shootout.

One of the strangest westerns of the seventies is a British-made film called *Hannie Caulder* (Paramount, 1972). The film was directed by Burt Kennedy, who co-wrote the screenplay with David Haft under the single pseudonym Z. X. Jones. *Hannie Caulder* is a comic fairy tale—its title sounds like an incantation and some of its plot elements are vaguely Arthurian—and although it is about revenge, its real concern is the price paid by the revenger. The film begins with the gory, comical, but thoroughly unsuccessful attempt by the three Clemens brothers (Jack Elam, Ernest Borgnine, and Strother Martin) to rob a bank. The three outlandishly demented villains manage to escape with their lives. They stop at a stage relay station to steal some horses and end up killing the owner, Jim Caulder, and raping his wife, Hannie (Raquel Welch). Tortured by nightmare visions in which she relives her terrible experience, Hannie vows revenge on the Clemenses. She meets an old bounty hunter named Thomas Luther Price (Robert Culp), a philosophical man with a gray beard and rimless glasses. Her mentor takes her to Mexico, where a special gun is made for her by a master gunsmith named Bailey (Christopher Lee). When the barrel of the gun is test-fired, a mysterious horseman appears, a lone gunfighter dressed in black who never utters a word (the part was played by Stephen Boyd; he is not given screen credit). Holding classes by the sea, Price, sage graybeard, instructs Hannie in the use of her weapon. (Young Max Sand in *Nevada Smith*, also thirsting for revenge, was schooled in gunplay by a wise tutor, but not at the beach.) Price is eventually killed by one of the Clemenses, but Hannie is rarely alone—each time she is about to use her gun, the phantom rider materializes. Is he there to protect her? Or is he there to collect from her the price for her lethal knowledge? (As Price has warned her, "Win or lose, you lose, Hannie Caulder.") Even viewers intrigued by the symbolism of the film may find themselves distracted by Hannie's outfit: above her tight, shrink-to-fit pants she wears only a loose-fitting poncho. Slight breezes and her own body movements frequently promise revelations.

Men, women, and guns

Just as the incidence of rape out West increased during the seventies, the number of wayward wives increased. Sexual freedom has no traditional place in the old West, but attempts to establish it in modern America had effects on westerns. In *Shane*, the attraction of Mrs. Starrett to the gunfighter Shane is subtly underplayed—she would never leave her home. Women have more options in the westerns of the seventies, but in the traditional manner, they still "find themselves" through a man's love. They get to leave home, but they seldom go far alone.

The Hunting Party (United Artists, 1971), directed by Don Medford, is about a wealthy cattleman named Brand Ruger (Gene Hackman), a cruel and impotent man whose wife, Melissa (Candice Bergen), is unhappy. He leaves her to go on a hunting trip with four

Left to right: Strother Martin, Raquel Welch, Ernest Borgnine, and Jack Elam—Welch is Hannie Caulder *(Paramount, 1972), and the three men are in trouble.*

Opposite: *Richard Romancito, John Wayne, and Katharine Hepburn in* Rooster Cogburn *(Universal, 1975).*

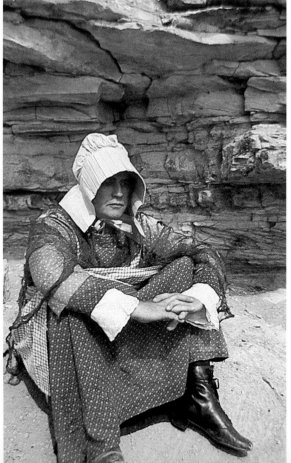

Above: The Missouri Breaks
(United Artists, 1976). Left:
Marlon Brando in The Missouri
Breaks. Opposite top: *Peter
Fonda and Warren Oates in*
The Hired Hand *(Universal, 1971)*.
Opposite bottom: The Great
Northfield Minnesota Raid
(Universal, 1972).

Above: McCabe & Mrs. Miller *(Warner Brothers, 1971)*. Opposite top
left: *Robert Redford in* Jeremiah Johnson *(Warner Brothers, 1973)*.
Opposite top right: *Bob Dylan in* Pat Garrett and Billy the Kid *(MGM, 1973)*.
Opposite bottom *(left to right)*: *David, Keith, and
Robert Carradine; Nicholas and Christopher Guest; Dennis and Randy
Quaid; and Stacy and James Keach in* The Long Riders *(United Artists,
1980)*.

Above: *Sondra Locke
and Clint Eastwood in*
Bronco Billy *(Warner
Brothers, 1980)* Right:
*Publicity photograph
of Eastwood marking
the beginning of his
directing career.*
Opposite: *Eastwood
in* Joe Kidd *(Universal,
1972).*

Above: Heaven's Gate *(United Artists, 1980)*. Left: *Willie Nelson on the set of* Barbarosa *(Universal, 1982).*

friends. The sportsmen have a special train—complete with a bordello—and high-powered rifles with telescopic sights. While her husband is away, Melissa is kidnapped by an outlaw named Frank Calder (Oliver Reed), who takes her because he mistakenly believes she is a schoolteacher, and he wants to learn how to read. Melissa does not try to escape and opts to stay with the outlaw. Mr. Ruger learns of his wife's abduction and, with his companions, goes after her, ruthlessly stalking his prey. When his friends realize that Ruger is insane, they leave him. He continues the hunt. (*The Hunting Party* shows up in *The Honkers*; it is the movie being shown at the theater where rodeo rider Coburn's wife works.)

Molly Parker (Vera Miles) is married to Sheriff Parker (John Anderson). Molly is meek, her husband is not, and when an attractive young outlaw named Johnny Lawler (Sam Elliott) is put in Sheriff Parker's jail, Molly is attracted to the lawless youth. Johnny dupes Molly into freeing him, and the two run away together. *Molly and Lawless John* (IND, 1972), directed by Gary Nelson, is about a woman on her way to a sort of liberation. Dissatisfied with Johnny, Molly kills him and returns home, where she explains to her husband that she was kidnapped and claims the reward money for the dead outlaw.

The screenplay for *The Man Who Loved Cat Dancing* (MGM, 1973), directed by Richard C. Sarafian, was written by Eleanor Perry based on a novel by Marilyn Durham, an Indiana housewife turned author. The story concerns a discontented, whining wife (Sarah Miles) who runs away from her husband (George Hamilton) and becomes a member of an outlaw gang led by Jay Grobard (Burt Reynolds). Grobard once

loved an Indian named Cat Dancing. Cat Dancing is dead, and Grobard wants to buy back their children from the Shoshone. He robs a train to get the money; the prissy wife, running away from home, gets in the way of the robbery and is taken along by the fleeing outlaws. When her husband is apprised of these events, he joins a posse (led by Lee J. Cobb), and the chase is on. Being intimate with Grobard has a salubrious effect on Miles—she loses her selfishness and becomes a different woman altogether.

Zandy's Bride (Warner Brothers, 1974), written and directed by Jan Troell, is the third film in Troell's trilogy about the American frontier experience—the first two films are *The Emigrants* (1972) and *The New Land* (1973). Like the other two, *Zandy's Bride* stars Liv Ullmann, but unlike the other films, it is not a very compelling story. Zandy Allan (Gene Hackman) has a ranch in Big Sur. He wants sons to help him run it, so he orders himself a wife through the mail. His mail-order bride (Ullmann) does not meet his expectations, however. She claimed to be 26, but it turns out that she's really all of 32. That is the least of their squabbles.

Another Man, Another Chance (United Artists, 1977), directed by Claude Lelouch, is probably the only western that begins with the Franco-Prussian War. The plot of the film—a widow and a widower are brought together by their children—is more than very much like Lelouch's popular film *A Man and a Woman* (1966). Lelouch wanted to tell the story of *A Man and a Woman* out West. His working title for the film was *Un Homme, Une Femme et des Fusils* ("A Man, a Woman, and Guns"); that was changed to *Another Man, Another Woman*, and, finally, *Another Man, Another Chance*.

The film really does begin with the Franco-Prussian War. Genevieve Bujold and her photographer husband leave France and travel west; her husband is killed, and she is left alone with their daughter. James Caan is a frontier veterinarian, a widower with a son. The children go to school together, the man and the woman meet, and, as in the original French film, they fall in love. The film has a quiet, offhand feel to it, probably the result of Lelouch's working technique. He is famous for not showing actors complete scripts—not even when they are being asked to consider taking a part. Lelouch moves through his films in small chunks, requiring the actors—who never know what is going to happen next—to memorize only the lines necessary for each scene.

James Caan stars in another western about a man and a woman: *Comes a Horseman* (United Artists, 1978), directed by Alan J. Pakula. The other stars of the film—Jane Fonda and Jason Robards, Jr.—knew each other and the director well. Fonda and Pakula worked together on *Klute* (1971), for which she won an Oscar; Robards won an Oscar for his performance

Sarah Miles as a wife on the run who has the good fortune of encountering Burt Reynolds as The Man Who Loved Cat Dancing *(MGM, 1973).*

in *All the President's Men* (1976), directed by Pakula; and Robards won an Oscar for his performance with Fonda in *Julia* (1977).

Comes a Horseman didn't win any Oscars. The title of the film comes from a song by Gordon Lightfoot, "Don Quixote," which includes the line, "Comes a horseman, wild and free." The story of the film is set in Montana in 1945. Two small ranchers (Fonda and Caan) are united in their fight against a vicious rancher (Robards) and an oil man (George Grizzard), who has the foresight to recognize the need for oil. The plot is very much like the traditional cattlemen-versus-homesteaders story, the only change being the dimension of ecological consciousness. The oil companies are ruining the land, and the small ranchers want to stop them.

The ways in which big companies have ruined or at least corrupted America are examined in *The Electric Horseman* (Columbia, 1979), directed by Sydney Pollack. Robert Redford stars as Sonny Steele, a five-time All Around World Champion rodeo rider who has fallen on hard times and taken to strong drink. Thanks to his former fame, he has a job promoting a breakfast cereal called Ranch Breakfast ("A champ's way to start a better day"). His picture is on the front of the box, and he performs an advertising routine at various events. He and a horse are wired and covered with light bulbs; he rides around a ring, the horse rears up, and the "electric horseman" doffs his hat, a living advertising sign. His business manager (Willie Nelson, in his film debut) tries to keep Sonny sober from event to event. Trouble arises when the company that produces the cereal supplies Sonny with a special horse, a Triple Crown-winning thoroughbred stallion named Rising Star (the horse playing the part is actually named Let's Merge). The horse is being shot full of harmful drugs by the sponsors, and Sonny decides to save it. He steals the horse, intending to set it free in the wilds, and his flight draws national attention. He is joined by a citified reporter (Jane Fonda) who eventually understands what the lone cowboy is doing and even falls in love with him. The film is frequently compared, unfavorably, to *Lonely Are the Brave*, but as good as that film is, it doesn't have Willie Nelson's songs, and *The Electric Horseman* does.

A former rodeo rider and his concern for a valuable stallion provide the simple plot for Joel McCrea's last western, *Mustang Country* (Universal, 1976), written, directed, and produced by John Champion. McCrea, who at that time was 70, teams up with a runaway Indian boy (Nika Mina) in a hunt for a wild horse. This was McCrea's first film since 1962, when he had starred with Randolph Scott in Peckinpah's *Ride the High Country*.

"Some men die for money, and some die for causes."

Five Man Army

By 1970, the "spaghetti" western had given way to a thoroughly international species of the western genre. Polyglot teams of bold professionals were assembled, usually in Spain, to perform daring capers, usually located in revolutionary Mexico. *Five Man Army* (MGM, 1970), directed by Don Taylor, unites Peter Graves (Jim Phelps of "Mission: Impossible," a wise choice for any dangerous job); James Daly (the dynamite expert); Bud Spencer; Nino Castelnuovo; and Tetsuro Tamba, a Japanese samurai capable of slicing a man in half. Castelnuovo, a revolutionary, rounds up these pros to steal a $500,000 gold shipment being sent by train to a vicious general. Their mission is to take possession of the gold, skim a little off the top as their retainer, and deliver the rest to the revolutionaries. "Some men die for money, and some die for causes," explains one of them.

Samurai swordsmen and western gunfighters had been exchanging screenplays for more than a decade; it seemed only natural that they should meet. *Red Sun* (NGP, 1971), directed by Terence Young, joins Charles Bronson with Toshiro Mifune, the star of a series of

The West in 1945: Jane Fonda and James Caan in Comes a Horseman (*United Artists, 1978*).

samurai films. The two of them get involved in an effort to recover a golden sword (a gift from the emperor of Japan to the president of the United States). Although their partnership is at times uneasy, they enjoy similar pastimes (they have a good time together in a whorehouse), and they learn to respect each other. Bronson commiserates with Mifune when the talented swordsman laments that changing times have ended his way of life. "You can't live by the sword anymore," says Mifune. "I think you're one hell of a man" is Bronson's judgment of his foreign ally.

In *The Stranger and the Gunfighter* (Columbia, 1976), directed by Anthony Dawson, Lee Van Cleef teams up with kung-fu master Lo Lieh. The film is a comedy.

An astonishing number of foreign-made westerns appeared during the sixties and early seventies. Sergio Leone's films were not the only Italian westerns, nor were Italians the only foreigners to make westerns, but Leone's films were the most international and the most acceptable to American audiences. Such directors as Sergio Sollima, Enzo Castellari, Damiano Damiani, and Sergio Corbucci made films similar to Leone's—many of these films have American actors and musical scores by Ennio Morricone, but they were frequently more "political," having as a common theme the incessant struggle against U.S. imperialists. Some of these Italian westerns have an odd divided structure, for while purporting to be political, they are ludicrously violent, as though they were made to please an audience composed of young terrorists and their working-class parents. Leone did not avoid the topic of revolution, but he treated it in a less political way, earning the criticism of some Italians.

Duck, You Sucker (United Artists, 1972) is also known as *A Fistful of Dynamite*, but its original title was *Once Upon a Time, the Revolution*. The revolution is the Mexican Revolution, the year is 1913, and the story of the film concerns a peasant named Juan Miranda (Rod Steiger) and an IRA terrorist and dynamite expert named Sean Mallory (James Coburn). Each wants to use the other—the idealistic Irishman wants to get the bandit involved in the revolution; the bandit wants to profit from the expertise of the explosives expert. "I don't want to be a hero. I want the money," exclaims Juan; Sean, one of the men who die for a cause, learns that the revolution is not what he thought and ends up throwing away his copy of Bakunin, the Russian revolutionary and proselytizer.

In *The Wrath of God* (MGM, 1973), written and directed by Ralph Nelson, another Irish terrorist on the lam (Ken Hutchinson) shows up in Mexico during a revolution in the 1920s. The later date explains the number of machine guns, one of which is employed by a defrocked priest (Robert Mitchum). Frank Langella plays a cruel despot whose anti-Church activities enrage his religious mother (Rita Hayworth).

Tonino Valerii, a disciple of Sergio Leone's, directed *My Name Is Nobody* (Universal, 1974), a comedy western starring Henry Fonda as Jack Beauregard, a famed gunfighter who is pestered by an enthusiastic promoter of legends named Nobody (Terence Hill, whose Italian name is Mario Girotti). Nobody wants to make a name for himself and to turn Beauregard into a national monument; Beauregard wants to sail away to a peaceful retirement in Europe. Thanks to Nobody, the aging gunman has to face a gang called the Wild Bunch—all 150 of them (they ride into battle to the strains of Wagner's "The Ride of the Valkyries"). Nobody understands, like Sergio Leone, the importance of legend in westerns and American history. (Everybody says that Sergio Leone is now working on a film about gangsters called *Once Upon a Time, America*.)

Feo, fuerte y formal

The habit of identifying John Wayne, the man, with the characters he plays in his films is hard to break, particularly since he promoted the idea himself. Wayne was a wealthy man and a political conservative. He talked about his politics, and politicians talked about him. Richard Nixon was very fond of *Chisum* (Warner Brothers, 1970), directed by Andrew V. McLaglen. He mentioned the film in a famous speech in which he praised *Chisum* for its treatment of the law, saying of the old West, "The law eventually came, and the law was important from the standpoint of not only prosecuting the guilty, but also seeing that those who were guilty had a proper trial" (he presumably intended to say "those who were accused").

Chisum is about the law, about the difference between revenge and justice, but it is also about America, and the difference between honest and dishonest capitalists. The film is interesting because at a time when other filmmakers were manipulating the "real" history of the West to indict American society, *Chisum* used a historical character to create a new legend in the old tradition. The name of John Simpson Chisum (1824–1884) is frequently heard in the story of Billy the Kid, Pat Garrett, and the Lincoln County War, but before this film, no one had thought to make Chisum a hero. He was a big-time rancher, one of the biggest landowners in New Mexico, a wealthy man who employed Billy the Kid for a short period. But he was not a saintly figure—he was a powerful man, a ruthless empire builder. In Peckinpah's *Pat Garrett and Billy the Kid*, Chisum is referred to as "Chisum and every other landowner that's trying to put a fence around this country"; he is identified as one of the big businessmen who are changing the country. Wayne, as Chisum, would agree, but Wayne's Chisum is in favor of progress.

"Things usually change for the better," says Chisum early in the film. According to *Chisum*, big business is not bad if it is governed by fair and honest men.

Both Billy the Kid (Geoffrey Deuel) and Pat Garrett (Glenn Corbett) have important roles in *Chisum*, but the film avoids entirely the most important aspect of their relationship—that Garrett killed Billy. Rather, they seem like the two sons every cattle baron should have, one bad (Billy, who seeks revenge rather than legal justice) and one good (Garrett, the honest lawman). Henry Tunstall (Patric Knowles), the learned, pipe-smoking Englishman who befriended Billy and whose murder inspired Billy's lust for revenge, appears as Chisum's friendly neighbor. The two are good businessmen and take care of the people in their domains. When a crafty, land-grabbing newcomer named Lawrence Murphy (Forrest Tucker), in cahoots with corrupt officials, raises the prices in the local stores, Tunstall and Chisum, beneficent capitalists, open their own store, in which the prices are fair. When Murphy cuts off the water from the local Mexican ranchers, Chisum offers them his water, free of charge. Chisum tries to deal with his crooked competitors legally, but in the end he is forced to resort to the old ways. "Let's break out some Winchesters," says Chisum to his foreman, Pepper (Ben Johnson). "You bet," snaps back Pepper, and the battle is on.

One of the villains they go off to fight is a bounty hunter named Dan Nodeen (Christopher George), a despicably avaricious character obviously modeled after the Man With No Name, the bounty killer played by Clint Eastwood in Sergio Leone's first three westerns. Such foreign mercenaries had no place in Wayne's West, and Nodeen is exposed as a coward. "The hell

with this," he says, runnning away as soon as the battle gets rough.

Chisum begins and ends with the same scene—a view of Chisum sitting on his horse surveying his expansive holdings. He is motionless, like a statue, a monument to American individualism, a powerful man who carved an empire for himself out of the wilderness and ruled it with justice for all. Chisum believes in the law. Perhaps Richard Nixon was inspired by Chisum's statement late in the film that "No matter where people go, there's always the law—and before that, they'll find out that God's already been there."

Big Jake (NGP, 1971), directed by George Sherman (this was Sherman's last film), is about a wealthy cattleman named Jacob ("Big Jake") McCandles (Wayne), a man very much like Chisum. He is even more like George Washington McLintock (of *McLintock!*)—he has the same wife (Maureen O'Hara—this was her fifth film with Wayne, and her name in *Big Jake* is Martha) and, like McLintock, McCandles is such an important man that his town is named for him. The opening sequences of the film establish the date as 1909. A narrator explains that it is the Edwardian "golden age," a modern era with airplanes and motorcars, Einstein and science, culture and refinement (the Morgans and the Vanderbilts)—there is even a scene from *The Great Train Robbery*. Although life in the East is civilized, life out West is still rough. It is 1909, however, and everyone believes that the pioneer empire builder Jacob McCandles is dead. He isn't, but he has been estranged from his wife for a decade and has been away from home so long that he doesn't know he has an 8-year-old grandson (played by Wayne's son John Ethan Wayne). He is, therefore, far away when his enormous ranch near the Mexican border is attacked by a gang of outlaws led by John Fain (Richard Boone).

The outlaws kill ten people and kidnap the grandson, leaving a note demanding a ransom of $1 million in twenty-dollar bills. Both the U.S. Army and the Texas Rangers offer Mrs. McCandles their services, but she turns them down, saying, "This is not a job for the Rangers or the army. It is going to be an extremely harsh and unpleasant business and will require, I think, an extremely harsh and unpleasant man to see to it." The man she has in mind is her husband. He arrives with his ferocious dog named Dog, recruits his Apache friend Sam Sharpnose (Bruce Cabot), and they set off on the trail of the gang. Big Jake and Sam Sharpnose are joined by two of Big Jake's sons (played by Patrick Wayne and Christopher Mitchum, son of Robert Mitchum)—sons he has not seen in a decade. He wins back

Richard Boone as the murderous outlaw John Fain in Big Jake *(NGP, 1971).*

their love and respect, and even though he has to abide such modern paraphernalia as a motorcycle, automobiles, an automatic pistol, and bolt-action rifles with telescopic sights, it is Big Jake's old-fashioned cussedness that wins the day.

Wayne was 65 years old in 1972; an old man, he did best as an actor when he portrayed old men. He had proved that at age 40 in *Red River*, and he had demonstrated it again at age 62 in *True Grit*. In *The Cowboys* (Warner Brothers, 1972), directed by Mark Rydell, Wayne plays a 60-year-old Montana cattleman named Wil Andersen. Andersen has 1,500 head of cattle to move 400 miles along the Bozeman Trail to Belle Fourche, South Dakota, but his hired hands all quit to take off for a gold rush, leaving the old man alone. A friend (Slim Pickens) suggests that he hire schoolboys, and Andersen takes on eleven of them, ranging in age from 9-year-old Hardy Fimps (played by Clay O'Brien, who had just turned 10) to 15-year-old Slim (played by Robert Carradine, son of John Carradine, who was 15). One of the boys is plump ("They call me Fats," he announces); one wears glasses and is called Four Eyes; one, named Charlie Schwartz, is Jewish. A group of mangy drifters applies for work, but Andersen turns them down when he catches their leader (Bruce Dern) in a lie, so the only other adult on the cattle drive is the cook (Roscoe Lee Browne).

In a scene that echoes *Red River*, Andersen shouts, "Move 'em out!" and the youthful cowboys get the herd moving. The scenes of the trail drive (like those in *Monte Walsh* and *The Culpepper Cattle Company*) are beautifully composed, like Remington paintings brought to life. The incidents along the trail include the usual dangers and some initiation rites for the boys. In a scene condemned by some critics, Andersen cures one of the boys of stammering by getting the boy angry; one of the boys is killed in a stampede; the youths have their first experience with whiskey; and they narrowly avoid a close encounter with a traveling bordello (Colleen Dewhurst is the madam). Whenever they pause too long, Andersen is there to speed the boys along with his favorite phrase: "Come on, we're burning daylight."

Andersen and his youthful cowboys are followed by Dern and his cutthroat gang. The gang leader eventually kills Andersen (this was the first movie in which Wayne had been killed since *The Alamo*). The cowboys bury Wayne on the trail and, with the help of the cook, dispose of the murderous thugs and take the cattle on to the railhead. On their way home, they search for Andersen's grave, but cannot find it—it has become part of the land.

John Ford, who visited Wayne while he was working on *The Cowboys*, died in 1973. Wayne himself did not have long to live, but he didn't stop making films.

"I got a saddle that's older than you are," says

Ricardo Montalban as a mysterious stranger in The Train Robbers *(Warner Brothers, 1973).*

Wayne to Ann-Margret in *The Train Robbers* (Warner Brothers, 1973), directed by Burt Kennedy. This was Kennedy's first film after *Hannie Caulder*, and it shares some of that film's gimmicks—the bad guys are a faceless, leaderless group; Ricardo Montalban appears and disappears without explanation. The story concerns an aging cowboy (Wayne) who is hired by a young widow (Ann-Margret) to recover a treasure in gold stolen from a train by her dead husband. She wants to clear her name for her son. Wayne puts together a small gang, including two of his Civil War cronies (Rod Taylor and Ben Johnson) and, chased by the anonymous villains, looks for the gold. Comparing this film to *The Great Train Robbery*—made exactly seventy years earlier—provides an interesting sense of the changes that have taken place in the western—very few.

Wayne made another western in 1973, *Cahill, United States Marshal* (Warner Brothers, 1973), directed by Andrew V. McLaglen, in which he plays a lawman so dedicated to his duty that he neglects his two sons (Gary Grimes and Clay O'Brien). The boys "go bad" and join an outlaw gang led by George Kennedy. Just as Big Jake was accompanied by an Indian, Cahill is accompanied by a half-breed (Neville Brand). Both men are portrayed as exceptional (both get killed). Wayne stated many times his strong feelings about American Indians—that they had had a good way of life but that it had had to change—but he never escaped being called, by some critics, a racist. "I ain't got a bigoted bone in my body," he states as Marshal Cahill, while holding a gun on a black man. "I'll blast

you to hell as quick as any white man."

Wayne repeated his role as the crusty, one-eyed marshal of *True Grit* in *Rooster Cogburn* (Universal, 1975), directed by Stuart Millar. *Rooster Cogburn* owes as much to *The African Queen* as it does to *True Grit:* Cogburn is teamed with a missionary's spinster daughter named Eula Goodnight (Katharine Hepburn) in a search for her father's killers. The two of them end up taking a ride on a very shaky raft that is piled high with nitroglycerin (the villains intended to use the explosives in a bank robbery). They also have the use of a Gatling gun and the aid of a young Indian (Richard Romancito). Eula calls Rooster "Reuben," and says to him at one point, "You're a credit to the male sex." *Rooster Cogburn* was not really a credit to Wayne's career, but it was not his last film.

The Shootist (Paramount, 1976), directed by Don Siegel, was Wayne's last film. Although he plays a character named J. B. Books, there is no doubt that Books is Wayne, and the film is John Wayne's valedictory. *The Shootist* begins with a series of scenes taken from some of John Wayne's other westerns, beginning with *Red River.* The scenes are presented as though they were incidents from the life of J. B. Books, but they reinforce the idea that no matter who Wayne played, it was always the same man—John Wayne. Wayne was once quoted as saying that there were some parts he wouldn't play: "I won't play anybody dishonest or cruel or mean for no reason. I've killed men on the screen, but it was always because they didn't follow the code." As Books in *The Shootist,* Wayne has a chance to voice his personal code: "I won't be wronged; I won't be insulted; and I won't be laid a hand on. I don't do these things to other people, and I require the same from them." (This code resembles the code Wayne's druggist father taught him: "Always keep your

word; a gentleman never insults anybody intentionally; and don't go around looking for trouble, but if you ever get in a fight, make sure you win it.") As a western, *The Shootist* is somewhat slow-moving and talkative, but as a farewell to John Wayne, it is poignant and suitably solemn.

The film begins on January 22, 1901. A new century is beginning, and as J. B. Books arrives in Carson City, Nevada, he rides past newsboys hawking papers with headlines about the death of Queen Victoria (these are modern times, and news travels fast—she died on January 22). Books is in Carson City to see a doctor (James Stewart)—he has been told he has cancer, and he wants a second opinion. Stewart confirms that Books has cancer (just as Wayne had cancer) and gives him two months to live. The doctor also tells Books that the end will not be pleasant and suggests to him that he take his own life. Books decides to die according to the way he lived, and the film is about his last week of life, from his arrival in Carson City to his death, in a gunfight, on his birthday, January 29.

Books takes a room in a boardinghouse run by a widow named Bond Rogers (Lauren Bacall). His presence doesn't please her, and his refusal to leave makes her angry, eliciting from Books the line, "You have a fine color when you're on the scrap," a rewording of Wayne's oft-heard "You're beautiful when you're angry" (in 1956's *The Conqueror*—in which Wayne plays a Mongol warrior named Temujin—the line is rendered, "Thou art beauteous in thy wrath"). Books is visited by a lawman (Harry Morgan) named Thibido who is delighted to hear that Books is dying. He is also visited by a newspaper reporter named Dobkins who wants to write a series of stories about Books, "the most celebrated shootist extant," getting down to the true story and answering such psychological questions as, "Are you by nature bloodthirsty?" and "Do you brood after the deed is done?" Books gets rid of Dobkins, only to be visited by a former girlfriend named Serepta (Sheree North) who wants to co-write with Dobkins a book called *The Shootist: The Life and Bloody Times of J. B. Books.* "Woman," says Books, "I still have some pride."

Books identifies himself with "old Queen Vic." "Maybe she'd outlived her time, maybe she was a museum piece"—but she never lost her style. He knows that he is an anachronism. Thibido tells him that "The old days are gone . . . we've got some weeding to do, but once we're rid of people like you, we'll have a goddamn garden of Eden." (Not only do they have automobiles, telephones, and bathrooms—dry cleaning has been introduced.)

"The most celebrated shootist extant" goes through his final days preparing for his death. He bargains with a stable owner (Scatman Crothers) over the price of his horse and saddle; he outsmarts an ingratiating and underhanded undertaker (John Carradine), whose credo is "The early worm gets the bird"; and he teaches Bond's son, Gillom (Ron Howard), about guns and being a man, including the observation that "Bat Masterson always was full of sheep-dip."

On his birthday, a beautiful day of "false spring," Books hops aboard a trolley for the ride to a saloon, where three gunmen (Richard Boone, Hugh O'Brian, and Billy McKinney) await. The way he dies—no one could ever take John Wayne in a fair fight—is fitting, and the brief violence of the film is far outweighed by some of its conversations, particularly those in which Books says his good-bys. "In general, I've had a hell of a good time," he says. Wayne meant it.

Wayne never made another film. In 1978, he underwent open-heart surgery; in 1979, his stomach was removed. He died in 1979, having already supplied his own epitaph, saying in a 1969 interview for *Time* that he wanted to be remembered by a Spanish phrase: *Feo, fuerte y formal* ("He was ugly, strong, and had dignity").

"A man's got to know his limitations."

Magnum Force

Budd Boetticher, who wrote the original screenplay for *Two Mules for Sister Sara*, planned to direct the film with John Wayne in the lead, but when it was finally made into a film, following a screenplay that

Albert Maltz based on Boetticher's story, ***Two Mules for Sister Sara*** (Universal, 1970) was directed by Don Siegel (who directed *The Shootist*), and it starred Clint Eastwood. Eastwood's second western after ending his career with Sergio Leone (*Hang 'Em High* was the first), *Two Mules for Sister Sara* finds Eastwood playing a character similar to the Man With No Name—a squinty-eyed, cheroot-smoking loner—but the character is changing, evolving into Clint Eastwood's personal version of the western hero, a man who lives by a code. It is a cynical code, but it makes sense in Eastwood's West.

In *Two Mules for Sister Sara*, Eastwood has a name (Hogan), and even though he is primarily interested in "dollars"—in getting paid for his services—and even though he still displays his superman, "spaghetti" prowess with his weapons, he is a recognizable man who is, at times, likeable. He is stubborn, however, as stubborn as a mule.

The opening scenes of the film establish Hogan's place in his environment. Alone, he rides through beautiful but threatening nature, past a variety of wild animals—a rabbit, snakes, a tarantula, a puma—past the bones of a man. This reverie of man in nature is ended abruptly when Hogan's horse steps on and crushes a tarantula. Neither Hogan nor the horse notices a thing. In the midst of potential violence, Hogan is the most dangerous creature around. His journey is interrupted when he comes upon three men in the pro-

Juarista guerillas and French soldiers in the final battle of Two Mules for Sister Sara *(Universal, 1970).*

215

cess of raping a woman. As in the world of the Man With No Name, evil is active everywhere—there is an ongoing struggle to survive. Hogan understands that—only his lethal instincts keep him alive—but the knowledge doesn't keep him from expressing weariness with the irritations brought about by villains and their villainy—they waste time. He saves the woman and is surprised to find she is a nun, Sister Sara (Shirley MacLaine). She is not surprised that he has happened along and saved her—God provides for His children. Hogan is not at all pleased with the notion that God might have "provided" him. He believes in a world ruled by random violence. It transpires that the unlikely couple are going the same way, so they travel together, Sister Sara on her mule, her other mule scanning the horizon for the enemy he knows is there.

There are lots of enemies around. The story of the film takes place in Mexico during the period of Maximilian and Juarez. Hogan, having spent two years as a Confederate soldier during the Civil War ("Everybody's got a right to be a sucker once"), is south of the border for a lucrative business deal with the revolutionaries; Sister Sara (who is really a whore) is an active *juarista* (revolutionary) wanted by the French. Her role as a nun doesn't prevent her from taking an occasional slug of whiskey or from blowing up bridges (the Church, she explains to Hogan, grants special dispensation in cases of need). There is a lot of humor in *Two Mules for Sister Sara*, humor that is spoiled by scenes of excessive violence. The final battle includes a Gatling gun—essential to mass carnage—and the obligatory use of dynamite for hand grenades (one of the appeals of the Mexican Revolution to filmmakers must have been the ease with which its battles could be made to resemble modern warfare).

In 1971, Eastwood made his first appearance as Inspector Harry Callahan, the brutally iconoclastic cop known as Dirty Harry because of his ruthless methods of law enforcement (he is a man with whom Rooster Cogburn would enjoy having a drink). *Dirty Harry*, directed by Don Siegel, was only the first of three films starring Eastwood as Harry Callahan; it was followed by *Magnum Force* (1973) and *The Enforcer* (1976). (It is at the end of *Magnum Force* that Callahan, surveying the final defeat of his enemies, delivers his opinion of their efforts: "A man's got to know his limitations.") Attentive viewers of *Dirty Harry* may notice that in one of the film's early scenes Inspector Callahan, chasing a criminal down a crowded city street, passes a movie theater—the film advertised on the marquee is *Play Misty for Me*. A suspenseful film about a disc jockey and a deadly fan, *Play Misty for Me* was Eastwood's first film as director. He didn't forget Don Siegel—he cast him as a friendly bartender named Murphy.

Eastwood's next western was directed by John Sturges. *Joe Kidd* (Universal, 1972) takes place in New Mexico after the turn of the century (there are automatic pistols in evidence). Eastwood plays the title character, a town drunk who is hired by a powerful landowner (Robert Duvall) to help track down a revolutionary named Luis Chama (John Saxon), leader of a group of Mexican-Americans who are fighting to regain land illegally taken from them. Kidd eventually changes sides, joining Chama. In the film's dramatic finish, Kidd drives a train off its tracks, through a town, into a saloon.

The first western directed by Clint Eastwood was *High Plains Drifter* (Universal, 1973). To emphasize the individuality of Eastwood's effort—and to put his past behind him—a publicity still was taken of him standing in a graveyard beside two tombstones—on one is written "S. Leone," on the other "Don Siegel." Eastwood had not shaken off all the vestiges of Leone, however, and the character he plays in the film has no name—he is called The Stranger. But *High Plains Drifter* is a very unusual western with a very unique style. The Stranger (Eastwood) rides into the mining town of Lago and is hired by the townspeople to protect them from a gang of outlaws, the Belding boys, who have been released from prison and are on their way to the town seeking revenge. The Stranger himself is in Lago for revenge. The townspeople once stood by and did nothing while their sheriff was whipped to death; the Stranger is troubled by dreams of being whipped. Is he the sheriff, returned from the dead for vengeance? He never says who he is, and the action of *High Plains Drifter* goes well beyond the boundaries of traditional westerns, becoming almost surreal. The Stranger prepares the townspeople for their battle with the Beldings, makes a dwarf (Billy Curtis) mayor, and has the citizens paint the town red. He renames the town Hell and ends up burning the whole place to the ground, while the craven townspeople meet justly suitable deaths.

More than a dozen westerns were released in 1976, but only one of them was even remotely related to the Bicentennial celebration: *The Outlaw Josey Wales* (Warner Brothers, 1976), directed by Clint Eastwood. Eastwood stars as Josey Wales, an ex-Confederate soldier who, looking for revenge, finds a new home. The Civil War is not the American Revolution, of course, but in the tradition of American filmmaking it has become the birth of the nation, and *The Outlaw Josey Wales* is about attempts, following the cataclysm of war, to construct an American society. Josey Wales is out plowing a field when he hears what sounds like a storm—the storm is a gang of border raiders, the so-called Redlegs, and they kill his wife and son and burn down his farm. Josey fights for the Confederacy and is a member of the last group to surrender; his companions are slaughtered, but Josey escapes, becoming an outlaw with a price on his head. Pursued by both his former enemies and bounty hunters, Josey takes off on an epiclike journey, gathering around him a small family. The first person to join him is a comical Indian (Chief Dan George) who explains that his tribe was never very warlike: "They call us civilized because we're easy to sneak up on." As the two of them (plus a dog who doesn't mind it when Josey spits tobacco on his head) make their way into Texas, they are joined by an assortment of misfits and losers, castoffs of society. This peculiar family finds a home and makes peace with the local Indians. Even the outlaw Josey Wales eventually makes peace with the world.

The scenes of violence in *The Outlaw Josey Wales* have some of the comic-book quality of "spaghetti" westerns, but Eastwood manages to use the unreality of the situations to create the ambience of a legend. Just when things are looking their worst, at the moment of greatest peril, the immortal Josey Wales appears on the horizon, usually with the sun at his back. As he says, "It sure pays to have an edge."

"The only things not on my diet would be the green top of the beet and okra."

The Missouri Breaks

Joseph Heller, author of *Catch-22*, was one of the three scriptwriters for **Dirty Dingus Magee** (MGM, 1970), directed by Burt Kennedy. The film stars Frank Sinatra as Dingus, a sly con man operating around the town of Yerkey's Hole, New Mexico. Served by a stageline called the Jackass Mail, Yerkey's Hole has only one industry, its whorehouse, which does a thriving business with the troopers from nearby Fort Horner. The film is full of the worst kind of humor: a girl holding a chicken calls out to a soldier on his way out of the brothel, "Wait, you forgot your cock." Dingus makes the mistake of stealing $400 from Hoke Birdsill (George Kennedy). Birdsill goes to the mayor of Yerkey's Hole, Belle Kops (Anne Jackson), who just happens to be the local madam. She makes him sheriff, and he pursues Dingus. Jack Elam makes an appearance as John Wesley Hardin, but it doesn't help.

Whorehouse humor provides most of the jokes in **The Cheyenne Social Club** (NGP, 1970), directed by Gene Kelly. Billed as a "western sex comedy," the film stars James Stewart and Henry Fonda as two aging cowpokes who have been together longer than either can remember. They travel along, Fonda delivering a nonstop string of reminiscences, Stewart silently tolerating his friend's palavering. Stewart's brother dies, leaving him a business in Cheyenne. It seems only natural that Fonda should tag along when Stewart goes to assume ownership of the firm. It turns out that the business is a whorehouse (run by Shirley Jones). When Stewart realizes what he has inherited, he wants to

close the place (his sidekick is busily working his way through the establishment, room by room, visiting with the staff). The humor is sometimes tired, but the film is worth watching if only for a scene in which Fonda and Stewart sing a song: "Rolling Stone."

The music in *Zachariah* (CIN, 1971), directed by George Englund, is of a different sort. Ads for the film showed a cowboy wearing mirror shades and earphones with a joint hanging from his lips; the caption read, "A head of his time." Billed as "the first electric western," *Zachariah* has music by such groups as Country Joe and the Fish, The James Gang, The New York Rock Ensemble, and White Lightnin'; the screenplay was written by Joe Massot and The Firesign Theater (Philip Austin, Peter Bergman, David Ossman, and Philip Proctor). It stars John Rubinstein (Arthur's son) as Zachariah. Zachariah's best friend is Matthew (Don Johnson). Pat Quinn (who played Alice in the film *Alice's Restaurant*) appears as Belle Starr. Trouble begins when a man in a bar, annoyed at the length of Zachariah's hair, calls him a "fag"; the gold our heroes seek is called "Gold de Acapulco."

The Skin Game (Warner Brothers, 1971), directed by Paul Bogart, is a comedy western with a very serious message about the roles of blacks and women in the West and the adaptations they have to make to survive. The story takes place around Kansas and Missouri before the Civil War. James Garner, a sly con man, pretends to be a ruined plantation owner forced by destitution to sell his loyal slave (Lou Gossett). Having sold Gossett, Garner then helps his friend escape, and the two move on to the next town, where they repeat the hoax. The two friends are joined by a con woman (Susan Clark) playing a role of her own.

The "something big" in **something big** (NGP, 1972), directed by Andrew V. McLaglen, is what an

Scene from something big *(NGP, 1972). Center: Harry Carey, Jr. Second from right: Dean Martin. Right: Don Knight.*

outlaw named Joe Baker (Dean Martin) has been planning to do for years. He came out West with the intention of doing "something big," but thus far he hasn't succeeded, and he is getting anxious. A colorful sort of outlaw, Baker travels with a yapping dog (the dog rides in a bag strapped to Baker's saddle) and has as his sidekick a Scotsman named Tommy who wears the obligatory tam-o'-shanter and plays his bagpipes on request. As the film begins, Baker has finally decided on his plan, and everyone in the territory, including the soon-to-retire commander of a nearby fort (Brian Keith) has heard the rumor that "Baker is plannin' something big." Baker wants to steal a treasure in gold from the villa of a Mexican bandit. What he needs to pull off the job is a Gatling gun in the possession of an oafish murderer (Albert Salmi) who is willing to trade the gun for a woman. So Baker sets about locating a suitable female, holding up (in novel ways) four stagecoaches. He never harms anyone or takes anything—he simply examines the women. On the fifth stage there is a woman (Honor Blackman) to his liking. Unfortunately, she turns out to be the wife of the retiring commander, a woman known for her frigidity. Baker pulls off his heist, and everyone seems to end up happy.

"What's a dazzling urbanite like you doing in a rustic setting like this?" asks the Waco Kid (Gene Wilder) of Black Bart (Cleavon Little). With his Gucci saddlebags and his very black skin, Black Bart does seem more than a little out of place as the sheriff of the all-white cattle town of Rock Ridge, but then nothing seems quite right—when a black road gang is ordered to sing "a good ole nigger work song," they break out in "I Get a Kick Out of You." The subtitle of *Blazing Saddles* (Warner Brothers, 1974), directed by Mel Brooks, is "never give a saga an even break," and the film doesn't, sending up westerns, the black exploitation films of the seventies, and all of Hollywood. The screenplay (by Brooks, Norman Steinberg, Andrew Bergman, Richard Pryor, and Alan Uger) manages to leap destructively and acrobatically in and out of every standard western formula, pausing only to underline every stereotype with alarmingly funny and frequently scatological bad taste. The plot of the film, glimpsed occasionally, concerns attempts by a crooked lawyer named Hedley Lamarr (Harvey Korman) and a corrupt governor named William J. Lepetomane (Brooks, who also plays an Indian chief) to pull off a land swindle. They hire Black Bart as part of their scheme to take over the town of Rock Ridge, but their plans backfire, and they decide to get rid of the lawman. They employ the blonde seductress Lili Von Shtupp (Madeline Kahn), a character based on Marlene Dietrich's role in *Destry Rides Again*. In and out of this story travels a crowd of unrelated Johnsons: Olson Johnson,

The ride across the desert in The Shooting *(IND, 1972).*

Reverend Johnson, Howard Johnson, Van Johnson, Gabby Johnson, Harriet Johnson, and Dr. Sam Johnson. In the end, all of these characters—who never seemed at home in the saddle—burst out of their set into the filming of another movie, a musical starring Buddy Bizarre (Dom DeLuise). *Blazing Saddles* was Mel Brooks's first hit movie, and it remains his best.

The Duchess and the Dirtwater Fox (20th Century-Fox, 1976), directed by Melvin Frank, is a slapstick comedy about an inept cardsharp (George Segal) and a Barbary Coast dance-hall girl (Goldie Hawn) who get involved in a series of humorous escapades.

The Great Scout and Cathouse Thursday (AIP, 1976), directed by Don Taylor, is set in Colorado in 1908 (automobiles and the presidential campaign of William Jennings Bryan against William H. Taft provide the historical setting). Sam Longwood (Lee Marvin), "the great scout"; his sidekick (Strother Martin); and a Harvard-educated half-breed (Oliver Reed) are trying to get back their shares of a gold mine, shares that they were cheated out of by a former partner (Robert Culp). They kidnap his wife (Elizabeth Ashley), but he doesn't want her back (she's got a very foul mouth). Cathouse Thursday (Kay Lenz) is a young whore; the half-breed Harvard grad is spreading venereal disease throughout the West in an effort to exact revenge on white society. The film is a comedy.

In the summer of 1965, Monte Hellman and Jack Nicholson coproduced two westerns, *The Shooting* and *Ride in the Whirlwind*. Hellman directed the films; Nicholson starred in them and wrote the screenplay for one. Roger Corman financed the two westerns, which were filmed back-to-back in Utah on a combined budget of $150,000. It took only three weeks to film each of these low-budget movies, but they have become cult favorites, praised for their existentialist themes. Although they were shown in Europe during the sixties, they were not released in the United States until 1972, by which time Nicholson's career had soared following his roles in both *Easy Rider* (1969) and *Five Easy Pieces* (1970).

Adrien Joyce, who wrote the screenplay for *Five Easy Pieces*, wrote *The Shooting* (IND, 1972), in which a man named Gashade (Warren Oates) and a man named Coley (Will Hutchins) are hired by a woman (Millie Perkins)—who never mentions either her first or last name—to help her cross the desert. She offers them a large sum of money, and ie seems to be seeking revenge—she occasionally fires her revolver. Gashade and Coley realize that they are being followed, and the three travelers are soon joined by a stranger named Billy Spear (Jack Nicholson). The four continue along until their journey ends with a very strange twist.

Ride in the Whirlwind (IND, 1972) was written by Nicholson. Nicholson and two pals (one of whom is Cameron Mitchell), on their way to a roundup, happen upon an isolated shack inhabited by a group of vaguely suspicious characters, one of whom is wounded. The three cowhands accept the invitation to eat some beans and biscuits and spend the night in the corral. The men in the shack are actually thieves being pursued by a posse of ruthless vigilantes. The next morning, the shack is surrounded. The posse sets fire to the building and shoots the men inside. The three cowboys in the corral, mistaken for members of the outlaw gang, are caught in the crossfire. One of them is killed; the other two (Nicholson and Mitchell) escape and break into the cabin of a settler, holding the settler's wife and daughter hostage. The posse arrives and kills one of the two cowboys. The last (Nicholson) escapes, riding away alone into the whirlwind.

Another film that has become a cult favorite is *Rancho Deluxe* (United Artists, 1975), directed by Frank Perry, a comedy western about two cattle rustlers in the contemporary West. Jeff Bridges and his Indian pal, Sam Waterston, are thoroughly modern outlaws in a garishly modern Montana. "Did you ever see *Cheyenne Autumn*?" asks Waterston. "Well, in another twenty years, they're going to make *Aluminum Autumn*." The two friends shoot cows and cut them up with chain saws. They also use an old buffalo gun to blast mighty holes in a Lincoln Continental Mark IV. The wealthy rancher who suffers these depredations (Clifton James) hires a range detective (Slim Pickens) to track down the two rustlers. Rancho Deluxe is the name of the prison camp they end up in. (Bridges and Waterston were destined for very different roles in 1980's *Heaven's Gate*.)

Rancho Deluxe was written by Thomas McGuane, who is the first American novelist to direct a film version of one of his own books (92 *in the Shade*, a film about fishermen in the Florida Keys). McGuane used the basic plot of *Rancho Deluxe*—a wealthy rancher who hires a specialist to get rid of rustlers—for another screenplay, *The Missouri Breaks* (United Artists, 1976), directed by Arthur Penn and starring Marlon Brando and Jack Nicholson. Enormous amounts of money were spent on the film—Brando received $1,250,000 for his fee; Nicholson, $1 million—and when it failed to earn a profit, it was attacked as an example of everything that was wrong with the Hollywood system of moviemaking, particularly the dependence on big names and the willingness of producers to let agents talk them into spending fortunes. (This same criticism, redoubled and redoubled again, was soon to be leveled at *Heaven's Gate*.) *The Missouri Breaks* was assailed for other reasons. McGuane attacked Brando and Nicholson for rewriting the script to suit their own tastes; critics denounced the film for both failing to make sense and for being offensive while doing so.

But *The Missouri Breaks* has also been praised and enthusiastically studied for its mythlike symbolism. It is visually beautiful, and most of the dialogue is outrageously poetic. Like *Blazing Saddles*, it seems ready to burst out of its borders and stumble into another reality.

The "breaks" in the title are the badlands of Montana, where the rapids of the Missouri River break up the land; they are also the fate dealt to those who live there. (McGuane has a ranch in Montana called the Raw Deal Ranch.) "First time I saw this country, it had buffalo grass and bluejoint right up to the stirrups," remarks a rancher early in the film. A rustler is about to be hanged, and he is asked, "Anything you care to say before we pass judgment? We would prefer something colorful, life on the frontier being what it is." The rustler (who makes the feeble plea that he would like to be remembered as the Lonesome Kid) is a member of a gang led by Tom Logan (Nicholson). Logan and his men steal horses from a wealthy rancher named Braxton (John McLiam). Braxton catches and hangs one of Logan's men—Logan hangs Braxton's foreman. The rancher then sends for a range detective, a "regulator," to take care of the horse thieves. The regulator is Robert E. Lee Clayton (Brando), the most comically terrifying hired gun in any western. "The only things not on my diet would be the green top of the beet and okra," announces Clayton (a believable statement: Brando then weighed over 240 pounds). Clayton disposes of the horse thieves, one by one, in viciously personal ways (he shoots one in an outhouse, another is killed while making love). He changes his outfit to suit his mood, appearing as an Indian, a preacher, a sweet old granny (in a dress and bonnet), a frontier scout in fringed buckskins, and various other characters. He also changes his accent (though not necessarily to match what he's wearing). Clayton is not without affection for the men he kills, commenting to one, "You're about the last of your kind, old man. If I was a businessman instead of a man hunter, I'd put you in the circus."

Jack Nicholson played another horse thief in *Goin' South* (Paramount, 1978), a film which he both directed and starred in. Nicholson's second movie as director (his first was 1972's *Drive, He Said*), *Goin' South* was the film debut of John Belushi (his second film, *Animal House*, was released first, however). The comedy western is set in Texas in 1866. Henry Moon (Nicholson) is about to be hanged for horse thievery when he is saved by a local ordinance providing that any male guilty of a crime other than manslaughter can escape hanging if a property-owning woman agrees to marry him. (The Civil War only recently ended, there is a serious shortage of man power.) The woman (Mary Steenburgen) who saves him is not interested in a husband—she wants a laborer to work in her gold mine. The title of the screenplay for *Goin' South* was *The Conjugal Rights of Henry Moon*, and most of the film

involves the couple's marital problems.

Another man is saved from hanging in *China 9, Liberty 37* (IND, 1978), directed by Monte Hellman, the title of which refers to a signpost giving the distances to two nearby towns. Warren Oates's life is saved when he agrees to kill a former gunfighter (Fabio Testi). The gunfighter and his lover (Jenny Agutter) flee, and in their flight they encounter a man who wants to write a dime novel about their exploits—the writer is played by Sam Peckinpah.

"I don't want to hurt you—I just want to make you kosher," calls a hungry Avram (Gene Wilder), chasing a chicken. *The Frisco Kid* (Warner Brothers, 1979), directed by Robert Aldrich, is a comedy western about a young rabbi who, in 1850, is sent from Poland to take charge of a San Francisco congregation. His money is stolen in Philadelphia, so rather than take a steamship to California, he has to set off on foot. En route, the bungling foreigner teams up with a young outlaw named Tommy (Harrison Ford), and the two share sundry adventures.

Kirk Douglas made his debut as a director with *Scalawag* (1973), a sort of *Treasure Island* out West tale in which Douglas plays a peg-legged pirate. In his second film as director, *Posse* (Paramount, 1975), Douglas plays a Texas marshal named Howard Nightingale who wants to run for the U.S. Senate. As part of his law-and-order campaign, he travels around Texas with a six-man posse in a special train quashing villainy. The publicity-conscious lawman even has a traveling photographer. Nightingale is the villain of the film—his crimes, in true post-Watergate style, are his political aspirations; the hero is an outlaw named Jack

Strawhorn (Bruce Dern), a murderer who has the misfortune of becoming the symbol of Nightingale's campaign. Strawhorn's gang (which plays a mean game of baseball) is no match for Nightingale's professional gunmen with their well-pressed uniforms. The six men of the posse eventually find it hard to side with their boss; reviewers found it hard to side with Strawhorn as the hero in this very political western.

The villain is easy to spot in *The Villain* (Columbia, 1979), directed by Hal Needham. Needham, the famous stuntman turned director whose first film as director was *Smokey and the Bandit*, described *The Villain* as "a cartoon with live actors." In fact, *The Villain* is a Roadrunner cartoon set in the West. The cast includes Cactus Jack (Kirk Douglas), a tireless bad guy who gets his villainous ideas from a book called *Bad Guys of the West*; Charming Jones (Ann-Margret); Handsome Stranger (Arnold Schwarzenegger); Damsel in Distress (Ruth Buzzi); and an Indian named Nervous Elk (Paul Lynde).

The Villain was in good company. Many cartoon characters staged successful comebacks during the seventies and early eighties. Such heroes as *King Kong* (1976), *Superman* (1978), *Popeye* (1980), and *Flash Gordon* (1980) resurfaced, as alive as ever. But the most popular place to set a film during the seventies was outer space. The first performances of *Star Wars* (1977) resembled the first showings of *The Great Train Robbery*: audiences were enthralled with a new spectacle, and they enthusiastically embraced the opportunity to once again see the bad guys clearly distinguished from the good guys. Like Edwin S. Porter's

film, which had made use of all the newest tricks of photography, *Star Wars* was the result of brilliant special effects. Critics quickly decided that outer space was the new frontier, the new setting for westernlike action.

Perhaps *Star Wars*—like *The Great Train Robbery*—is really about current events. Longing for the future, we no longer live in the present, and although interplanetary travel is not yet a reality, we already suffer its side effects—the weariness that comes of having seen it all, and the uneasy suspicion that other people are potentially dangerous aliens. The past—all of history—has become legend.

The seventies ended without a film like *The Wild Bunch*, but Butch Cassidy and the Sundance Kid reappeared, like comic-book heroes, in a "prequel" to *Butch Cassidy and the Sundance Kid*. *Butch and Sundance: The Early Days* (20th Century-Fox, 1979), directed by Richard Lester, stars William Katt (who resembles Robert Redford) as Sundance and Tom Berenger (who resembles Paul Newman) as Butch. The film recounts the comic adventures of the two youths as they begin a life of offbeat but amiable crime.

Left: Ride in the Whirlwind *(IND, 1972).* Top:
Chaos in Goin' South *(Paramount, 1978).*
Above: *William Katt (left) and Tom Berenger as the two famed outlaws in* Butch and Sundance: The Early Days *(20th Century-Fox, 1979).*

Living Legends
1980–

> **"It's getting dangerous to be poor in this country."**
>
> *Heaven's Gate*

Ronald Reagan, born the year of *Broncho Billy's Christmas Dinner* (Essanay, 1911), was elected president in 1980, but having a former star of western movies in the White House did nothing to help the genre. The beer-drinking crowds at Gilley's in *Urban Cowboy* (1980), waiting for their turns on the mechanical bull, wear cowboy hats, cowboy boots, and tight-fitting jeans, but they don't pay to see westerns. To the strains of country-and-western music, the heads of studios—studios owned by conglomerates interested only in finding "this year's *Star Wars*"—casually agreed that westerns were dead. No one seemed to believe in the West anymore.

No one, that is, except Bronco Billy McCoy. *Bronco Billy* (Warner Brothers, 1980), directed by Clint Eastwood, is an affectionately funny film about a modern-day cowboy and his traveling Wild West show. Bronco Billy (Eastwood) was a shoe clerk in New Jersey until, at age 31, he decided to head West and change his life. He and his troupe of actors perform their tricks—exciting events like "rattlesnake rassling"—before small audiences of children and their grandparents. Bronco Billy, who calls the children "little cowboys and cowgirls" and "little pards," performs his own act, firing sixguns and throwing knives at attractive female assistants. Unfortunately, Bronco Billy's aim is poor, and he has trouble finding willing targets. The part is finally taken by a New York heiress (Sondra Locke). "Are you for real?" she asks Bronco Billy. He is as real as any of his acts. When he goes to a bank to cash a $3 check, he ends up foiling a bank robbery, going into action only after one of the would-be robbers frightens one of his "little pards." Loraine Running Water (Sierra Pecheur), the resident Indian maiden, delivers the film's theme: "You can be anything you want to." That, at least, is the dream.

Steve McQueen always wanted to make a movie about Tom Horn—McQueen thought Horn had been the last true western hero. Robert Redford was interested in making a film about Horn, too, and for a while Redford, with scriptwriter William Goldman and director Sydney Pollack, and McQueen, with Thomas McGuane and Don Siegel, were both working on similar projects. Redford eventually dropped the idea; he and Pollack made *Electric Horseman*, and Goldman's script was used in a television movie, *Mr. Horn* (1979). Siegel left McQueen's project and was replaced by William Wiard. *Tom Horn* (Warner Brothers, 1980), directed by Wiard, is Steve McQueen's penultimate film (*The Hunter*, also made in 1980, was his last film).

Preceding pages: *Charlton Heston (left) and Brian Keith in* The Mountain Men *(Columbia, 1980). Right: Isabelle Huppert and Kris Kristofferson in* Heaven's Gate *(United Artists, 1980).*

Tom Horn was a cowboy, a deputy sheriff, a Rough Rider in Cuba, a Pinkerton detective, a frontier scout, and a range detective. Before he was 20, he learned to speak Spanish and Apache and served with the army as an interpreter—the Indians called him Talking Boy. He helped track down renegade Apaches and is sometimes credited with bringing in Geronimo. A crack marksman, he was a famous hunter, but the game he stalked was usually human—he was one of the most feared stock detectives, or "regulators," a hired killer employed to eliminate rustlers. (The character Marlon Brando plays in *The Missouri Breaks* was probably modeled after Horn.)

The screenplay for *Tom Horn*, written by Thomas McGuane and Bud Shrake, is based on Horn's autobiography, *Life of Tom Horn, Government Scout and Interpreter, Written by Himself*, a book that Horn dictated during his last days, while he was in jail, accused of killing a 15-year-old boy. The film covers the last three years of his life, 1901 to 1903. Horn, an aging legend, is hired by an association of Wyoming cattlemen to get rid of some rustlers. He goes about the task with his usual efficiency, blasting away with his .45-60 Remington single-shot rifle. But it is no longer the old West, and Horn's murderous methods embarrass the cattlemen—who represent law and order—and they frame him for the murder of a young shepherd.

The film is visually beautiful—Wyoming has rarely looked so cold—but its plot doesn't always make sense. Among its other actors are Linda Evans as a schoolteacher friend of Horn's, and Slim Pickens as a sheriff. Pickens was well-suited to playing the sheriff—he claimed that during his rodeoing days he had met the sheriff who had hanged the real Tom Horn.

There were plenty of rustlers in Wyoming during the 1890s—plenty of big cattlemen and plenty of small homesteaders. After the terrible cattle-killing winters of the late 1880s, the big cattlemen were acutely aware of rustling and—not completely without reason—they blamed the small homesteaders. The big cattlemen wanted to keep the range open—after years of using it freely, they felt it belonged to them—and they wanted to get rid of the rustlers. The conflict in Wyoming can be told from either side—Tom Horn, a gunman hired by wealthy ranchers to eliminate rustlers, resembles Wilson, the character played by Jack Palance in *Shane*, a gunman hired to frighten off homesteaders—and its most famous incident—the Johnson County War of April 1892—is still the source of controversy. The big cattlemen, including members of the Wyoming Stock Growers Association, put together a list of the men they believed were involved in the rustling and hired fifty regulators for an invasion of Johnson County, the area they believed was the rustlers' base. The fifty gunmen, traveling in a special train, entered Johnson County and killed two men. They got no farther. Sur-

rounded by a 200-man posse assembled by a Wyoming sheriff, the hired gunmen would have been themselves exterminated had they not been saved by the cavalry. The subsequent trial settled nothing.

The Johnson County War provided the background for Owen Wister's landmark novel, *The Virginian* (1902). A wealthy easterner, Wister sided with the big cattlemen. To him, the small ranchers were "thieves"; to Michael Cimino, they were revolutionary heroes—he presented his case in *Heaven's Gate*.

Heaven's Gate (United Artists, 1980), written and directed by Michael Cimino, was not an easy film to see—it was not easy to get into a theater to watch it, and it was not easy to sit through. The film was first released in November of 1980 with a running time of 219 minutes. The initial reviews were so terrible that it was withdrawn. It was rereleased five months later with 70 minutes cut, but it was still considered a disaster and was again withdrawn. It may someday be rereleased under a new title (*The Johnson County War* has been suggested); it will need a new title, for *Heaven's Gate*, like Watergate, has become a national synonym for disaster.

Great things were expected of the film. Cimino, who won the Academy Award for best director in 1978 for *The Deer Hunter*, spent two years making *Heaven's Gate*. He also spent nearly $40 million, and when the film failed, it was declared to be both the end of westerns and the end of the film industry. It wasn't, but the disaster of *Heaven's Gate* led to the sale of United Artists to MGM.

In *Heaven's Gate*, the Johnson County War becomes a symbol of class struggle in America: the thesis is that the rich kill the poor. Kris Kristofferson stars as James Averill, a federal marshal and graduate of Harvard (class of 1870). Out in Wyoming, he meets a classmate who is a member of the Stock Growers Association. His classmate tells him, "It's getting dangerous to be poor in this country." "Always was," responds Averill. The immigrants to Wyoming are Eastern Europeans, who arrive clinging to train cars. The wealthy landowners (led by Sam Waterston) want to get rid of these foreign newcomers. True to history, they make up a "hit list" of the people they want to do away with, and they hire mercenaries to invade Johnson County. The mercenaries and the immigrants (led by Jeff Bridges) collide; the conclusion of the film has nothing to do with history.

Heaven's Gate is magnificently beautiful (the photography is by Vilmos Zsigmond), the musical score (by David Mansfield) is excellent, and the details—the attention to period articles—makes a dazzling display. Some of the scenes, in particular a scene of roller skating in a Grange hall, are both unexpected and skillfully composed. But there is no story to follow. There is too much to look at and not enough to think about.

In *The Long Riders* (United Artists, 1980), directed by Walter Hill, the photography (by Ric Waite)—scenes of rainy, lush woodlands, alternately dark and brilliant green—and the musical score (by Ry Cooder)—a combination of banjos, guitars, and Jews' harp—help tell the story, contributing a suitably tense atmosphere. *The Long Riders* is about the James gang; the film covers a period of nearly fifteen years in the career of the gang, including the ill-fated bank robbery in Northfield, Minnesota (the subject of 1972's *The Great Northfield Minnesota Raid*). This film differs from all the many previous films about the gang in its casting—it uses real brothers to play the brothers that made up the gang:

Cole Younger: David Carradine
Jim Younger: Keith Carradine
Bob Younger: Robert Carradine
Jesse James: James Keach
Frank James: Stacy Keach
Ed Miller: Dennis Quaid
Clell Miller: Randy Quaid
John Younger: Kevin Brophy
George Arthur: Harry Carey, Jr.
Charlie Ford: Christopher Guest
Bob Ford: Nicholas Guest

Left to right: *Rod Steiger as Bill Tilghman; Burt Lancaster as Bill Doolin; Steven Ford as a deputy in* Cattle Annie and Little Britches *(Universal, 1981).*

Dressed in identical white shirts and long dusters, the members of the gang look pretty much alike, but the sense of family is very strong, and the knowledge that the actors really are brothers who care for each other makes the violence in the film even more effective. And the violence is awesome: the bloody battle in the streets of Northfield is filmed in slow motion—even the flying bullets are slowed down, allowing the audience to hear each one whizz toward its victim. *The Long Riders* was produced by Tim Zinnemann, son of director Fred Zinnemann.

Fraser Clarke Heston, son of Charlton Heston, wrote the screenplay for **The Mountain Men** (Columbia, 1980), directed by Richard Lang. The film stars Charlton Heston as Bill Tyler and Brian Keith as Henry Frapp, two grimy and grizzled fur trappers who get possession of an Indian woman named Running Moon (Victoria Racimo). A wicked chief named Heavy Eagle (Stephen Macht) doesn't like the idea—he wants to have Tyler's head decorating the point of his spear. The ensuing battles are ridiculously bloody.

A much more unusual treatment of Indians is **Windwalker** (IND, 1980), directed by Keith Merrill, a film in which all the characters are Indian and all the dialogue is in Crow or Cheyenne—with English subtitles. Not all the actors are Indian, however: Trevor Howard stars as an aging Cheyenne warrior who saves his tribe from its enemies.

The title of **Comin' At Ya!** (IND, 1981), directed by Ferdinando Baldi, refers to the exciting sensation of 3-D; this was the first 3-D movie in a long time. Although *Comin' At Ya!* is in some ways similar to a "spaghetti" western, it is really a horror movie, delighting in gruesome close-ups of death and endeavoring, whenever possible, to spurt blood into the audience's lap (not to mention the bats and rats, rape, and people chopped to pieces).

Sometimes referred to as "*High Noon* on Io," **Outland** (Warner Brothers, 1981), written and directed by Peter Hyams, is an example of how science fiction can use western themes. Io, third moon of Jupiter, is the site of a mining camp; Sean Connery is a federal district marshal charged with keeping the peace. The lawman discovers that workers are being manipulated with drugs. No one wants to hear about it, and no one helps the marshal in his struggle against the outlaws. He is alone—and hired killers are arriving on the next shuttle. There are no ticking clocks, of course: time flashes by on digital clocks as he awaits their arrival.

Cattle Annie and Little Britches (Universal, 1981), directed by Lamont Johnson, begins with a train robbery in the Oklahoma Territory around 1893. The outlaws are the notorious Doolin-Dalton gang. They stop the train in fine style, but the gold shipment they are after is not to be found, and they end up with some pigs and a load of baseball equipment (which they later

make comic use of). The passengers are not perturbed by the holdup—they are delighted, and as the engineer calls out the names of the famed outlaws, the passengers applaud and the outlaws nod their heads in recognition. On the train is a cargo even more valuable to the gang than gold: two teenage girls on their way west to experience the exciting life they have read about in dime novels. When they finally join the gang and are given appropriate nicknames, Cattle Annie (Amanda Plummer, daughter of Christopher Plummer and Tammy Grimes, in her film debut) and Little Britches (Diane Lane) find that the outlaws are not the heroic gentlemen they had read about. Led by Bill Doolin (Burt Lancaster) and Bill Dalton (Scott Glenn), they are a scruffy, pathetic rabble, forever arguing and complaining. The enthusiasm of the two girls changes the gang into the legendary heroes they never were.

There is a lot of humor and a lot of sweetness in *Cattle Annie and Little Britches*. Cattle Annie, speaking in the ironically polite diction of a dime novel, changes Bill Doolin into a hero, even to himself and even though he is old and getting a little heavy around the middle. Bill Tilghman (Rod Steiger), hunting the Doolin-Dalton gang, doesn't want to hear about how good Doolin is. "He may be the best," says Tilghman. "All the rest are dead." (Tilghman's deputy is played by Steven Ford, son of former president Gerald R. Ford.) "All legends end in bullshit," says one of Doolin's men. "Well," responds Doolin, "I'll just try and see if this one works." With the help of the two girls, it does.

Cattle Annie and Little Britches is based on a story that is supposedly true, and the film ends by relating the lives of the two girls after they left the outlaws (Little Britches didn't have far to go—she died during an influenza epidemic at 17 while working as a domestic in New York; Cattle Annie lived a long life in Kansas City). Based on fact, the film recounts the birth of a legend.

The West of the seventies was dusty and dirty—"realistic"—physically and spiritually soiled, and peopled by mangy outlaws and equally mangy nonoutlaws. There were no more heroes or villains, and the westward movement was portrayed as nothing more than massive urban sprawl, the ominous expansion of the corporate state. The West became a pretty depressing place to be (westerns, of course, have always mirrored contemporary American society). The attempts during the seventies to debunk the myth of the West gave way to the decision during the eighties that the West was a fairyland. To avoid the unacceptable taint of history, some westerns have adopted the aspect of fantasy. The towns are still dusty, but the dust—like everything else—sparkles.

The Legend of the Lone Ranger (Universal, 1981), directed by William A. Fraker, is not the children's

Diane Lane (left) as Little Britches and Amanda Plummer as
Cattle Annie in Cattle Annie and Little Britches (Universal, 1981).

movie one might expect—it is far too sanguinary, as though the masked man had tumbled from the airwaves into a seventies western. Even with its bloodshed, the film has a plot that belongs to the make-believe world in which anyone can be anywhere at any time. *The Legend of the Lone Ranger* begins, like *Superman,* by covering the history of the hero, explaining the Lone Ranger's (Klinton Spilsbury) relationship with Tonto (Michael Horse) and why he wears a mask. The film then gets the hero involved in a plot to kidnap U.S. Grant (Jason Robards, Jr.). Grant appears in a train car accompanied by General Custer (Lincoln Tate), Wild Bill Hickok (Richard Farnsworth), and Buffalo Bill Cody (Ted Flicker). The film makes use of many traditional stunts, including the stagecoach trick—letting the coach pass over and then climbing up the back—made famous by Yakima Canutt in *Stagecoach.* In *The Legend of the Lone Ranger,* the stunt is made into a self-conscious spoof—it doesn't work. In *Raiders of the Lost Ark* (1981), a much more exciting film, the stunt works wonderfully.

Barbarosa (Universal, 1982), directed by Fred Schepisi, is about the birth and perpetuation of a legend. The film begins, like countless westerns before it, with a lone man riding through the desert. Karl (Gary Busey), carrying his hat on a stick, is a farm boy. Dressed in his overalls, he looks like an auto mechanic. He does not belong in the desert, but he has had to run away from home after killing his brother-in-law. Out of the sunlight appears Barbarosa (Willie Nelson), an inhabitant of the desert and a living legend. He, too, has been cut off from his family, having killed a few members of his bride's Mexican family on their wedding night. Wearing an enormous cathedrallike hat that keeps him forever in the shade, Barbarosa, with his beard and his tattered clothing, looks like the desert he lives in, but—like Karl—he would rather be home. The two outcasts are pursued by revenge-seeking relatives: farmers are out after Karl; there is an endless stream of young men out after Barbarosa. It is a difficult life, and Barbarosa has been living it for a long time. For thirty years, he has suffered and survived the attempts of his wife's family to kill him, and his invincibility has turned him into a legend. His various escapades become the subject of folksongs overnight, and his story has become a popular bedtime tale for the young, a fairy tale in which his beard, once the golden

color of honey, drips red with blood. "Barbarosa!" the spellbound children chant. "Barbarosa!" Many of the youths sent out to kill him have never seen him, but they recognize him. As one says, "I will know him from the songs we sing and the stories we tell."

Wise old Barbarosa, scanning the desert through his collapsible telescope, becomes Karl's mentor, teaching him how to catch armadillos for dinner and voicing some folksy philosophy. "What cannot be remedied must be endured," he says. He treats his fate with tender affection, understanding and sympathizing with everyone, even those who try to kill him. Karl learns well; he begins to grow a beard. So it is that when Barbarosa is finally killed, he reappears, risen from the dead, riding his horse in a circle before disappearing alone into the desert.

Although it was filmed in Texas, the landscape of *Barbarosa* is unearthly. Barbarosa and Karl ride through constantly changing patterns of ethereal light; they ride past unreal—or unrecognizable—forms. The violence in the film is unnervingly awkward: people stand just about nose to nose and shoot at each other, invariably missing with the first few tries. Both Nelson and Busey are native Texans (as is scriptwriter William D. Wittliff), and both are musicians as well as movie stars. It is Nelson's gravity, his steady sense of himself and other people, that makes him a believable hero.

Director Schepisi is Australian, and Australia—a nation not unlike the United States in many ways—has become the source for many films that resemble American westerns. *The Man from Snowy River* (20th Century-Fox, 1983), directed by George Miller, tells the story of a boy (Tom Burlinson) reaching manhood in an atmosphere very much like that of the American West. The title of the film comes from a well-known poem by A. B. Paterson. The film stars Kirk Douglas (who plays two parts) and Jack Thompson (who appeared as a lawyer in Bruce Beresford's *Breaker Morant*). *The Man from Snowy River* is so much like a western—including a final chase scene—that it prompted some American reviewers to express longing for westerns, for films with straightforward, optimistic plots and rugged, individualistic heroes. Perhaps Butch and Sundance survived their encounter with the Bolivian army and made it to Australia. Perhaps their grandchildren may yet give us back the dream of riding free through a beautiful world.

Reviving old legends and creating new ones. Opposite top: *Scene from* The Legend of the Lone Ranger *(Universal, 1981). Left to right: Jason Robards, Jr., as President Grant; Michael Horse as Tonto; Klinton Spilsbury as the Lone Ranger.* Opposite bottom: *Willie Nelson as* Barbarosa *(Universal, 1982).*

Afterword

Violence is not the secret of the western, just as violence is not the lone truth behind the history of the American West. The galloping horse at which Eadweard Muybridge aimed his cameras became the galloping horses in the first western, the first film. Action, exciting physical movement, is both the secret of the western and the heart of filmmaking.

In the same way that the galloping horse was a perfect target for movie cameras, the history of the West—as viewed by Americans and American filmmakers—was ideally suited to films: it was full of potential movie stars. Thanks to Wild West shows, dime novels, and our national willingness—even desire—to believe that important events are the result of the courage of individuals, the West had become the story of rugged characters, men with memorable names and fancy outfits. The history of the West embraced by early filmmakers still smacked of tall tales and the bragging of proud men. It was a part of our national history told just the way we wanted to see it—full of excitement and heroism.

Historical accuracy was not the primary ingredient of Wild West shows and western novels, and historical individuals—men like Wyatt Earp and Wild Bill Hickok—had become separated from their true histories long before they made their way into movies. No one can be blamed if, in the thrill of telling that spectacular story of heroes and villains, cavalry and Indians—the taming of a great land—the names of those real men got mixed up with the names of fictional heroes. The makers of westerns inherited an endless supply of names, and they used them as they pleased. Contemporary viewers of westerns cannot be faulted if they sometimes have trouble distinguishing the Ringo Kid from Billy the Kid or Rooster Cogburn from Bat Masterson. They are all characters played by actors in films, and those who actually drew breath are joined forever to those who were created from the spirit of the times.

Telling the story of the American West proved to be a perilous undertaking, but the early makers of westerns had no way of knowing that the heroes they were celebrating would someday lose their dignity. Until quite recently, the makers of westerns had a very dramatic story to tell, a story full of nostalgia for an exciting past, a time when civilization and all its blessings had not yet changed America. In thousands of separate incidents in thousands of films, individual courage proved itself stronger than gangs of criminals or groups of unscrupulous businessmen. Whether pushing longhorns north to a railhead or fighting off swarming Indians, the heroes did what had to be done, and did it not just for themselves, but for the benefit of others. True heroes, loping along and not saying much, they were always ready to protect the innocent and always full of a fervent belief in the future. In the real West, it was the horses that became anachronistic, replaced by automobiles; in the filmed West, it was the heroes and their mythical interpretation of a period of history that became anachronistic, replaced, thus far, by nothing.

Heroes and saints, adventurers and scoundrels: as hard as it is today to look back and believe, some of their stories are true. The original power of westerns was not all Wild West showmanship and dime-novel dramatics—it was based on a heroic past that we should all be proud of. The physical movement that is the secret of westerns is an American spirit brought to life: long, proud strides across an endless land of promise.

Even the showmanship of westerns was, in the beginning, a powerful force for audiences. It is a wonderful experience to read the reviews of *The Great Train Robbery* that were printed in newspapers around 1903. The film was quite exciting in its day, and one enthusiastic reporter noted that there was a great amount of shooting in the film and that the smoke of the pistols was "plainly seen." He expressed surprise that although the film was silent women put their fingers in their ears to shut out the noise of the gunfire. The thrill of it all was very real. When, in the last scene, the actor George Barnes raised his gun and fired directly at the audience, grown men ducked and females screamed.

The image of Barnes silently aiming his revolver out of the screen is still with us. His aim has remained true through all the years, but his gun no longer frightens anyone. We have other things to worry about.

George Barnes in The Great Train Robbery *(Edison, 1903).*

Index

Acknowledgments

Special thanks to Walter Seltzer; Jane Novak; Elmo Williams; Jet Fore; Elliot
Silverstein; Jerry Pam; Clarke Reynolds; Bernie Abramson; the staff of the Margaret Herrick Library, Academy of Motion Picture Arts and Sciences; the staff of
the Museum of Modern Art/Film Stills Archives; Peter Bateman and Jeff Dighton
of Larry Edmunds Cinema Bookshop, Leith Adams and Lindy Narver at USC;
Joe Hyams (no proven relation to the author), Jess Garcia, Judith Singer, Jack
Kingsley, and Dennis Walman at Warner Brothers; Dore Freeman at MGM;
Corine DeLuca and Maureen Angelinetta at Universal; Rich Kelley (for an act of
remarkable faith); Margaret Schiller; Stephen Weitzen; Lynn Bond; Francis
Wintle; Laura Dempsey; Cynthia Parzych; Sara Clio Nicolis (for inspiration);
Allan Mogel; Laurie Orseck; Eric Marshall; Linda McClow; Jane Waldman; Fred
and John Sammis; Hedy Caplan; Jan Westervelt; and my father, Joe Hyams,
without whom I never would have dared.

Picture Credits

l (left); *r* (right); *t* (top); *c* (center); *b* (bottom)
The photographs in this book appear courtesy of the following:

Columbia Pictures: 72; 74-75; 81 *(b)*; 128 *(t)*; 159; 163 *(b)*; 164; 165; 172; 189; 222-23 **Larry Edmunds Cinema Bookshop:** 27; 31; 36-37 *(t)*; 41 *(b)*; 42; 43 *(t)*; 47 *(br)*; 53; 59; 60; 63 *(t)*; 65 *(t)*; 67; 72; 73 *(b)*; 74-75; 81 *(c* and *b)*; 88-89; 93; 94-95; 99; 108; 110-11; 114; 118; 121; 122-23; 127; 128; 135; 136; 143; 144; 146-47; 153; 155; 157; 158; 163; 166; 172; 184 *(b)*; 186 *(t)*; 188; 191; 194-95; 197 *(b)*; 198; 209; 213; 215; 217; 218; 220-21; 222-23 **Margaret Herrick Library, Academy of Motion Picture Arts and Sciences:** 2-3; 11; 16-17; 19; 25; 26; 28-29; 41 *(t)*; 45; 47 *(t* and *bl)*; 51; 61; 63 *(b)*; 81 *(t)*; 83; 84; 91; 104; 107; 116; 117; 138; 159; 160; 164; 170; 174; 177; 178-79; 184 *(t)*; 186 *(c* and *b)*; 189; 197 *(t)*; 200; 210; 212; 214; 221; 224-25; 233 **MGM:** 81 *(c)* © 1953 Loew's Inc. Copyright renewed 1980 by Metro-Goldwyn-Mayer Inc.; 93 © 1956 Loew's Inc. Copyright renewed 1983 by MGM/UA Entertainment Co.; 163 *(t)* © 1964 Metro-Goldwyn-Mayer Inc. and KHF Productions; 186 *(t)* © 1971 Metro-Goldwyn-Mayer Inc.; 191 and 205 *(tr)* © 1973 Metro-Goldwyn-Mayer Inc.; 209 © 1973 Metro-Goldwyn-Mayer Inc. **Museum of Modern Art/Film Stills Archives:** 14; 15; 21; 23; 24; 32-33; 34; 35; 36-37 *(b)*; 38-39; 43 *(b)*; 47 *(tr)*; 48; 48-49; 54-55; 56-57; 65 *(b)*; 69; 70; 73 *(t)*; 79; 85; 97; 100; 113; 141; 165; 171; 180; 182; 190; 192 **New York Public Library:** 12, 13 **Jane Novak:** 30 **RKO General Pictures:** 2-3; 73 *(b)*; 88-89 *(t)*; 97; 121 *(b)* **Twentieth Century-Fox Film Corporation** (all rights reserved): 11 and 177 © 1969 Campanile Productions, Inc., and Twentieth Century-Fox Film Corporation; 63 *(t)* © 1942 Twentieth Century-Fox Film Corporation; 63 *(b)* © 1948 Twentieth Century-Fox Film Corporation; 65 *(t)* © 1941 Twentieth Century-Fox Film Corporation; 69 © 1946 Twentieth Century-Fox Film Corporation; 83 © 1950 Twentieth Century-Fox Film Corporation; 104 *(b)* © 1952 Twentieth Century-Fox Film Corporation; 153 *(b)* © 1966 Twentieth Century-Fox Film Corporation; 186 *(c* and *b)* © 1972 Twentieth Century-Fox Film Corporation; 221 *(b)* © 1979 Twen-

tieth Century-Fox Film Corporation. **United Artists** (all rights reserved): 70 © 1948. Monterey Productions. Renewed 1975 by United Artists Corporation; 84 © 1954. Linden Productions. Released through United Artists Corporation; 107 © 1954. Flora Productions. Released through United Artists Corporation; 108 © 1956. Russ-Field Corporation. Released through United Artists Corporation; 129 © 1958. Donald Hamilton. Released through United Artists Corporation; 130-31 © 1960. Mirisch-Alpha. Released through United Artists Corporation; 136 © 1961. Seven Arts Productions, Inc. Released through United Artists Corporation; 141 © 1960. The Alamo Company. Released through United Artists Corporation; 143 *(t)* © 1967. Harold Hecht Company. Released through United Artists Corporation; 150 *(b)* © 1966. Rainbow Productions, Inc. and Brien Productions, Inc. Released through United Artists Corporation; 151 © 1968. Leonard Freeman Productions. Released through United Artists; 157 © 1962. E. C. Productions. Released through United Artists Corporation; 160 © 1969. Three Pictures Corporation. Released through United Artists Corporation; 192 © 1970. Woodfall Limited. Released through United Artists Corporation; 197 *(t)* © 1975. United Artists Corporation; 202 © 1976 United Artists Corporation; 205 *(b)* © 1980. United Artists Corporation; 208 *(t)* and 224-25 © 1980. United Artists Corporation; 210 © 1978. United Artists Corporation **Universal Pictures:** 4-5; 6-7; 27; 51; 59; 61; 81 *(t)*; 91; 94-95; 99; 132; 143 *(b)*; 150 *(t)*; 166; 174; 185 *(t)*; 198; 201; 203; 206 *(b)*; 207; 208 *(b)*; 215; 227; 229; 230 **Warner Brothers** (all rights reserved): 1 and 204 © 1971 Warner Bros. Inc.; 85 © 1956 Warner Bros. Inc.; 149 © 1969 Warner Bros. Inc.; 152 © 1974 Warner Bros. Inc.; 205 *(tl)* © 1972 Warner Bros. Inc. and Sanford Productions, Inc.; 206 *(t)* © 1980 Warner Bros.; 213 © 1973 Warner Bros. Inc. **Weiss Global Enterprises:** 117